When I see what Ron Martoia is now doing, it makes me proud to be called one of his teachers. In fact, in this book, he has become my teacher. Ron takes biblical terms such as *salvation* and *kingdom,* dusts off the cobwebs of routine, and finds under them fresh expressions for a new day.

—Scot McKnight
author of *The Jesus Creed* and professor at North Park University

Ron Martoia is a sparkling, creative, brilliant thinker and a crisp, extraordinary, engaging communicator. His new book, *Static,* will help you think in fresh ways about familiar words that are crucial to your faith. You'll never hear or read key words like *gospel, Christ, kingdom,* or *repentance* the same way again. As a result, you'll be able to communicate your faith more effectively with others—and your own faith will be deeply enriched. A beautiful book!

—Brian McLaren
author/speaker/activist (brianmclaren.net)

NEWSFLASH: Ron Martoia's phenomenal retelling of the story of Jesus will change the way you think about . . . well, nearly everything in the Bible. *Static* will provide you not only with new insights into the mission of Jesus, but also with a fresh, new vocabulary to communicate this breaking news in a much more meaningful way than before. This fascinating book by one of the leading spiritual architects for our generation sets the pace for a relevant new way to articulate our faith in today's world. Read it, and you will see why.

—Stephan Joubert
editor of eKerk (echurch.co.za) and extraordinary professor in New Testament Studies at the University of Pretoria, South Africa

Ron Martoia's unique ability to help us navigate the deep waters of cultural change is a great asset to today's church leaders. He gives us fresh perspective on our need to understand and translate the ancient language of the church to a generation who currently only hear us speaking gibberish. Ron gives us new tools to communicate Jesus' message with great clarity. *Static* will serve the church as a catalyst to help us think differently about many issues of our faith and liberate us from the prison of the status quo.

—Ted Baird
pastor of Fellowship Church@Anthem

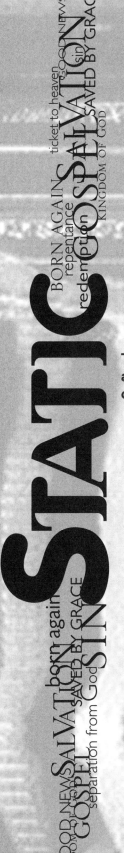

STATIC

Tune out the "Christian noise" and experience the real message of Jesus

Ron Martoia

TYNDALE HOUSE PUBLISHERS, INC.
CAROL STREAM, ILLINOIS

Visit Tyndale's exciting Web site at www.tyndale.com

Static: Tune Out the "Christian Noise" and Experience the Real Message of Jesus

Designed by Beth Sparkman

Edited by Dave Lindstedt

Library of Congress Cataloging-in-Publication Data

Martoia, Ron, date.
Static : tune out the "Christian noise" and experience the real message of Jesus / Ron Martoia.
p. cm.
Includes bibliographical references.
ISBN-13: 978-1-4143-1213-2 (sc)
ISBN-10: 1-4143-1213-X (sc)
1. Witness bearing (Christianity) I. Title.
BV4520.M375 2007
248'.5—dc22 2006038423

Printed in the United States of America

13 12 11 10 09 08 07
7 6 5 4 3 2 1

To RJ, Skyler, and Ari, my three amazing teenagers, whom I love with everything in me and who keep me laughing hilariously about the language changes I need to make to stay fresh and culturally current

CONT

ENTS

Acknowledgments

Like all books, I suppose, the genesis of this volume has a feel of serendipity. I met Ken Petersen, senior acquisitions director at Tyndale, while he and I were at a small meeting of cultural creatives outside Washington DC. I was facilitating a conversation about how the language we use creates a cultural container for understanding. My role was to help this group reflect on the religious language so often used in media and the arts, and how that often shuts down spiritual conversation instead of enhancing it. Ken grabbed me after the group conversation and said, "We need to talk more about this." That talk wasn't to happen for a couple more months.

A number of weeks later, at Catalyst, I was doing a workshop on a similar topic. I was in a large ballroom, doing the typical post-talk question-and-answer time with a group of people, when out of the corner of my eye, I saw Ken again. His statement was an echo of what he had said before: "We need to talk." That "talk," more than anything else, is responsible for *Static*'s birth into the world of print media. I have Ken to thank for taking the initiative, and Gabe Lyons, the founder of Relevate, to thank for hosting the Axiom Conversation that brought Ken and me together.

Influencers in a book like this are legion, but I want to honor my primary "Gospels and Teachings of Jesus" mentor, Scot McKnight, with whom I studied and helped as TA for a semester during my master's program. Scot has had more influence on my love of and engagement with the Gospels and with the Jesus in those Gospels than any other person. Though I quote him and reference him at times, do not hold him responsible for any craziness you read in these pages. His teaching, writings, and the subsequent lunch he invited me to share with him and N. T. Wright at an SBL conference some ten years ago have had a seminal impact and a profound shaping influence on me.

Several people have been idea clarifiers and sounding boards in the process of this project. Tom Morrissey, the outstanding Christian novelist, has been a part of a faith community with me for a number of years. His challenges to me to write dialogue and communicate in a way that feels quite foreign at times have been a good stretch. I hope I have become a better writer for it. Our times at Beaners, in front of the fireplace, were critical and formative for Static.

At a crucial junction in my ministry, I had the opportunity to meet, and then more deeply connect with, Chuck Smith Jr. His long-distance support and friendship, as well as his theological dialogue, were life giving—and even nurturing—at a time when these ideas were just starting to ripen. Chuck, I have learned from your humility and acumen; thank you for modeling that blend for me.

Ted Baird and the amazing staff at Fellowship Church@ Anthem have played a significant role in the *Static* discussion. Our monthly one-day theological retreats were influential in helping me think out loud about these concepts and how they might translate into a local church context. Ted, you are a dear friend, and with deep gratitude I thank you for who you are and all you have done for me. Thanks, Peg, for letting him be such a close friend to me. You are the great woman behind the great man.

I also want to express my appreciation to Joe Lengel, a fellow journey partner, who not only honestly "gets it" but is willing to push to the very edge for a glimpse of elegance and beauty that can be seen only from that vantage point. Your soundings on these ideas have been helpful and at times catalytic, and your friendship a treasure. Karen and Joe, our dinners together are great memories and foretastes of more to come as we share the sacrament of food.

To the Vortex Learning Community of Jackson—the place where these ideas were initially roughed, refocused, and refined—and to each Velocity Learning Conversation that sounded off around these concepts I want to express my deep appreciation. The groups of people all over the country that have given input into this volume are impossible to number, but to all of you—thanks.

This book wouldn't have made it to completion without the work of acquisitions director Jon Farrar and senior editor Dave Lindstedt at Tyndale House. Thanks, you guys, for pushing and taking push back. All our tussling has made this a better book and, I hope, me a better writer. Thanks.

This book represents a journey in progress. My guess is that it raises as many questions as it attempts to explore. But instead of creating a sort of aimless agnosticism so common in the world of rethinking theological ideas, I hope that this points the way toward fruitful possibilities—possibilities worthy of further exploration, and possibilities that help us all become better followers and communicators of the message of Jesus.

Ron Martoia

Foreword

"Read your Bible every day to know Christ better."[1]

Do you agree or disagree with the above statement? Millions of Christians agree that Bible reading is necessary for spiritual growth. But after reading a few chapters of Leviticus or some of the strange logic in Romans or a few of the comic book–like scenes from Revelation, we realize that it is not enough to just *read* the Bible; we have to do some work at interpreting what we read as well.

Without having the luxury of acquiring tools for biblical study—such as learning Hebrew and Greek, being familiar with the geography of Bible lands, or exploring the culture of the ancient Mediterranean world—many Christians give up and trust their preachers to study the Bible for them. However, not all Bible teachers are created equal, and once we get a wrong idea lodged in our heads, discerning the real meaning of Scripture becomes more difficult.

In the following pages, you will recognize errors that are commonly assumed to be accurate reflections of what the Bible teaches. You will also see how the religious vocabulary of evangelical Christians tends to create confusion about what the Scriptures actually teach.

Why is it so difficult to properly interpret the Bible? What has happened to the message since the time that the scribe's pen was first put to paper (or papyrus) that makes it so easy to read our own ideas *into the text* rather than extract the text's inherent meaning? Ron explains that the central problem is "static." Regardless of the quality of the transmission of God's truth, the many significant differences between yesterday and today, the culture of the Middle East and our contemporary Western world, and the original languages of Scripture and English (including usage and idioms), the interference is great enough to distort our reception of its meaning.

Ron Martoia has done a great service for everyone who loves the Bible and wants to see its truth in the hands and hearts of people who have never heard it in their own language, even though their language is English. He explores the cultural static—both historical and contemporary—that makes the message of the Bible more difficult to hear the further we get from the time of its composition. He also explains how static is increased when we read the Bible as if it were written by an author living today and writing specifically for our times.

Ron's book is a gift for believers who are discontent with superficial interpretations of Scripture, cliché evangelism, and a bad news version of the gospel. Guiding us back through original language in its original setting, Ron brings us to a gospel that is a divine newsflash, as compelling today as it was in the first century. He suggests a revision of our evangelistic lexicon so that the invitation and truth of God become more accessible to people in our own time, both inside and outside the church. Finally, Ron shows us how looking through a clearer lens will enable us to receive the biblical message as it was intended. As a result, when opening the Bible, we encounter a livelier text, a more profound revelation, and a compelling meaning that applies God's Word to our deepest needs, desires, and aspirations.

Chuck Smith Jr.
January 2007

1

Pheidippides Was a Wimp

Jackson County, Michigan, where I live, is not for the faint of heart. Not if you're a runner, that is.

It's not that the hills are exceedingly steep, or excessively long. They're just everywhere. It seems you're always on a grade, either huffing toward a rise or coasting gingerly down the other side, planting your feet carefully because it's a whole lot easier to mess up a knee or an ankle running downhill than it is when you're climbing.

It was on a rare stretch of sun-dappled flatland that my friend Jess said to her husband, Phil, "You need to tell him. Tell Ron."

Hearing my name, I glanced back.

Conversation during our early morning training runs was not uncommon. And really, they weren't *our* training runs. They were Jess's. She was in her first year of marathoning and still trying to get a handle on the whole issue of *pace*. Distance running is all about pace—run too fast and you'll burn out early; run too slow and you will quite literally be an also-ran. So Phil and I, who have been running for years, were there for the same reason there is a mechanical bunny at a greyhound track. We were pacesetters.

An important key to pacesetting—one that just about every endurance athlete knows—is that the ideal pace is generally the most rapid one at which you can still comfortably carry on a conversation. So talking is good.

And that's why I fell back into stride with my two friends and asked, "Tell me what?"

Phil shrugged. At least I think he shrugged. Either that or he'd just stepped funny on a seam in the blacktop.

"It's that guy at work I told you about. Marty."

"The one you brought to Westwinds a couple of weeks ago?"

"That's the one."

It was not unusual for our conversation to turn to church and spirituality. I had pastored a large church for nearly a decade and a half before taking on an international speaking and consulting ministry. I had even baptized Phil, for that matter.

"He seemed like a pretty nice guy," I said. "Pretty garrulous." I pulled in a breath, a deep one, through my nose. The roadway was starting to rise again, and *garrulous* was a bigger word than I wanted to use at our present speed. Did I mention that Jess had finished tenth in her last marathon? So we were going at a pretty good clip.

I caught my wind. "You work with Marty, right?"

"Uh-huh. He's in the office next to mine. We usually grab lunch together. But lately, he's been—well—ducking me. I've asked him to get together with me several times over the past few days, and he's always had something else going on."

I knew where this was going.

"You didn't shove him a gospel tract or something, did you?"

Phil snorted. "Of course not. But I did . . . well, I did *tell* him about the gospel."

Jess surged slightly ahead. Taking the hint, Phil and I picked up our pace a little. We rounded a turn and met with a slight headwind. I pulled ahead and let Jess and Phil fall in behind me. We'd be running in this direction all the way back to my place, and we would take turns pulling and drafting—either blocking the wind or running in the lee of the lead runner.

"So," I called back over my shoulder, "what did you tell him?"

"You know," Phil said, "that . . . um . . . that he was a sinner and Jesus died for his sins, and how . . . well, how he needed Jesus."

I glanced back again. "In other words, you told him he's totally inadequate, and you've got the cure."

"Now, come on . . ." Phil blustered. But after a long moment of silence, he conceded, "Well—yeah. I guess I did."

"Then no wonder."

"But Phil's *got* to do that," Jess pointed out, her voice steady. I envied her. Even without looking, I could tell that she was fresh, not even slightly winded. The woman has lungs. "We're commanded to do that. It's in the Bible."

"It is?"

"Mark 16:15."

She said it so quickly that she must have been primed for this conversation. I wondered why it had taken her 4.7 miles to bring it up.

"Jesus said to go into all the world and preach the good news to everyone, everywhere," she concluded.

"Okay." I nodded out of habit, even though all they could see was the back of my head. "And what's the good news?"

"That's a silly question, Ron. It's in the next verse," Jess said. "Anyone who believes and is baptized will be saved, but anyone who refuses to believe will be condemned. Jesus died for your sins. That's the good news. Everybody knows that."

"Everybody does," I agreed. "But what if everybody's wrong?"

I sensed a change in our running formation and glanced back over my shoulder.

I was running by myself.

I stopped and turned around. Fifty feet back, Phil was bent over with his hands on both knees, huffing, and Jess was just sort of standing there, glaring at me.

"It's cool," I assured them. "I haven't turned atheist. I haven't even turned universalist. And I can explain. But first, come on, you two; we have another half mile. Let's pick it up again before we cool down."

There's a secret to making a decent egg-white omelet. To start with, forget the milk. No, not even skim milk, or *organic* skim milk. Milk in any form has no business—ever—in an omelet pan.

The temperature is vital, too. So is aeration. You have to whip the eggs like there's no tomorrow, but not so much that you wind up with a pastry topping.

Jess and Phil have long since learned to leave me alone in the kitchen. So, before I fired up the stove, I walked into my study, pulled down a couple of different Bible versions, and gave one to each of them, saying, "Have a run through these while I get breakfast ready. You're looking for two verses: one saying that the gospel—the *good news*—is that Christ died for your sins, and another one saying you're supposed to buttonhole people and say, 'Okay, there are these four spiritual laws . . .'"

I heard the two of them muttering as I sautéed some onions, mushrooms, and cilantro. There was a "here" from Jess and an "uh-huh" or two from Phil as I poured the beaten egg whites into a couple of omelet pans. By the time I set their plates before them, they both had a pencils-down, test-over look on their faces.

"Okay," Jess said, tapping a page of the New Testament. "It says here that—"

"Hang on a sec," I told her. "I need to get my omelet off the stove."

I came back with my plate, set it down, sat myself down, and said, "Let's pray." As I offered thanks for the food, my two friends had a look of relief on their faces. I could almost read their thoughts: *Well, he's still praying, so he can't be* that *far gone.*

"Let's eat this while it's still hot," I said. "Then we can tackle the deep theological questions, okay?"

We discussed the morning's run while we finished our breakfast, but I hadn't even set my fork all the way down before Jess said, "First Corinthians 15:3" (NLT).

"All right." I nodded. "What does it say?"

"'I passed on to you what was most important and what had also been passed on to me. Christ died for our sins.'"

"And the end of that second sentence?"

"Huh?" Jess glanced down. "Oh, '. . . just as the Scriptures said.'"

“Which may be the most important part of the verse,” I said. I turned to Phil. “What did you find?”

Phil skewed his mouth to one side, the way he does when he’s thinking things over. “Well, I was looking here in the third chapter of John. You know, the part about Nicodemus? This is verse 3, in the NIV: ‘I tell you the truth, no one can see the kingdom of God unless he is born again.’ Seems to me that Jesus is witnessing there.”

“Is he?” I asked. “Or is he just answering a question—or was there even a question asked? I think the Nicodemus passage may be a discussion for another morning run; we need to talk about that passage sometime.”

Jess and Phil looked at each other.

“In the stories of Jesus’ life, the salvation parts—all of them—are answers to direct questions,” I said. “People ask Jesus or a disciple to tell them about salvation, and they get an honest answer. But if *salvation* is the ‘good news’ that we read about, then why do people have to drag it out of Jesus and the disciples? Or look at Acts 16:17, NLT. In that account, a girl is tagging along behind Paul and Silas, and she is shouting, ‘These men are servants of the Most High God, and they have come to tell you how to be saved.’ But Paul, instead of saying, ‘Uh-huh—sing it, sister; we got the power,’ turns around and commands an evil spirit to leave the girl. So, apparently, Paul recognizes that emphasizing salvation is a misdirection—not to mention an irritant. Which it is.”

“It is?” Jess and Phil responded in stereo.

I gathered the plates and took them to the sink. “We need to think of these verses in the context of the time when they were written. We need to think in the mind-set of the ancients.”

“They were wimps,” Jess said.

Okay, this requires an explanation. As most schoolkids and all marathoners know, in 490 BC, the fate of ancient Greece hung on the outcome of the Battle of Marathon because Marathon was the final obstacle between the invading Persians and the city of Athens. Naturally, the Athenian rulers were on pins and needles, waiting to hear how the battle would turn out. And because this news was so crucial, a Greek warrior named Pheidippides was dispatched from the battlefield to bring the news of the Greek victory to Athens. He ran the roughly twenty-five miles from Marathon, gave his report, and then promptly died of exhaustion.

When Jess had run her first marathon, Phil and I were waiting for her as she crossed the finish line. She had been tired, but was by no means totally exhausted. After she'd caught her breath from the finishing sprint, she looked happily at Phil and me and declared, "Pheidippides was a wimp!"

When Jess made her remark about the ancients being wimps, I laughed and said, "Okay, agreed. All wimps. Every one of them. But wimps with their own cultural roots, which were very different from ours."

Setting the dishes in the sink, I walked back into my study, retrieved a book from my shelf, and came out reading the text:

> The providence which has ordered the whole of our life, showing zeal and concern, has ordained the most perfect consummation for human life by giving it to [him] . . . by filling him with virtue for doing the work of a benefactor among men, and by sending in him, as it were, a savior for us and those who come after us, to make war to cease, to create peace everywhere. . . . The birthday of the god was the beginning for the world of the gospel that has come to men through him.[1]

I looked up. "That's a pretty good translation of a birth announcement that was written in *koine* Greek, the same form of basic, universal Greek used in the New Testament. Whose birth do you think it announces?"

Jess gave me a look like, *What kind of softball question is that?* "The birth of Jesus, of course," she said.

"Wrong," I said with a smile. "It's the official birth announcement of Octavian—otherwise known as Caesar Augustus—written almost six decades before the birth of Christ."

I showed them the page and they scoured it, looking for an error, a footnote, anything that might lessen the confusion. Finally, Phil looked up. "But it says *savior.*"

"Which, in ancient times, meant about the same thing as *victor,*" I said. "You probably know that when a king or a general in those days captured a city or defeated an enemy at war, it was his right to burn the city to the ground and kill everyone in it. A quick survey of the Old Testament shows that such things happened with absolutely numbing regularity. But as victor, he could also decide to spare the city and its inhabitants, which made him their *savior*. In other words, he kept them from a death they deserved."

"Exactly," said Jess. "Which was why people had to know about Jesus. They knew they needed to be saved from the consequences of their sins."

"Did they?" I sat down at the table again. "Let's think about this. Jesus conducted a roving ministry, walking around Palestine—a Jewish state occupied by a foreign power. The final destruction of the Temple had not yet taken place. In fact, Herod the Great—the same Herod who tried to hunt down Jesus when he was an infant, and the father of the Herod who was ruling when Jesus was crucified—had rebuilt the Temple as a means of pacifying the Jews to make them more accepting of their Roman rulers. So, if you had been in an argument with your neighbor, or you hadn't met with your *minyan,* your synagogue leaders, for a few days, you could set things right by going into the Temple and making a donation or offering a sacrifice."

I turned to Phil. "What would you say if I told you I had a great device to keep the elephants off your lawn. Would you be interested in one?"

"I'd say I don't have a problem with elephants on my lawn."

"That's right. And a Jew in the first century would have given a similar reply to someone who said, 'I've got the remedy for your sins.' Jews of this period didn't see themselves as sinful. They were doing a pretty good job of living by the rules; and when they broke one, they could offer a sacrifice at the Temple. That's why Jesus and the disciples didn't lead with the salvation story, as in 'This is how you get to heaven.' They knew they wouldn't find any takers."

"But Jesus died for our sins!" Phil insisted.

"He did," I agreed. "But stay with me for a second." I looked at Phil and Jess and asked, "Is slavery wrong?"

They nodded.

"Would you agree that it's a sin?"

They nodded again.

"So the plantation owners of the antebellum American South—were they sinners?"

"Sure," Phil said.

"Then, in that case, every Union soldier who perished during the Civil War died for slave owners' sins. Does that make all those soldiers the same as Jesus?"

"Of course not!" Jess realized she had almost shouted her reply, and added, "Sorry."

"Jesus was not the only Jew to die on a tree in those days," I said. "Thousands did. It was the most common means of executing people who were seen as enemies of the Roman state—non-Romans, at least. So, although his death gained some notoriety, it didn't make him unique. And even though John 3:16 makes it clear that Jesus died to create a pathway to God, that isn't the good news we're talking about when we read the New Testament. In fact, I'm not even sure 'good news' works as a translation in this day and age. It's more of a 'breaking story' or 'headline news.'"

Jess and Phil looked at each other, and then at me.

"So," Jess asked after a moment of silence, "what *is* the headline news?"

Not many people ask Jess's question: "What is the headline news?" or even "What is the gospel?" In fact, I had never asked either question myself. I assumed I knew the answer.

I was part of the church. I was studying Scripture. I thought I knew it all. But when I talked to people outside the Christian bubble, people who didn't believe or who were searching for a deeper spirituality, I hit a brick wall every time. It was as if I had a weak cell-phone signal and static was chopping up my words. Does that sound familiar to you? That's what Jess and Phil were experiencing with Marty.

When you hit so many brick walls, eventually you've got to question whether you truly understand the message yourself—or whether you really know how to communicate it. When I found myself hitting brick walls, I started a search to understand what was going on. I read. I talked to people. I listened. This book contains the results of my search.

Maybe you're on the same journey I've been on. You know something isn't working, but you're not quite sure what. I invite you to see what I've learned. On the other hand, maybe you're on a much different journey than I am. Maybe you're burned out by church. Or maybe you've experienced a lot of *static* when you've talked about God or spirituality with other people. Maybe you're searching for something, but you're not sure what. I hope that some of the lessons I've learned on my journey will help you see more clearly what you're ultimately searching for in life.

2

Baggage

My conversation with Phil and Jess is one I've had many, many times, in one form or another. It is the same conversation I've had with several mentors in my life who helped me make sense of some things that just didn't add up for me. Not long into my formal studies, it became obvious to me that much of what I had unquestioningly adopted as "gospel truth" contained all sorts of anomalies, unexplained loose ends, and far too many trite and thin explanations. The Bible, as I had come to understand it, even in the context of earning a biblical studies degree at a Christian university, didn't seem to sing with the richness and depth I thought would be consistent with the heart of God, the Creator of the universe.

Many of my questions were intensely personal. I wanted to understand how we could have such good news, yet have it come across so poorly. So I had lots of conversations, during lots of late nights with lots of professors and mentors, who I'm sure at times were sick and tired of seeing me come yet again with all my questions that wouldn't yield to easy answers. But, for me, so much was at stake in those dialogues.

I had come to recognize that we as Christians used language that other people either did not understand, or that pushed all the wrong buttons with them. As a result, we had little opportunity to have extended conversations about spiritual things with our friends and neighbors.

Let me illustrate what I mean by language that pushes all the wrong buttons.

First of all, we have to understand that language, by its very nature, is subjective. When you hear the phrase *old barn,* for example, what image comes to mind? Instantly, and without any prompting from me, you began searching your memory banks for a "photo" of an old barn. The exact picture that you accessed in your memory archives depends on your past and current life experience.

So, what does the phrase *old barn* bring to your mind? Is it a memory from childhood, when you and a friend explored an abandoned old barn that became a secret clubhouse or a place for hiding treasures? Maybe you grew up on a farm and have firsthand knowledge of old barns, or perhaps you pictured a photo spread in *Architectural Digest* showing a spectacular home created from a renovated old barn. Maybe the first image that came to mind was from last night's rerun of *Little House on the Prairie* that your seven-year-old daughter was watching, or the DVD rental of *Cold Mountain* you watched this past weekend. The point is that whatever image came to mind, your understanding of the phrase *old barn* is based entirely on your life experience. If you had never seen an old barn, your memory banks would be empty, and the phrase would have no meaning to you. The words we use have no raw definitions. Instead, from our life experiences we fill up "mental containers"—containers of understanding and meaning—that we call words. And because your life experience is different from my life experience, the connotations of words—our understanding of what those words mean—will vary from person to person.

Some definitions and images from the past are innocuous or pleasant. But others conjure up a whole range of uncomfortable emotions. For example, if you were visiting your grandparents' farm when their barn caught fire, and you watched it go up in flames, killing some of your grandpa's prized cattle, then the phrase *old barn* will evoke entirely different images and emotions for you than it does for me.

So here is an important lesson: Not only do words and phrases evoke images from our complex archives of experience, but they also tap into our emotions and, in some cases, create involuntary responses.

What is true for an old barn is also true for the words and phrases we use to talk about Christianity. When we use words such as *gospel, salvation, repentance,* and *sin,* we need to be aware that the people we're talking to may not have the same understanding of these words that we do. If we grew up in a conservative Baptist home, for example, the views we have toward various Christian concepts will be different from the views of someone who grew up in a Catholic home or who was agnostic toward God but rigorously committed to logic, rationality, and high integrity. For someone who has had a bad experience with Christians or Christianity, these words may evoke negative emotions that get in the way of our ability to talk to them about Jesus. At the very least, we have to be aware that our differences in understanding may create *static* in our communication.

Before we take a closer look at some specific examples of this type of static, I need to mention another issue that is just as important as the idea that the language we use is loaded with baggage—namely, that many times our own understanding of the concepts we are trying to communicate is flawed, incomplete, or downright wrong. This may be hard to swallow, but frankly, it's true.

I came to an interesting *aha* moment a few years ago that was both liberating and quite embarrassing. I realized one day that I had come to believe I was about 97 percent accurate in what I held to be doctrinally true. In other words, I acknowledged that I may have been wrong about a few details, but certainly no more than about 3 percent.

Can you believe it?

I am totally ashamed to admit it today, but I really thought I had God figured out. So, there's lesson number one: When pursuing knowledge—especially knowledge about the infinite God—arrogance must be carefully guarded against.

I quickly recognized that I was not alone. I was a product of the academy, where a premium was placed on being right, ready, and full of insight. At some level, I was merely reflecting the values commonly taught at Bible schools and seminaries around the globe. The problem with this sort of posture—this sort of "certainty"—is that over time it becomes impervious to change, fresh insight, or new understanding. Before long, we move from being learners (which is the real meaning of the Greek word for *disciple* in the New Testament) to becoming protectors—protectors of "what we have always believed."

In retrospect, my attitude was completely laughable. How could I, a mortal and finite person, be 97 percent right about anything, much less about the mind and actions of an infinite God? Yet that is the view of reality I held. When I came to realize that my need to be right or to have it all figured out could be replaced by the far better and more humble disposition of *curiosity,* my entire life changed, and the biggest changes were spiritual ones.

I once heard the eminent New Testament scholar N. T. Wright say he is pretty certain that 70 percent of what he believes is wrong; he just isn't sure which 70 percent. Now that's liberating. We can all admit that we are human, which means we get things wrong and we don't completely understand God or our world. That is something I wish I had learned prior to pursuing my biblical studies degree, but better late than never.

All genuine learning requires a tentative disposition—tentative in the sense that I must hold open the possibility that the thoughts I have and the positions I hold may need to be adjusted, revised, or even discarded in favor of more complete understandings. Preserving this level of openness is exceedingly difficult, and yet it is the basis of all true learning. I need to be open to the possibility that God may want to teach me new things—things I hadn't considered or even imagined in the past.

God is bigger than my thoughts. That sounds rather obvious, but I have to admit it's a relatively new posture for me. Over the past several years, I have come to realize that I am primarily a reactive listener. I hear what someone says, and if it doesn't basically square with what I already believe, which of course is *the truth,* I either dismiss what they've said as irrelevant or go inside myself to start crafting a rebuttal.

Are you laughing? C'mon, you've done it a million times yourself, just as I have. We do it in marriage, with our kids, with our friends and neighbors, and with anyone else we're trying to convince. We're not very good listeners. But we are consummate correctors and persuaders. To let someone else's position seep into our thought structure and potentially topple one of our core beliefs? Well, that would be disconcerting and uncomfortable. To look at challenging ideas and thoughts as tools that God is using to refine our thinking? For many of us, that would be painful to do.

Phil and Jess were feeling some unsettling emotions about some of the ideas we were talking about. I was beginning to crowd some of their long-held positions and traditions, and as a result, they were experiencing a little vertigo. I had a pretty good idea how they were feeling because I had experienced a lot of disorientation myself as I began to grow and learn how to be more adept at the whole "spiritual conversation" thing. And in the process, I have come to understand better who Jesus is, how the New Testament presents the Big Story, and how I can communicate it best. The biggest adjustment in my learning process has been the move from reactive listening to suspending judgment. Now when I hear new things, things that don't square with my current understanding, I have to pause and say to myself, "Ron, stop! These people are intelligent, and they are sincere about what they believe. Not only that, but they seem to have great insights and motives. So with all that going for them, if they hold this position, maybe you need to dig into their thinking a little bit to understand why."

Notice this doesn't mean I check out mentally or am uncritical or undiscerning. What it does mean is that I make a commitment to be sure I understand what people are saying, instead of instantly assuming it's my duty to demonstrate why their thinking is all wrong.

I admit that this has been a big step for me, and a very humbling one. It has also brought about a powerful shift in my own personal journey. When I decide to fuel my curiosity with the question of why someone else would hold or believe something so totally outside my comfort zone, I find whole new ways of seeing the world. Some of these new ways I can accept and integrate into my thought world, whereas others I place on the shelf for possible future consideration.

Nowhere is this posture more important or powerful than in the area of our relationship with God and our understanding of him. Of all the topics we could talk about that would include vast amounts of information, complex ideas, and texts from other cultures and historical periods, we could hardly pick a more rich subject than God and the Bible. A lifetime of learning would never be enough to understand the mysteries of God. Would it?

3

The Not-So-Good News

Some years ago, perhaps as far back as the 1960s, it became clear that the word *gospel* had become little more than a Christian code word that had picked up all sorts of extra baggage in the culture at large. In light of this trend, some Christ followers began substituting the term *good news,* a modern phrase that captures the essential meaning of *gospel.* This substitution was an effort to move the conversation about the gospel into an arena of greater initial neutrality. The idea was that using terminology without a lot of negative connotations attached would help people keep their reactions at bay so they might continue listening and be open to learning more about God.

The same principle is equally valid today. If we use words that provoke reactions based on definitions or connotations of those words that are inaccurate or even wrong, then we are doing a poor job of communicating. If, rather than turning people off right away with our opening remarks, we can use a word or phrase with less freight and negative baggage, then I'm all for it. However, we have to make sure that the words we substitute haven't themselves become so defined by our culture that they instantly ring "churchy" or negative.

For many people, the words *gospel* or *good news* don't sound all that good. That's because the gospel message, as it is often presented, goes something like this: "You are going to hell unless you respond to this good news."

Let's face it, that's not very persuasive, and it's a bit oxymoronic.

How is that good news?

I have struggled with that question for a long time, and I have grappled with an even more insidious version that is tantamount to a bait and switch: "God loves you and has a wonderful plan for your life—but if you don't respond appropriately, you will burn in hell when you die." Wow, that softens the blow a bunch, doesn't it? I'm no different from any other Christ follower, trying to understand what Jesus came to do and the message he came to communicate. But if the gospel truly is good news, then it ought to be good news for everybody—for you, me, the Muslim guy at the gym, the Hindu doctor from India whose kids play with yours in the neighborhood, and the single mom who escaped from an abusive relationship and is struggling to make ends meet.

I can remember being exposed to the writings of Leonard Ravenhill, the great prayer warrior, during my college days in Oklahoma. I deeply respected his writings, and on numerous Friday evenings I would drive down to Lindale, Texas, to attend a prayer meeting he held. Ravenhill was big on holiness, and big on the fire and hell that would befall those who didn't respond. At one post-prayer-meeting talk at his house, he introduced me to the sermons of Jonathan Edwards. Though I had heard of this great revivalist and well-known preacher of the 1700s, I had never read any of his sermons. In response to a question that one of us students asked about the harshness of the holiness message and how that was actually good news, Ravenhill pulled out of a drawer a tattered and yellowed document that looked as if it could have been the original sermon (though I knew it couldn't have been). He began to read passionately what is arguably the most famous of Edwards's sermons, "Sinners in the Hands of an Angry God."

> The God that holds you over the pit of hell, much as one holds a spider or some loathsome insect over the

> fire, abhors you and is dreadfully provoked; his wrath towards you burns like fire; he looks upon you as worthy of nothing else, but to be cast into the fire; he is of purer eyes than to bear to have you in his sight; you are ten thousand times more abominable in his eyes than the most hateful venomous serpent is in ours. You have offended him infinitely more than ever a stubborn rebel did his prince; and yet it is nothing but his hand that holds you from falling into the fire every moment.

I wonder how much this sort of depiction of God has influenced the view of the gospel that is now prevalent in our American cultural conversation. Though no single sermon has the power to set the tenor of 250 years of history, I can't help but wonder whether "Sinners in the Hands of an Angry God" has had an impact—a negative impact—that people like Marty, Phil's colleague from work, feel in a trickle-down sort of way.

My own story of first hearing the gospel is quite simple and not at all unusual. The details I am about to recount are the recollections of an impressionable nine-year-old. But of course, that is how all history is recorded, isn't it?—our personal perspectives on events that molded and shaped our opinions and our lives, sometimes permanently.

I grew up in a nominal Presbyterian and Catholic family. We attended services at both churches every weekend, which was pure torture for me as a kid. When I was nine, I had an opportunity to attend a new camp that had just been built in Michigan. (Today, some thirty-five years later, this camp is one of the coolest Christian camps in the nation. People fly in from all over so their kids can chill there for a week.) This camp was all about "making the gospel known" to young boys and girls. As this was my very first exposure to any of these ideas, whatever they told me was, quite simply, going to be swallowed hook, line, and sinker as the gospel truth (yes, pun intended). After a couple days of camp, the gospel and how you entered into it was quite clear.

The setting is also important. Although Christian themes were interspersed through the other things that went on during the day, it was in the evening, around the campfire, when we were given the full story—the story of the gospel, that is.

And so the story goes . . . even as a young child, you were a sinner. Though you had probably done nothing outlandish or horrible, like kill anyone, the fact that you wanted to be nasty to your brother or sister, or stole a piece of gum from the corner store, was proof positive you were already a sinner. And those childish things, it was noted, were really not any different from killing someone, because it was all sin in God's eyes. The selfish little boy who didn't accept the gospel and the killer on death row who didn't accept the gospel were in exactly the same boat, going to hell.

The wages of sin were illustrated in dramatic fashion. The campfire itself was a mini-illustration of the sort of thing that God had prepared for those who chose to persist in their sin. Thus, I later came to understand, the campfire setting was designed for dramatic effect. You see, there was a huge lake of fire that everyone would be cast into at the end of their lives unless they knew Jesus. Knowing Jesus was the only way not to be banished to the fires of hell. Knowing Jesus was important because he came and lived a sinless life, died on a cross—a death I should have died—and then was raised from the dead so that I, too, could be resurrected and go to heaven instead of hell.

This incredibly dramatic story was presented as the gospel. After we had listened to the story and sung a few songs, our cabin counselor would ask us whether we wanted to go to heaven or to the lake of fire called hell. If we wanted to go to heaven, we were asked to pray a particular prayer, which we recited back to the counselor, and that would seal the deal.

Question: How many nine-year-old boys do you think preferred the lake of fire to the prospect of heaven? Well, your guess is right—not one. Why would anyone choose death, suffering, and horrible torment? They had illustrated the horrors of hell by inviting us to inch ever closer to the campfire to see how much just getting close to it could hurt, let alone considering what it would be like to actually live in the fire forever. You can get even the most ADHD-afflicted nine-year-old's attention with that experience.

If you are at all familiar with what I now refer to as conversional, point-of-sale Christianity, you know that various forms and degrees of what I have just recounted play out in churches, at summer camps, and over the airwaves every week of the year.

If you come from an evangelical Christian background, you may have similar categories in your mind. For many, the gospel has been defined as a message about the world's sinful state, God's remedy in sending Jesus, and the need to repent at an altar of some sort, followed by the culminating act of reciting a prayer. Many have heard this rendition of the gospel and responded to it, and it has been a life-altering experience. For others, the same experience was a decisive, and even nasty, turnoff.

I could imagine what had stopped Marty from wanting to hear any more about Jesus. But I wanted to know exactly why he was so opposed to talking about God. So the next time Phil and I met for our favorite steak fajita lunch at Chili's, I asked him what he knew.

"Well, I think his family was pretty much antagonistic about things spiritual and about God," Phil said, "so Marty was left to his own devices. He lived with his mother after his parents split up, and she was apparently hostile about the idea of God. His father, on the other hand, was highly intellectual and had for the most part reasoned God out of existence. He had some friends in high school who tried to share the gospel with him, but he was kind of turned off by the high-school youth group. He said they just confirmed what his father had always said about Christianity being narrow."

"And what happened in college?"

"Well, I think that when he attended Northwestern, he was approached by two sharp athletes who appeared to be friendly and supportive. But it didn't take long for them to try to recruit him for their campus ministry group. I think that made him pretty skeptical about Christians who seem friendly but have an agenda."

"So Marty had no church attendance or Christian camp experience to shape his understanding of Christian concepts," I interjected, "but he did have the life experiences of those around him, some uncomfortable encounters with a few Christians, and probably the influence of media."

"Oh, yeah. Big time. On more than one occasion he has told me his opinion of TV evangelists, which is not good. And he has his perspectives on other so-called Christian media. The problem is that few if any of these outlets portray a balanced, positive view of things as they are."

"Or maybe that *is* how things really are in the Christian world," I said as I reached for my glass of iced tea. "Whatever the case, that's Marty's archived experience, and it influences him every bit as much as my campfire experiences influenced me when I was a kid. If his parents were antagonistic or indifferent toward the idea of God and his friends were always trying to sell him on the gospel, the fair and factual assumption is that Marty isn't coming into the conversation with even a neutral ear; he is definitely biased and skeptical."

"Yeah, I guess I didn't think about that." Phil stared past me. I could tell he was mentally re-creating his first conversation with Marty.

"What's important to acknowledge, Phil, is that there is no 'neutral ear.' Everybody's perspective is biased, filled with history and background, and loaded with personal experience. This is something I think we all struggle to acknowledge. I know I have."

"So, are you saying there's no objective truth?" I could hear in Phil's voice that he was starting to wonder about me again.

"No, what I'm saying is that nobody has an objective perception of things. We all have our assumptions based on where we've come from, and we hold on to those assumptions as if they were objective truth. I think I've learned more about God and Jesus and more about how to communicate that knowledge in the last several years when I have been most willing to fully embrace my ignorance and lack of knowing. There's a great line I heard from Daniel Boorstin, who was the Librarian of Congress for several years and who wrote several great books about human history. He said that barriers to progress in human history were never due to ignorance but to 'illusions of knowledge.'" I took a bite of my fajita to allow Boorstin's phrase to sink in.

"Think about it, Phil. Don't you want to live and act as if you *know*? I lived my life that way. I always thought I had it all figured out and had every angle on any issue. But the truth is, I'm prideful. Pride prevents learning, and refusing to learn calcifies my thinking so I become hardened and arrogant. I believe this attitude about knowledge is one of the greatest impediments to progress in our spiritual lives, and not just that, but it also prevents learning how to help people like Marty on their spiritual journey."

"I'm not saying I have it all figured out," Phil said, "but isn't it important that we share the truth of the gospel with people? I mean, how else is Marty going to find the truth?"

"The problem is that when Marty hears the word *gospel* it doesn't conjure up images of anything good, positive, necessary, or helpful. If anything, he sees this gospel thing as militant, imperialistic, intolerant, and arrogant—which makes every Christian sound to him like Archie Bunker on *All in the Family*—remember that show?"

"I used to watch it every week when I was a kid," Phil said.

"On the other hand," I continued, "what little bit Marty has heard about Jesus the person probably sounds to him more like Gandhi: patient, loving, nonjudgmental, open, tolerant—in short, all the things the Christians he has run into aren't. So it's not surprising that he concludes *gospel* is shorthand for 'run the other direction as fast as you can.'"

I can't say I blame Marty. I can't even say he lives with an inaccurate characterization of Christianity. I can't say his judgments are unfair, skewed, or off base. Marty sees

Christianity and the gospel in the way we have presented it, in the way *I have presented it.* In many respects, I empathize with Marty *and* with those who tell that rendition of the gospel story. Because you know what? They are only retelling the very same story they themselves have heard. How do I know? Because it is what I and countless other pastors have been doing across the country and around the world for years. We pass on what we have received. Unfortunately, we come to find out, the people from whom we learned this version of the story were doing the same thing—passing on what *they'd* been told. And pretty soon we realize we are just like the first graders in the line of kids who are whispering in the ear of the person in front of them. What starts out being, "Please pass the pepper for my hamburger" becomes, "Peas placed on paper make a hand burn" by the time it has been whispered down the line. The resulting sentence has portions that are understandable, but as a representation of the original statement? Well, there are at least some letters in common.

I wish I could say that Marty is simply a victim of immature campus ministry initiatives or unfair TV portrayals or an overzealous youth pastor in high school. But we all know that isn't true.

I would also love to say that my own camp experience and Marty's cultural observations are unique. But after pastoring a large church for nearly twenty years and working with other church leaders for several more years, I am convinced that these are common experiences, common understandings, and common ways of perceiving what modern, Western Christianity calls "the gospel."

4

Of Kings and Kramer

When missionaries are called to work with a distant people group, the first thing they realize is that the message they want to convey must be translated into terms the people will understand. It is up to the missionaries to learn the language, customs, metaphors, and culture of the people so that they can translate the message in the proper ways. The missionaries have two distinct goals: (1) to accurately communicate their message, and (2) to make sure the message is accurately understood by the people. Even if they faithfully articulate their message, they can still be 100 percent *ineffective* if the people hearing the message understand something different from what the missionaries intend to communicate.

The same principle applies in our own culture, even when both parties are fluent in English. If *they* don't understand what *we* are trying to communicate, then what we are saying is ineffective.

Let me propose a "what if."

What if the meaning of the Greek word *euangelion,* which is translated in most English versions of the Bible as "gospel," is more accurately reflected in the phrase *breaking headline* or *newsflash*? Think about what this would mean to the conversation between Phil and his colleague Marty. Let's say that Phil has never uttered the word *gospel* because he knows that Marty has all sorts of background and baggage surrounding it that would short-circuit any conversation Phil tried to initiate. Instead, what if Phil spoke of a newsflash or a breaking headline? Would his conversation with Marty have a greater chance of getting off the ground? Without getting ahead of ourselves too much, shouldn't the message we share *feel* like a newsflash? Shouldn't it have the intensity of "We interrupt this program for a breaking news story . . . "? Unfortunately, for many people—and I include myself here—the gospel as currently defined does not hold that sort of intensity or riveting interest.

Let me suggest why. We have reduced the gospel and abbreviated the story. We have decided that "the gospel" is all about getting people a seat in the heavenly stadium. But what if tickets on the fifty-yard line in heaven are at best a by-product of the gospel and the newsflash is something quite different? Is it possible that the breaking headline has a lot more backstory to it than we've been letting on?

To understand the urgency of a newsflash, we have to know the backstory. You know what I mean, the juicy details that fill in the background so the story has some depth. Think here of the personal interviews and hometown stories of Olympic athletes that are shown on TV before the athletes perform; or the video features that tell us a little bit about the people auditioning on *American Idol;* or the stories of crisis and challenge in the lives of the family chosen for this week's *Extreme Makeover: Home Edition.* These are the backstories, the background details that make the *full* story more real and understandable.

So, instead of asking, "What does the word *gospel* mean to me?" or, "How should I share the gospel today?" I'm suggesting that we pursue the question from the viewpoint of where it all began. Before we try to figure out what the word means to us today, let's discover the backstory.

I have to confess that at first it was very difficult for me to get a clear view of the backstory of certain biblical words. I had been to seminary. I had a systematic theology that directed me toward certain interpretations and understandings. I thought I had it all figured out. I had immersed myself in learning Greek, for crying out loud. So this was some tough sledding. It wasn't until I realized that there is always more to learn and that unless I was willing to acknowledge that much of what I believed or understood was, at best, incomplete and provisional, I would never learn anything new, never grow, never experience what it is like to have new insights that would set me free.

When we look at the words in the Bible, we are actually dealing with at least two different worlds that are coming together: the biblical world and the cultural world into which Jesus came. In other words, there were two converging backstories. When Jesus spoke, there were details that would be understood easily by his first-century audience, figures of speech and other nuances that they would automatically be familiar with. For us, being removed from the first century by two thousand years, a different language, and a totally different culture, we have a lot of missing pieces to uncover before we can reasonably say that we're getting the whole story. And we have a lot of gaps to fill in before we can say we're even close to being on the same footing as those who heard Jesus' teaching firsthand.

In the case of the word *gospel,* we have to start with an understanding of the Old Testament world before we can get a handle on what was going on in the New Testament when Jesus arrived on the scene. This idea throws some people for a loop. "How can we talk about the gospel in the Old Testament," they ask, "when the gospel is that Jesus died for our sins?"

Of course, this is exactly what we are investigating. Does Jesus' dying on the cross for our sins so that we can go to heaven reflect the story that people in the first century would have told when explaining the word *gospel*?

Let me quickly say that I am perfectly comfortable with the idea of people using the word *gospel,* from an in-house perspective, and having in mind some way of getting to heaven.

But let me add just as quickly that getting to heaven is not what Jesus, John the Baptist, or the apostle Paul seemed to have in mind when they used the word.

To say it another way, I don't want to imply that I think the "way of salvation" (to use the phrase so common in conservative Christian culture) is unimportant or that the use of the word *gospel* as shorthand for that is wrong. But I do want to say that because Jesus and Paul didn't use the word that way, we are creating unnecessary confusion, a confusion that often manifests itself in an abbreviated, incomplete story of what the word *gospel* actually means. Are you with me so far?

Most New Testament scholars would agree that the background for the word *gospel,* as used in the New Testament, is rooted in Isaiah 40–66, notably in chapters 40 and 52. Here's an example:

> Comfort, comfort my people, says your God. Speak tenderly to Jerusalem, and proclaim to her that her hard service has been completed, that her sin has been paid for, that she has received from the LORD's hand double for all her sins. A voice of one calling: "In the desert prepare the way for the LORD; make straight in the wilderness a highway for our God. Every valley shall be raised up, every mountain and hill made low; the rough ground shall become level, the rugged places a plain. And the glory of the LORD will be revealed, and all mankind together will see it. For the mouth of the LORD has spoken."
>
> A voice says, "Cry out." And I said, "What shall I cry?" "All men are like grass, and all their glory is like the flowers of the field. The grass withers and the flowers fall, because the breath of the LORD blows on them. Surely the people are grass. The grass withers and the flowers fall, but the word of our God stands forever." You who bring good tidings to Zion, go up on a high mountain. You who bring good tidings to Jerusalem, lift up your voice with a shout, lift it up, do not be afraid; say to the towns of Judah, "Here is your God!" See, the Sovereign LORD comes with power, and his arm rules for him. See, his reward is with him, and his recompense

> accompanies him. He tends his flock like a shepherd: He gathers the lambs in his arms and carries them close to his heart; he gently leads those that have young. (Isaiah 40:1-11)

In the last half of Isaiah (chapters 40–66), the prophet makes an intentional effort to show that a time was coming when God would return to Jerusalem (sometimes also called Zion), and he would rule and reign. Of course, this had been Israel's hope and expectation for a long time. The promise of someone from the line of David sitting on the throne of Israel forever had been given by God through the prophet Nathan (see 2 Samuel 7, especially verse 16). But don't miss a very important detail and a critical backstory element.

Notice in the opening few verses of Isaiah 40 that the prophet is writing to a group of Israelites who are anticipating the end of their exile. Isaiah's prophecy links the end of Israel's exile with the appearance of a figure who will announce himself as a "way preparer." Most of us are familiar with this passage in Isaiah because these are the verses quoted by John the Baptist as he prepares to baptize Jesus.

Isaiah is setting the stage for an incredible story climax: Israel has been in exile, scattered and away from their homeland, but that won't be forever. There will come a time when they will return from exile and will be rallied by someone who prepares the way. The context, says Isaiah, will be one where others may be ruling, but Israel could know that all men are like grass, and rulers are like the flowers of the grass—they wither, fall to the ground, and are blown away. The "way preparer," says Isaiah, will have "gospel" (translated as *good tidings* or *good news* in many English translations of the Bible, or as we've been saying here, a very important newsflash or a breaking headline), and here it is: God is coming to Zion (Jerusalem), and he will reign.

Isaiah established an expectation that a day would come when a way preparer would emerge; this would coincide with the children of Israel being rallied from exile; and the breaking headline, the gospel, the newsflash would be that whoever was in charge would wither away like the grass and God would be the reigning king. So when John the Baptist arrived on the scene and quoted Isaiah 40:3, you can imagine the reaction of the people. This sort of newsflash had major political, social, and lifestyle implications.

Think about the story that John's proclamation would have conjured up in the minds of the people. When someone quotes a familiar line or uses a metaphor or other image in a story, the assumption is that the audience will connect it to a mental picture, a series of events, or a story line.

I have tested this connection in scores of conference settings. If I am talking about TV and mention Kramer, for example, what comes to mind? Anyone who has seen the show *Seinfeld* will instantly visualize a particular character with his wild hair, his quirky sliding entrance into Jerry's apartment, and his wild mannerisms and facial expressions—all this from simply mentioning a name in a specific context. On the other hand, after actor Michael Richards, who portrays Kramer, made headlines in 2006 for his tirade at a comedy club, the mention of the name Kramer might bring to mind an entirely different image.

The point is that the simple mention of a number or a name can conjure up all kinds of ideas, feelings, and emotions. We do this in families all the time. We look at each other and say "Uncle Harry," and all sorts of family stories, embarrassing moments, or crazy situations come to mind. The word, name, or phrase is embedded in a story that operates as a framework of understanding. These are the "old barn" archives in our minds, filling up our understanding of various words.

Let's return our attention to Israel for a moment. They have been waiting for roughly four hundred years for the way preparer to appear. This expectation is part of the backstory for the whole nation of Israel. So, when John the Baptist quotes the opening lines of the most hopeful section of the Old Testament prophets, you can bet that a whole complex of ideas, expectations, and hopes came rushing to the surface in the hearts of the people. But Isaiah 40 is merely a prelude to the real clincher in Isaiah 52:7, which is arguably the most important passage for understanding the content of the newsflash that we call the gospel.

> How beautiful on the mountains are the feet of those who bring *good news,* who proclaim peace, who bring *good tidings,* who proclaim salvation, who say to Zion, "Your God reigns!" (emphasis added)

We have already done enough background work to understand the importance of this verse in the unfolding story that Isaiah is telling. But many people in the church—and this was true of me for many years—never grasp the larger story. We're used to quoting a verse here and a verse there, but few of us have the broad sweep of the entire story in our minds. Consequently, a verse in the middle of Isaiah 52 conjures up no connections, no story lines, no character resolution or plot climax. But not so for first-century Jews.

Many people of a certain generation are familiar with Isaiah 52:7 because it was the basis of a popular worship song in the late '70s and early '80s. But even in singing it, they overlooked the actual content of the gospel. What are the "good tidings" or "good news" expressed in Isaiah 52? That someone is coming who will die for your sins so you can go to heaven when you finally leave this planet? No. The newsflash here is that someone is coming who will say to Jerusalem, "God reigns! He's the king!"

Now, before you start trying to figure out how all this fits into your personal experience, whether good or bad, just hit the pause button for a moment, take a deep breath, and let's reflect. We're talking about things we all hold near and dear, so this isn't a journey where emotions are absent. But remember what is at stake. We are trying to learn how to communicate with people like Marty—your neighbors, your family, your work associates, or maybe yourself. We are trying to figure out how to communicate clearly and in nonhostile ways the most important story in human history. Even more, we are trying to make sure we tell the real story—and the full story—not a CliffsNotes version that leaves out important, plot-altering details, or a *Reader's Digest* excerpt. We are trying to invite people into the greatest story ever told, a story that can help them make sense of their personal stories, alter their life's trajectory, and find a destiny and connection in loving God and loving others.

5

A First-Century Newsflash

What would the listeners of Isaiah's gospel have heard when the prophet proclaimed "good tidings"? Remember, this is the gospel now. They would have heard that salvation has finally arrived. But be careful what you import into your understanding of the word *salvation,* because for most of us salvation is some sort of possession we get after reciting a prayer that ensures we are saved from the fires of hell and are given a seat in the afterlife, usually called heaven. But you know what? Neither Isaiah nor his listeners had any sense of that idea of salvation. Neither did John the Baptist and his listeners, nor Jesus and his. What they heard was a newsflash that promised an end to their exile and, most importantly, an end to being ruled by foreign powers. That's what salvation meant to them. Their king would finally be restored to the throne, and they would be free and would experience peace and wholeness.

Before we can look at the practical implications of these observations for our conversations with people like Marty, we have to understand some additional background that contributes to our understanding of the word *gospel* as used in the first century. This is the second of the two converging backstories, the social and political setting of Israel in the first century, which was greatly influenced by Roman rule and Greek culture. In the Greek world, the word *euangelion* ("gospel") was used to announce a great victory, an important birth, or the enthronement of a new king. You can see how this would be good news—a newsflash. But it is sometimes difficult for us in our contemporary Christian culture to equate this definition of *euangelion* with "the gospel," because we have already filled up our word containers for the word *gospel* with a bunch of other ideas.

I think most Christians probably assume that *gospel* is essentially a Christian word, or at least a word unique to the Bible. But the truth is that *euangelion* is a word that is also significant in both pagan and Jewish cultures.[1]

The coming of a new ruler or emperor meant the beginning of a new world order, and perhaps a time of new peace and prosperity. Never was this more true than in 31 BC when Augustus became the first Roman emperor after a long civil war.

Imagine awakening to shouts of a first-century newscaster. The sun is just rising, a gentle breeze blows through the window of your stone-walled bedroom, and the silence is broken by a young man shouting an announcement: "Here is the gospel . . ."

From an old inscription on a stone tablet from the city of Priene (ca. 9 BC), we have just such an announcement. This is the same inscription commemorating the birth of Caesar Augustus that I read to Phil and Jess the morning we had omelets at my house. It opens with the statement, "This is the beginning of the gospel." Here's part of the inscription:

> The providence which has ordered the whole of our life, showing zeal and concern, has ordained the most perfect consummation for human life by giving it to Augustus . . . by filling him with virtue for doing the work of a benefactor among men, and by sending in him, as it were, a savior for us and those who come after us,

> to make war to cease, to create peace everywhere. . . . The birthday of the god was the beginning for the world of the gospel that has come to men through him.

This inscription uses the very same word for "gospel" that we saw in the Greek Old Testament text of Isaiah 52 and the same word used numerous times in the New Testament, *euangelion* (or one of its derivatives). This announcement typifies a common source of "good news" in the ancient Greco-Roman world: an event marking the initiation of a new situation coming into the world.[2] The gospel was an announcement. And the content of that announcement, though varying in detail, had to do with kings and kingdoms, empires and conquerors, who was in charge, who ruled and reigned, and what Isaiah called salvation. These were all possible scenarios that would have come to mind for someone in first-century Israel who heard the word *gospel.*

When Isaiah recorded his prophecy, Israel was in exile, without a king, alienated, alone, and very aware of not experiencing the blessings that should have been theirs. So when the prophet foretold a time when someone would appear on a mountain with the up-to-the-minute newsflash "*Finally,* God reigns! *Finally,* God is the king!" you can imagine that the anticipation was significant.

For Americans, our lack of experience with living in a literal kingdom presents us with a difficult challenge when it comes to understanding the context of the "good news" in the Old and New Testaments. To complicate matters, and because we don't really understand the backstory, most of us have been trained to spiritualize the word *gospel.* We'll return to that issue a bit later, but in the meantime, let's look at some examples of what the Jews in the first century were *not* thinking about when they heard the word *gospel.*

First and foremost, they were *not* thinking about Jesus dying for their sins. Let's remember that throughout the Old

Testament and the first four books of the New Testament—at least until the very end—Jesus hadn't died yet. And no one would have connected the Crucifixion with the idea of a king ascending to power.

Second, when they heard the word *gospel,* they didn't think of a personal moment of conversion where they could have a transformational experience with God. And they didn't think of eternal bliss in an undisclosed location called heaven. When they heard the word *gospel,* either they were reminded of Isaiah's prophecy about the coming reign of God, or they heard the newsflash, the breaking news story, that a new caesar was ascending the throne.

You may be inclined to ask which backstory is the more legitimate for understanding the word *gospel* in the New Testament—the Old Testament backstory or the Greco-Roman social and political backstory. Do Isaiah's words of comfort and encouragement win out, or does the imperial proclamation about a secular king? Such an either/or dichotomy is a product of our modern, Western thinking. We always seek the one right answer. But what if both backstories serve as a foundation for how the word *euangelion* is to be understood? What if from the Old Testament we came to recognize that the long-awaited reign of a king is finally dawning? And from the Greco-Roman world we realized that the announcement of Jesus as King is a direct statement challenging the claims of Caesar? I'm suggesting that both stories are legitimate backdrops—and both stories are actually reinterpreted by Jesus in surprising, unexpected ways.

The opening lines of Paul's letter to the Romans provide a very interesting commentary on the convergence of these two streams of thought.

> Paul, a servant of Christ Jesus, called to be an apostle and set apart for the gospel of God—the gospel he promised beforehand through his prophets in the Holy Scriptures regarding his Son, who as to his human nature was a descendant of David, and who through the Spirit of holiness was declared with power to be the Son of God by his resurrection from the dead: Jesus Christ our Lord. (Romans 1:1-4)

When Paul says that he was set apart for the gospel of God, many people instantly hear, "Paul was called to deliver the message of Jesus dying for our sins." But do you notice how he clarifies what he means by "the gospel"? The gospel, the good news, the newsflash he has in mind is the one promised long ago and found in the prophets. Pick up any commentary on the New Testament or on Romans and you will find agreement that the passage Paul is pointing to here is Isaiah 52:7, "How beautiful on the mountains are the feet of those who bring good news, who proclaim peace, who bring good tidings, who proclaim salvation, who say to Zion, 'Your God reigns!'"

Now think about the context into which this letter was delivered. It was written to the Romans, who were living *in Rome.* Forgive me for stating the obvious, but it's important because who else lived in Rome? Who was running the show in Rome? Who was called Lord and King and Savior? That's right—the emperor, Caesar. So when Paul says there is some good news, and in an oblique way makes it clear he is referring to the kingship of Jesus, we can see both streams of thought flow together in this passage to give it a particular punch.

Now, before we jump to any conclusions, let's pause and acknowledge that this story sounds a bit strange to us. In fact, for many of us, it sounds inaccurate and maybe even wrong. I confess that the first time I grappled with these concepts, I had a hard time. I felt there must be some mistake, that the people introducing me to these concepts must surely be misguided. I now realize that my knee-jerk response was informed by my "old barn" archive of experiences. My understanding of the gospel was based on what I had seen and heard in the past, and I had never seen or heard the full backstory before.

I know my experience is not unusual, because I have helped others take the same journey. In talking about this topic for the past several years, I have found that people have a lot of emotional investment in making sure that what they have believed in the past is in fact correct. I have seen person after person first get defensive, and then courageously examine and explore the archives of experience that are informing their definitions. Then they begin the process of exploring whether this thing they have never heard before is perhaps a better, richer, more nuanced, more beautiful, more complete and engaging way to tell the story. What if the story we have looked at in this chapter is the gospel that first-century hearers of the words of Jesus perceived and understood? What if reading the story this way is the beginning of discovering a richer, more complete understanding?

I realize that I am challenging some long-held assumptions. I also realize that I am dealing with topics that are considered central to the Christian faith, and therefore the scrutiny and gravity surrounding this discussion is considerable. But I also know that as followers of Christ—the church, the only voice that Jesus opted to leave on this earth—you and I and others have a very real responsibility. For every Jess, Phil, and Marty story I could tell, I have ten more, and I bet you have a dozen more yourself. The burden of these chapters isn't to create a new formula or a system of code words to help us converse with people. My desires are more profound and subtle. I am hoping that through these discussions you will emerge with a deeper understanding of the often volatile words we use in talking to people about Jesus. And I hope that this heightened awareness will inevitably require you to broaden your understanding of the story God is telling us and inviting us into. A deeper understanding of God's big story invites us into the creative place of becoming translators and not just transmitters. Maybe you can come up with a better word or phrase for *gospel*. Maybe, tuned to this new frequency and with static at a minimum, you will be able to come up with all sorts of alternative ways to communicate effectively what

Jesus is saying—ways that will allow you to enter conversations with all sorts of people who are interested in spiritual things.

Let me also suggest that the historical material interspersed throughout this book, though by no means exhaustive, can help you in conversation. It may allow you to clear up confusion, adjust misunderstandings, and even agree with people when they make correct observations about the way many Christians "beat people over the head with the gospel."

The first time I heard that phrase, I just froze. What do you say to that? Do you try to defend that approach in order to protect God in some way? No. The truth is, that accusation is correct. So for us to be able to agree with people who have witnessed militant, mean-spirited ranting about the gospel is a powerful and true concession. But then also to be able to say, "Let me help reframe that idea for you" can be extremely helpful if done with gentleness and respect (see 1 Peter 3:15).

So, far from merely trying to come up with one-to-one word exchanges throughout this book, I am trying to lay the groundwork for us to consider what may be a host of alternatives, so that we can connect with all the people around us who are instinctively yearning for a connection to God—and may not even know it. All we can do is continue the conversation, propose some directions for the discussion, and hope that others join in and creatively work on alternatives. If the gospel really is good news and it comes with the urgency of a late-breaking newsflash, then we need to have the stories, the concepts, and the language to reflect both realities.

6

Lust and Legionnaires

When Phil called and asked me to arrive two hours early for a four o'clock cookout at his house, it probably should have tipped me off that he had an ulterior motive.

I did as I was asked, expecting a nice, civilized two hours of conversation and refreshment before the feast commenced. Instead, Phil invited me out to the patio, where he had wheeled his NASCAR-size toolbox next to a big Char-Grill box marked "Three-burner, 80,000 BTU Gas Grill."

Uh-huh.

Phil's a mechanical engineer. My father is a mechanical engineer. And to Phil's way of thinking, this somehow makes me mechanically inclined, even though I have explained to him, over and over again, that either I never inherited the "handy" gene or it is terminally recessive in my case.

The cardboard box had a shaded area that showed the tools necessary for assembly: a pair of pliers and a Phillips screwdriver. I looked at Phil's big, red rollaway toolbox with its assortment of slide-out drawers and lift-out compartments. He probably had a pair of pliers and a screwdriver in there somewhere.

"Okay," I said, hoping there wasn't too much resignation in my voice, "should I open the box and look for the instructions?"

"Instructions? For this?" The look on Phil's face was pure pity.

Twenty minutes later, we had the gas grill in about 150 exploded-view parts on the patio paving stones and Phil in the Dumpster-diver position, rummaging through the packing materials we had tossed back into the box, looking for the instructions.

As the sound of the garage door closing reached us through the open glass doors to the kitchen, we heard, "Hey guys. Is this gonna be ready pretty soon?" It was Jess, back from the store, standing in the kitchen doorway holding a big foam tray of T-bone steaks.

"You bet." Phil emerged from the box, clutching a sheaf of standard, 8½ x 11 pages. He read silently for a minute or two, and then hefted a clear plastic bag of small parts and started rummaging though the big red toolbox.

I heard the refrigerator door open and close in the kitchen: It was Jess, wisely keeping the steaks cold. A minute later, she rejoined us on the deck.

"Phillip?"

"Uh-huh?" He was still opening and closing drawers on the toolbox, not looking up.

"What are you doing, dear?"

"Looking for my calipers. The parts list says we have both inch-and-a-quarter and inch-and-an-eighth bolts in here. I want to make sure I use the right bolts in the right places, so I have to measure 'em."

Jess held out her hand.

"Give," she said.

Twenty seconds later, she handed Phil a dozen screws. "These are the inch-and-a-quarters, and these"—she handed him two dozen more—"are the inch-and-an-eighths."

Phil looked at the two handfuls of screws. "How do you know?"

"Because an inch and an eighth is shorter than an inch and a quarter."

"Oh . . . thanks."

"Don't mention it." Jess smiled. "And Ron?"

"Yes?"

"What about repentance?"

"Pardon?"

"Repentance. Sinner's remorse. Sealing the deal. We still have to get 'em to do that, right?"

I laughed. "You don't believe in segues, do you?"

"That *was* a segue—proceeding from one topic to the next without interruption."

"Oh, excuse me. I forgot that you're a walking dictionary."

Jess gave me one of her knowing smiles, but didn't miss a beat. "So what about repentance, Ron?"

Phil looked up and said, "You can go ahead and answer her, Ron. I won't need you until I get to the part where I mount the, uh" —he looked at the instructions—"the, uh, tub-thing on the base."

"Tub-thing," I repeated. "I love it when you get all technical on me, Phil." Turning to Jess, I said, "Okay, where did that question come from?"

"Ron, we really want to get deeper into a conversation with Marty, but I'm just not going to start out with some crazy statement like, 'Hey Marty, I've got a CNN newsflash for ya, a news ticker from God.'"

Phil chimed in, "Ron we've been thinking that it's important to start with the problem. We need to start with the fact that Marty is screwed up—even if he doesn't see it, it's the truth. Don't we need to start with the repentance piece? After all, that was John the Baptist's opening line: *'Repent!'*"

"I see where you guys are on this," I said. "So let's get to the bedrock of what *you* think you are saying. Let's start with the word *repent*—what does that mean to you?"

Jess gave me a quick nod. "'To turn from sin and dedicate oneself to the amendment of one's life.' And that's not my own 'walking' definition; it came straight out of *Merriam-Webster's Collegiate Dictionary, Eleventh Edition*."

"All right." I tried not to grin at her obvious ambush. "And while you're at it, could you define the word *broadcast* for me?"

"From *Webster's*?"

"Just your own definition will do."

"To send a radio or TV signal," Phil muttered as he matched a pair of parts.

"Or to make generally known," Jess added.

"Very good. And would you agree that *overwhelm* means to dominate by force and that you, Jess, just *arrived* at the house a few minutes ago?"

"Sure."

"So would I," I said. "Yet in its original form, *broadcast* was an agricultural term for sowing seed by throwing it from your hand. And *overwhelm* meant to have a following wave overtake the 'whelm,' or 'helm,' of a ship. And a few hundred years ago, you couldn't 'arrive' anywhere except by ship, because the Latin root, *rive,* means 'the edge of a body of water.'"

"Like *Riviera*?" Phil asked.

"Listen to you," Jess murmured. "And I would have thought the only Riviera you knew about was a Buick."

Phil snorted.

"The point," I said, wanting to get it in while they still knew I *had* a point, "is that words migrate in their meanings as they get used in different contexts. And the word *repentance* comes from the same root as the word *pensive*. They're both about thinking."

"So to 'repent' is to 'rethink,'" Jess said.

"Right."

"As in rethink your priorities and start living a sinless life."

"Wrong."

Jess gave me a "here you go again" look.

"Including the Ten Commandments, how many laws did a Jew of Jesus' day have to adhere to?"

"Exactly 613," Phil said. "You covered that in a message a couple of years ago."

Impressed, I replied, "And how did Jesus up the ante on that? I think I covered this in the same message."

"Oh. Yeah." Jess looked up as if she were reading a celestial PowerPoint presentation. "Jesus said that even *considering* breaking a law was the same as breaking it. The Jimmy Carter 'lust in my heart' thing."

"You remember Jimmy Carter saying that?"

"I did a term paper on him," Jess answered. "In middle school."

Feeling suddenly ancient, I forged ahead. "So, pretty much, Jesus made it clear that, unless you're like him—all God and all man, both at the same time—living sinless is pretty much impossible."

"Uh-huh," Phil and Jess said in unison.

"So, if perfect sinlessness is not an attainable earthly goal," I said, "how can you start living a sinless life?"

Dead silence.

"Remember I read you Caesar's birth announcement a couple of weeks ago?"

They nodded.

"The word used in the New Testament that we translate 'repent' is from the root *metaneo*. Without going into detail, the word essentially means to change your mind, shift directions, change your course heading. When governments changed in Rome, an announcement would go out to the Roman Legion units stationed in the provinces, calling on them to 'repent,' using a form of the same word. Do you think it was calling on them to stop sinning?"

"Well," Phil grunted as he tightened a bolt, "they were pretty honorable guys, right?"

"By their own definition of honor, which was loyalty to the state, they were," I agreed. "But this was the Roman state. And Rome had, for instance, a law saying that a woman could not be put to death for a capital crime if she was a virgin."

"That's sort of sweet," Jess said.

"But the Legion's method of getting around that problem was not. The centurions would turn presumed virgins over to their men to be raped, so they could then be executed as nonvirgins."

Jess gasped.

"They were brutal times. The torture and mocking of Jesus by the soldiers before he was sent to the cross? That wasn't a bunch of bullies amusing themselves. Those guys would have been under orders. They were doing what they'd been told to do."

"So they weren't sinless," Phil said.

"Not by any definition we'd agree with."

"Then what would that 'repentance' announcement mean to them?" Jess asked.

"Think about it. These guys were the muscle with which

Rome ruled the world. If there was a coup in Rome and a new emperor was named, he needed to have the troops behind him or he would be powerless. So the announcement called for them to reconsider—"

"—their loyalties," Jess finished softly.

"Their loyalties to their ruler. Their king. And according to the New Testament, who is the ultimate king?"

"Jesus," they said together.

I nodded. "If I were an apostle writing an account of Jesus' life or a letter to a church today, I wouldn't use the word *repent.* The meaning's too fuzzy. Instead, I might say 'switch parties,' 'jump ship,' 'realign,' or 'sign with a different team'—something like that."

"So when we call on someone to repent, we ask them to change their allegiances," Jess said.

"Exactly. From the ruler of this world to the ruler of the greater world to which we actually belong. It still has the sense of coming out of rebellion, but the focus is not on *stopping* what we're doing—it's on *resetting our priorities* as to who ultimately has dominion over us, who ultimately is calling the shots in our lives."

I looked at Phil, who was wrestling with a big piece of cast aluminum.

"You want help with that tub-thing?"

"Help would be good," he said. As I helped him align the parts, he added, "And it's not a tub-thing, Ron. It's the 'firebox, lower half.'" He winked. "How's that for less fuzzy?"

7

Sealing the Deal

Do you feel any connection with Jess and Phil? Have you experienced spiritual conversations with coworkers or friends that end with an awkward silence when you bring up the subject of God? Or do you avoid such topics? Do you feel at a loss when you think of trying to bring up such topics in casual conversation?

Phil thought there was only one way to talk about his relationship with Jesus. He had been taught a formula, with four steps to the conversation. The starting point is the concept of sin and the remedy of repentance. That was where he was going to start with Marty, no matter how he thought it would be received.

The problem is that, at best, repentance is difficult to communicate to people today. By starting the conversation there, we almost always hit a dead end pretty quickly.

Phil assumed that the formula he'd been taught was the entire salvation story as presented in Scripture. Yet there is so much more to the full story. If we're honest with ourselves, there is so much we assume, so much we are comfortable with, so much we don't know, and so much we don't even know we don't know. Back in the eleventh century, Salomon Ibn Gabirol identified four types of people. Have you heard the saying?

There are those who know not and know not that they know not;

They are fools—shun them.

There are those who know not and know that they know not;

They are simple—teach them.

There are those who know and know not that they know;

They are asleep—awaken them.

There are those who know and know that they know;

They are wise—follow them.

I decided a long time ago that I really didn't want to be in the first category—a fool. It's a whole lot better to be simple, because at least then you can learn and eventually become wise. Still, when it comes to the very important topics of how we talk about God and how we think about God, it's hard for me to admit that I know that I don't know.

Hazy, unclear, foggy or fuzzy—call it what you want. The truth is, we probably aren't nearly as clear on a lot of things as we would like to think we are. Depending on where you sit in your relationship with God, and how you relate to him, *repentance* may have a variety of meanings.

My early Christian experience was littered with conversations I had with people about spiritual issues. My high school years gave me plenty of opportunities to open my mouth and insert my foot, offend scores of people, and be an outright jerk at times.

Why?

Repentance.

I have had little, if any, success using that word in spiritual conversations. But not because the word isn't important or the concept isn't central to the Christian experience.

I played trombone in high school with a guy named Arnold. Not only was he a good trombone player, he was also a standout on the swim team and quite the jock. I respected him, and one day decided I needed to bring him up to speed on my newfound faith. I hadn't had any coaching at this stage, no evangelism course, no training sessions by a seminar expert. I simply did what had been done to me and what I had seen on TV. I told Arn he needed to think about following God, and repentance was the first step. I will never forget his response: "Have you gone off the deep end and become one of those born-agains? God help you, Ron."

Ironic, huh? He had me pegged just by my simple opener. Now, granted, my approach wasn't very smooth, and I didn't have much of a lead-in to finally get us to the repentance conversation. But Arn's word container for *repentance* was already full. He was instantly suspicious of my conversion experience, placing me in the category of "born-agains," which in his mind was right up there with outer-space Martians with pink stripes. I was suspect, possibly unstable, and not to be trusted.

Let's face it, *repentance* is another one of those words with baggage. On the one hand, it is a big evangelism driver. When we see both John the Baptist and Jesus begin their preaching ministries by saying, "Repent, for the kingdom of heaven is at hand" (Matthew 3:2; 4:17, NASB), we realize this must be a critical component. On the other hand, the word *repentance* conjures up images of TV evangelists begging people, over a backdrop of dramatic music, to "come, repent, and make things right with God so you, too, can have a seat in the eternal stadium and forever sing praises to God."

For Thanksgiving one year, we went to Chicago for the week. The plan was to eat turkey, freeze ourselves nearly to death at the downtown parade, and get caught up in the post-Thanksgiving Friday shopping pandemonium on Michigan Avenue, which can be described only as off-the-meter nutty. The crowds were bad enough, but as my family and I exited one of the stores, lo and behold we ran into a lanky thirty-something shouting at the top of his voice, as if to compete with the Christmas music coming from every store's sound system and the zoom of traffic along the Magnificent Mile, that everyone needed to repent. He was on a rampage, yelling and screaming that unless repentance happened *now,* people were in danger of landing in hell. My teenagers looked at me and just shook their heads, grinning, like, "Come on, does this guy really think this is going to do anything?"

When we got into the next store, one of my kids said, "Dad, why don't you engage this guy in some conversation so we can spare at least some of these holiday shoppers from getting a bad view of Christianity?"

What a great observation and perceptive insight. Not only was this guy not doing any good, he was part of the reason why so many in our culture don't understand true repentance. He was filling their *repentance* word containers with wrong ideas.

If you're skeptical about Christianity and unconvinced about Jesus as a result of a bad experience with Christians who think that shouting about repentance is the most effective way to communicate, I apologize; your skepticism is well-founded. Unfortunately, you don't have the whole story—or in some cases, even the right story. Your wariness, and perhaps even cynicism, is evidence that we followers of Christ need to re-examine what we are trying to accomplish. I invite you to continue your investigation and to ask the hard questions. I believe that genuine seeking will be genuinely rewarded.

If your understanding of repentance hasn't been shaped by a self-appointed John the Baptist at the corner of Michigan Avenue and Ohio Street in downtown Chicago, perhaps what comes to mind are images of people kneeling at altars, weeping and confessing every sin they can think of, in search of the right combination of confession and contrition that will appease God's anger and set their lives on the right track.

You see, it isn't only society in general that has a skewed understanding of the message of Jesus and the real intent of his words. Countless numbers of Christians have filled their word containers for *the gospel* and for *repentance* with baggage-laden misunderstandings. Christians by the thousands are hopping from church to church or leaving the institutional church altogether, disappointed, disillusioned, and disheartened because their understanding of the gospel and repentance has not delivered the dramatic life change they were led to believe would happen. Further, their disappointment makes "sharing their faith" even more difficult because it seems they are making promises they can't deliver on, and neither can the church.

Part of the reason for this problem is our narrow and reduced understanding of repentance. The English word *repentance* is a fair translation of the Greek word in the New Testament, but as a concept to put forth in the forum of public conversation, it is, I believe, overloaded with baggage and therefore too volatile to be helpful in meaningful spiritual conversation.

Remember Jess's question about "repentance, sinner's remorse, and sealing the deal"? She hit the nail on the head. "Sealing the deal" is a mind-set that prevails in much of evangelical Christianity. Altar calls, counseling rooms, and the recitation of "sinner's prayers" are fixtures, often permanent fixtures, in many of our church services and evangelistic outreach efforts. Yet, despite our claims of being "people of the Good Book," none of these ideas are found in the Bible.

I will be the first to admit that much of what we do in the Christian church isn't found in the Bible. In theological circles, the word we use for these practices is *extrabiblical.* They are things that aren't specifically mentioned in the Bible, but neither are they *against* what the Bible teaches and may, in fact, be in line with certain biblical principles. As Christians down through the generations have sought to discover and pass along "what works," many of these ideas and practices have gained a footing in the church, to the point that many Christians may not even know that what they're doing and saying isn't actually biblical (that is, in the Bible). A whole lot of what we do—how we organize our worship services, how we celebrate Communion, how we design our buildings and our Sunday school programs, and how we staff our churches—is extrabiblical. Likewise, much of what we do in the name of getting people to "repent" is also extrabiblical.

Most extrabiblical practices are based on preferences, convictions, or practical experience (in other words, they are things that have been deemed *effective*). Of course, that doesn't mean that extrabiblical things are right or wrong; they could be either or neither. But what *is* decidedly wrong is mandating our extrabiblical preferences as the only right way. When we "baptize" and "canonize" extrabiblical rituals and practices, making them a litmus test for our standing (and the standing of other people) before God or a means of judging the orthodoxy of other churches, we are being unkind, arrogant, and just plain wrong.

We have to be careful. *Extrabiblical,* by its very definition, means we can't legislate what others do in areas that are outside the bounds of what the Bible directly teaches. We can't mandate that churches must have a pipe organ and wooden pews. Nor can we mandate that churches have a Communion table or a cross in the auditorium or sanctuary. And we can't decide that a congregation must follow a particular order of service or liturgy in order to have a *real* church service. These are all extrabiblical issues and, as such, are negotiable preferences, not necessary obligations.

Let's suspend judgment for a moment and enter the arena of dialogue. Let's go to a place of really trying to grasp an alternative to the current view—or the way things have always been done—and let's investigate the possibility of a fuller grasp and a deeper understanding of what Scripture is saying. What is at stake? Far more than the ideas we hold to as sacred cows. What is at stake is our ability—yours, mine, Phil's, and Jess's—first, to *live* the message that Jesus brought and, second, to use words, if necessary.[†]

Of course, if we are going to use words, it might be a good idea to investigate whether we have the right definitions for the biblical terms we are using. What is at stake is our ability to communicate with compassion and clarity. So, what if *repentance* actually means something fundamentally different from what we have commonly understood? The prevailing view in evangelical Christianity essentially says that not only was repentance a major theme of Jesus' ministry, it is the prelude to conversion, to being saved, to getting to heaven.

In a sense, repentance is seen as the negative side of the equation, the plus side being the resulting "salvation," which is a divine gift of grace and impossible to earn. This prevailing view of repentance is presented as essentially the opposite of what the Jews, and particularly the Pharisees, taught. The Pharisees are portrayed as teaching a path of connection with God that could be earned through a merit system. Jesus, it is said, came to undermine and challenge this view and to offer the alternative way of unmerited grace, to which we gain access through the process of repentance. In other words, this view sees repentance as belonging to the world of individual moral conduct, because Jesus and John the Baptist were preaching a timeless message about humankind's distance from God and how we could be converted.

But let's take another look.

What if we were to think about repentance from the perspective of the Jews in that place and time? What would they have heard in the call to repentance issued by John the Baptist and Jesus? Well, the first thing we would need to

[†] This idea borrows from a famous quote, most often attributed to St. Francis of Assisi: "Preach the gospel at all times. If necessary, use words." Of course, we first need to fully understand what "the gospel" is before we can preach it.

understand is that the characterization of the Pharisees outlined above (and which is a common view held in contemporary evangelical circles) is not very accurate. The Pharisees didn't really say that the way to God was by earning your way through a complex merit system. Consequently, when Jesus challenged the Pharisees, he wasn't challenging a merit system, as is so often supposed. Instead, Jesus was taking on something a bit more complex. He was telling the Pharisees, and the Jews in general, that their method of being Israel—of being distinct by keeping all the purity, dietary, and Sabbath laws—was unnecessary and did not in any way create for them a place of privilege. In other words, Jesus was trying to tell them that their understanding of being "chosen" didn't give them a special exemption from having to cultivate their hearts in connection to God.

8

Reorienting the Compass

As we consider how the Pharisees, and the Jews in general, would have understood the word *repentance* in the first century, it is important to note that when John the Baptist and Jesus said, "Repent, for the kingdom of heaven is at hand," they were speaking to Israel as a nation. The call to repentance is notably absent from Jesus' personal invitations to the twelve disciples to follow him. I'm not suggesting this diminishes the importance of repentance, but we need to pay attention to when and where it is mentioned in Scripture. The text may be assuming that all the disciples at some point in time repented, but it doesn't explicitly say that. So, repentance as a necessary first step in following Jesus is clearly an assumption that can be only inferred from the text. But even if it is a reasonable inference, the where, when, and how are pretty much left up in the air—for many of us, frustratingly so.

To understand the first-century context, we must remember that John the Baptist and Jesus came on the scene at the end of four hundred years of silence (speaking in terms of revelation from God through the prophets). The rabbis were certain that with the demise of Zechariah and Malachi, God had stopped speaking and the only thing left to be heard was the *bath qol* (Aramaic for "the echo of God's voice").

Israel as a nation was in exile, but the people were

looking forward to the day when, according to the last word of the prophets as recorded in Malachi 3:1, someone would appear on the scene to prepare the way for a Coming One. Israel had a real sense that she was living in the context of an unfolding story, a perspective that is largely absent from American evangelical renditions of the message of Jesus. That's why it's necessary to retell, restate, and reframe the story of Scripture.

All that historical sketching is helpful, but it's no substitute for helping people see that they are part of a still-unfolding story and that their personal stories have meaning and value in a larger narrative framework. The intersection of those two stories is what we are seeking.

When John the Baptist came on the scene, his words to Israel by the Jordan River were loaded with powerful historical significance. As the people listened, they must have been thinking, *Oh my gosh, this is what we have been reading about and waiting for; this is what Malachi talked about. This man even has the wild look of the prophet Elijah. Wow, something is afoot. Let's get ready for what is about to happen. Our exile must be coming to an end; foreign domination will soon be a thing of the past; God will finally establish his kingdom in Jerusalem. We need to be prepared.*

Another important piece we can't afford to miss is the powerful symbolism of John's location, the Jordan River. The Jordan was the river that Israel crossed to enter the Promised Land. For John to come out of the desert to the banks of the Jordan to announce that the kingdom of heaven was at hand was to invite the people to realize that they were being prepared to re-enter the Promised Land, signifying the end of exile. Just as the children of Israel had gone from the desert across the Jordan and into the Promised Land as part of the Exodus, here is John the Baptist, in the same setting, preparing the people for a second and final exodus.

What about the baptism of John—what is that all about? Often this is misunderstood as some precursor to Christian baptism. But there isn't much evidence to support that idea. John's call is to the nation of Israel, who has been waiting for the right moment in history when everything would come together. John is calling the nation to be cleansed and reconstituted as the people of God by reentering the Jordan River as a symbolic revisiting of the place of entry into the Promised Land.

This, too, is why Jesus was able to be baptized by John. Baptism has nothing to do with being saved, converted, or trying to find a personal way into heaven. It has everything to do with coming out of exile. In submitting to John's baptism, Jesus affirmed the end of exile, and he affirmed the need for Israel as a nation to prepare for the arrival of the Coming One. In his baptism, Jesus affirmed that John was the messenger they had been waiting for.

Can you see how this version of repentance meshes with the Jewish crowd's perspective and anticipation? They were not looking for a private pathway to an afterlife. They had no idea in their heads that God was going to send them a prophet, according to Malachi's prediction, so they could figure out how to ensure an eternal place with God. For them, repentance in this context was what Israel as a nation had to do if her exile and alienation from God were to end, and if God were to restore her fortunes.

Israel had not been the people they were called to be. They hadn't been a blessing to the world; they had become exclusive and elitist. They needed a change of mind as to what they thought they were all about, as well as a change of heart toward God. Only then could they become fully reoriented to their original purpose. In other words, repentance meant a full-scale *reorientation* to what it meant for Israel to be Israel.

What would this sort of reorientation mean to a Jew in the first century? At the very least, it meant that Israel needed to return to the *shema,* the clarion call to acknowledge and love Yahweh, the one God, with all their hearts, to return from exile and return to him.

If reorientation is the biblical idea behind the word *repentance* for Jews of Jesus' day, what was the connotation of *repentance* in a secular political and social context? Some Christians find this hard to believe, but the word *repent* had very definite nonreligious uses. In the writings of Josephus, a first-century Jewish historian, we find the word *repent* used to mean something like "abandon sword and spear and rethink your militant revolution."

If you're encountering these ideas for the first time, you may be having the same reaction as some of my Christian friends and many people I have met at conferences. Not long ago, I was in Florida speaking to a group of church leaders. When they heard me explain repentance in a first-century Jewish context, at first they were incredulous. However, it didn't take long for their incredulity to give way to anger.

"If this is true, why weren't we taught this in Bible school? Why didn't we learn this in seminary? Why isn't this common knowledge in the way we talk about these terms and concepts?"

Perhaps you share their frustration. If you've been around Christian circles for a while and yet are hearing these concepts for the first time, you might be feeling a bit cheated because the stories you were told before are now looking a bit thin. At least that's how they may seem in comparison to the incredible, fascinating, and complex version found in the pages of the first four books of the New Testament.

The message of Jesus and John the Baptist was not about a private, internal, spiritual experience; instead, it was something with huge national, political, and social implications. Of course, there are spiritual dimensions to it, but the first thing that came to the minds of the first-century Jews would have had nothing to do with how repentance related to securing an eternal seat in a heavenly location. Okay, but then what would have come to mind? To broaden our perspective, let's take a look at the use of the word *repent* in a nonreligious, political, and military context.

In the writings of Josephus, a Jewish aristocrat and historian, we find an account (ca. AD 66) of his attempt to persuade a faction of political revolutionaries to lay down their swords and spears and instead pursue quiet, nonmilitant means, which in Josephus's mind was a better way to achieve their aims.† He tells of confronting a Jewish brigand, coincidentally named Jesus, and exhorting him to "repent and believe in me." Obviously, Josephus was not expecting this revolutionary to drop to his knees, recite a sinner's prayer, and thereby find a way to spend eternity in heaven. Further, Josephus was not suggesting that the brigand "believe" in him in the sense that Josephus had nailed down an inside track to eternity. (It is interesting, however, and I think important to note that the word for "belief" used by Josephus is the same Greek word used in the New Testament for *belief* or *faith*). What Josephus was telling the man was, essentially, "repent and prove your loyalty to me.

Josephus wasn't asking for some sort of little heart change; instead, he was talking about an entire change of orientation or basis for action. Today, we might call it a paradigm shift.[1]

If we now take this richer, deeper understanding of repentance and belief back to the biblical context, we gain a slightly more nuanced understanding of what John the Baptist and Jesus meant when they said, "Repent, for the kingdom of heaven is at hand." It is now a bit easier to see that both John and Jesus were calling the nation of Israel to a paradigm shift to realign their priorities with the kingdom of heaven.

"But wait a second, Ron," I can hear Phil and Jess saying, "didn't you just say that repentance isn't about securing a seat in heaven? And now you're saying that it *is* about heaven. What gives?"

Well, first of all, the main point I'm making in this section is that many words that seem to be specifically "biblical" also have a much broader, secular, cultural arena in which they were used. And we need to understand *both* contexts in

† The date AD 66 is not inconsequential, for this is the same time period during which the Gospels of Matthew, Mark, and Luke would have been coming into their final forms.

order to understand the words as they're used in Scripture. Second, and more directly to the point of repentance and heaven, before we can conclude what John the Baptist and Jesus meant in their respective calls to repentance, we need to understand what Jesus said about the kingdom of heaven. It's beyond the scope of this book to delve into that discussion, but suffice it to say that Jesus spent about three years telling parables and other stories about the kingdom of heaven, and we would do well to understand those stories in both their biblical and first-century cultural contexts.

Another interesting context to help us understand repentance in a larger picture is the ancient community of Qumran. No doubt you've heard of the Dead Sea Scrolls, the oldest surviving biblical manuscripts (or fragments of manuscripts), which were found in eleven desert caves near Qumran and the Dead Sea. The scrolls have toured all over the world and have been touted as some of the most important archaeological finds of the twentieth century.

Qumran is an interesting test case for further understanding the concept of repentance because the inhabitants of the community felt they were the ones devoting themselves to full preparation for return from exile and the appearance of the Messiah. Some scholars believe it is possible that John the Baptist came from Qumran, given his dress, desert location, and message. Both the Qumranians and John used Isaiah 40:1-3 as their key passage for self-definition.

> Comfort, comfort my people,
>   says your God.
> Speak tenderly to Jerusalem,
>   and proclaim to her
> that her hard service has been completed,
>   that her sin has been paid for,
> that she has received from the LORD's hand
>   double for all her sins.

A voice of one calling:
"In the desert prepare
  the way for the LORD;
make straight in the wilderness
  a highway for our God."

I don't think it's coincidental that verse 3, "Prepare the way for the LORD; make straight in the wilderness a highway for our God," occurs in the context of verses 1 and 2, which talk about a time coming in the future when Israel's exile would be over.

In light of Isaiah 40, then, the call to repentance wasn't intended to bring the people into a private conversional experience with God, but rather to reset their orientation for the return of the Messiah and the end of exile.

Clearly, if we want to understand the deep, rich, and full dimensions of the word *repentance* (and any number of other key biblical words and concepts), we must consider all three streams flowing together: the New Testament context, the first-century secular and historical context, and the first-century religious context outside the Bible. When we do this with *repentance,* we find that the word has to do with the orientation, directional heading, and trajectory of an entire community, culture, or nation, not just the front end of a private, personal conversional experience that results in a guaranteed seat in heaven. So, when we hear an evangelist on the corner of Michigan Avenue and Ohio Street saying, "Repent, for the kingdom of God is at hand," he is saying something entirely different from what John the Baptist was saying.

Perhaps the best way to bring all this together is to realize that "repentance" or "reorientation," from the lips of Jesus and John the Baptist, was not a summons to a moralistic reform. It wasn't a timeless call to get your life together. It wasn't about cleaning up some personal foibles. It was a call for Israel to prepare for the end of her exile as a nation and to change agendas, specifically in the way she was not being the nation that God intended for her to be. It was a call to re-engage with God's original purpose for Israel, which was to be a blessing to the whole world. Did individual Jews have to respond to this? Of course, but the call to repent wasn't made to individuals. Jesus was calling an entire nation, not as a collection of individuals but as a collective organism. God had called Israel to be his people. He had called her and rescued her from Egypt. He had led her across the Red Sea. Now he was calling her to reorient her life as a nation back to his original purpose and agenda.

A further twist in the story helps to flesh out this idea. The reorientation that Jesus intended to bring about included offering the kingdom of heaven to lots of people who were outside the camp of ethnic Israel. Jesus included non-Israelites in the mix and treated them as equals, and yet they weren't circumcised, did not keep a kosher kitchen, and totally ignored the Sabbath laws. These were the things that most irritated the Pharisees and teachers of the law who were constantly challenging Jesus.

Okay, so what does all this mean to a conversation with people like Phil and Jess? Though the implications may not be immediately apparent, they are very significant. First, it means that when Phil is engaging a friend in spiritual conversation, he needs to know that the word *repentance* pushes all the wrong buttons. A word to the wise, then, would be, *Don't use it.* Pretty simple. Of course, many Christians react to that idea or quickly respond with a rejoinder: "But we do need to talk about repentance somehow, don't we?" Well, that all depends. This was exactly my friend Jess's point. She felt as if there was no way around making known this very critical bit of information: "You have to get the word of repentance out to people or they won't be saved—right?"

When we read the New Testament narratives carefully, we see that many people reoriented their lives to a new compass heading without ever being invited to do so, without ever reciting a sinner's prayer, and without ever hearing the word *repent.* For Phil and Jess, this realization required a reorientation of a different kind. They needed to alter their approach to spiritual conversations if they wanted to see those conversations continue and progress.

I can tell you how exciting life becomes when we interact with people about spiritual things without trying to push them through a factory-made, one-size-fits-all pattern. Let's allow the Scriptures to speak for themselves on this one. First, let's look at some stories that point to Jesus' national concern for Israel to reorient their lives because of their failure to be the sort of light he wanted them to be. Then let's turn to some individual stories in the Bible where full-scale reorientation occurred but with no sense of any formal invitation, or even discussion about it.

9

High Stakes and Juicy T-Bones

Phil stood attentively at the Char-Grill, keeping watch over the sizzling steaks and admiring the steel masterpiece he had spent the past few hours assembling.

I settled into one of the deck chairs, next to Jess and the pitcher of homemade raspberry iced tea.

"You know, Ron, I agree with you," Jess said, pausing to take a sip of her tea. "Marty wouldn't react too well if I started a conversation with 'You need to repent.' But isn't that a sign of Marty's *hardened heart*? I mean, isn't that how John the Baptist started his message—with 'Repent'?" Jess looked at me intently with a furrowed brow. "You can't deny that, can you, Ron?"

"Well, let's look at that Scripture passage. What does it really say?"

"Let me get my Bible." Jess set down her glass and headed toward the house. Just before she disappeared into the kitchen, she turned her head toward her husband. "Hey, Phil, don't burn those steaks."

"Don't worry about me," Phil said. "I've got all 80,000 BTUs under control."

Within seconds, Jess returned from the kitchen with Bible in hand.

"Go ahead and read Luke 3:1-6," I said, "the passage that describes John the Baptist's ministry."

"Okay, let's see . . . 'In the fifteenth year of the reign of Tiberius Caesar—when Pontius Pilate was governor of Judea, Herod tetrarch of Galilee, his brother Philip tetrarch of Iturea and Traconitis, and Lysanias tetrarch of Abilene—during the high priesthood of Annas and Caiaphas, the word of God came to John son of Zechariah in the desert. He went into all the country around the Jordan, preaching a baptism of repentance for the forgiveness of sins. As is written in the book of the words of Isaiah the prophet:

"A voice of one calling in the desert,
'Prepare the way for the Lord,
make straight paths for him.
Every valley shall be filled in,
every mountain and hill made low.
The crooked roads shall become straight,
the rough ways smooth.
And all mankind will see God's salvation.'"'"

"Do you know what Luke is quoting?" I asked Jess as I gazed at the streaks of orange and red that had begun to paint the evening sky.

"Well, it says in the notes 'Isaiah 40.'" Jess strained to read the note in the fading light.

"The first thing is that the Jews of Jesus' day would have known instantly the passage in Isaiah." I glanced over at Jess, who still had her face buried in the Bible. "But we have to strain to read the small margin notes to find out what Luke is quoting."

"Well, if Phil would put more lights out here, I wouldn't have to strain," Jess said with mock disgust. Phil just nodded. He was still engrossed with his steaks.

"Any practicing Jew worth his salt would have known that the opening lines of Isaiah 40 described a time when Israel would be called out of exile and her years of hard suffering would be over. But notice where Luke ends his quote." I leaned over and pointed at the passage. "He ends by saying 'all mankind will see God's salvation.' This would come as something of a surprise to the Jews of that day. They had a sense that because they were God's chosen people, no one else was included."

"I remember that. Weren't the Pharisees pretty much elitist snobs?" Phil said as he brought the sizzling steaks from the grill. "By the way, dinner is served."

"Don't be too quick to judge, Phil," I said while stabbing a sizable steak with my fork and sliding it onto my plate. "The more I study the Pharisees, the more I realize they were a lot like me."

Phil shrugged and cut into his steak. "I wouldn't say that, Ron . . ."

"Look at this. Right after this announcement, Luke describes John the Baptist running into people like the Pharisees. Jess, go ahead and read it."

"Okay, this is Luke 3:7-9: 'John said to the crowds coming out to be baptized by him, "You brood of vipers! Who warned you to flee from the coming wrath? Produce fruit in keeping with repentance. And do not begin to say to yourselves, 'We have Abraham as our father.' For I tell you that out of these stones God can raise up children for Abraham. The ax is already at the root of the trees, and every tree that does not produce good fruit will be cut down and thrown into the fire."' See, I told you, Ron. John the Baptist is calling people to repent. He's talking about the coming of fiery hell."

"I wouldn't jump to that conclusion, Jess. Who was John the Baptist talking to?" I looked at Jess and then over at Phil. They stared back at me with blank faces.

"Isn't he quoting the Pharisees themselves when he says, 'We have Abraham as our father'?"

"Well, of course, he was talking to the Israelites," Phil said.

"But why is he talking about *fleeing*? In John's mind, there was an impending doom, some event soon to happen that they needed to get ready for as a nation. And the readiness to which John was calling the Israelites was repentance—that is, a full-scale reorientation and recalibration of their compasses, something that would enable them to avert this coming disaster."

Jess rattled the ice cubes in her glass. "What's your point, Ron?"

"I'm getting there. Notice a couple of other things here. After telling the crowd as a whole, 'Produce fruit in keeping with repentance,' John says, in effect, 'Don't be smug about your skin color.' Literally, he says, 'Don't put any stock in your ethnic status as an Israelite.' Apparently, he was referring to what many in Israel at the time were doing—taking refuge in the fact they were 'children of Abraham.' But John's next statement makes it clear that Israel as a nation is in trouble. He says, 'Don't hide behind your ethnicity; don't claim that because Abraham is your father you are somehow exempt from having your hearts connected to God.' John was challenging their sense of entitlement. His real point was that a time was coming when their identity as children of Abraham wouldn't exempt them from having to bear the fruit of righteousness in their lives."

"How does this relate to Marty?" Phil stared at me. "I doubt he's a Jew. His last name sounds more Irish than anything else—and he doesn't even talk about being Irish."

"My point is that the verses we often quote so quickly about repentance don't easily support our simple salvation formula: Repent, say a prayer, and be assured you have a seat in heaven. First, notice how this passage is addressed more to the corporate nation of Israel than to an individual person's salvation. John was talking about the general direction of the nation Israel. Next, look how John is talking to people who are hiding behind their ethnicity as a way to get close to God. He is challenging the religious leaders of his day—the opinion leaders and influencers—to reorient their lives."

"So your point is that John the Baptist was preaching to the chaplain of the Senate, not to Marty?" Phil said with a puzzled look on his face.

"No, my point is that John the Baptist's message of reorientation was directed to the Israelites who were resting in their ethnicity instead of bearing fruit in keeping with their relationship with God. My point is also that we need to pay attention to what doesn't appear in this passage—namely, the easy formula we all learned for salvation." I savored the last bite of my steak as I looked up into the sky. The last vestiges of sunset had faded, and blinking stars were starting to appear against the darkening blue.

The journey into re-exploring old concepts like these is both exciting and disconcerting. At least it was for me. I remember the first time I heard a professor suggest some of the things we are talking about here, and I can remember the first word that came to my mind: *compromise.* I have since come to realize that my initial response had a lot to do with my mind's defense mechanism against anyone who said things I disagreed with. If you're wrestling with what I've been presenting, I want you to know I understand. My hope is that you are at least beginning to see what is at stake. And just because these are things you may not have heard before doesn't mean they're wrong or examples of compromise. I also understand what is at stake in the broader sense. These ideas aren't just challenging our thinking, they are also challenging us to reconsider what we *do* as a result of our new understanding.

The group of leaders I spoke to in Florida were quickly exasperated when they realized that the story they had been telling, the definitions they had been using, and the invitations they had been issuing would all need reconsideration. They had already concluded that the practical and extrabiblical things they were currently doing weren't working. So they had been hoping to find some new program "fixes" to help them along. Little did they expect a rereading of the Bible to bring them to a place of new ideas and understanding. New programs generally aren't too threatening; new ideas often are. Paradigm shifts are often disturbing, but they can also be exhilarating.

Wow! Can you imagine the effect that a fresh perspective on the Scriptures would have on your spiritual conversations?

Recently, I was invited to speak at a church in California. The pastor and I had become friends over the past couple of years and he was on a sabbatical. So, for two consecutive weekends, I had the opportunity to share this reconsideration of what real repentance is. I have to tell you that what I shared the first week about a very well-known Bible story was so disruptive to some people that they wrote letters and posted on a Web site that I was a heretic. It was, honestly, a very, very small minority, but it does illustrate what I have been trying to communicate throughout this whole process. When we challenge the way people think the world works or should work, we tread on some very holy ground for a lot of people.

So, what was the fuss all about? Let's look at a story that you've probably heard before. It is found in Luke 19:1-10.

> Jesus entered Jericho and was passing through. A man was there by the name of Zacchaeus; he was a chief tax collector and was wealthy. He wanted to see who Jesus was, but being a short man he could not, because of the crowd. So he ran ahead and climbed a sycamore-fig tree to see him, since Jesus was coming that way.
>
> When Jesus reached the spot, he looked up and said to him, "Zacchaeus, come down immediately. I must stay at your house today." So he came down at once and welcomed him gladly.
>
> All the people saw this and began to mutter, "He has gone to be the guest of a 'sinner.'"
>
> But Zacchaeus stood up and said to the Lord, "Look, Lord! Here and now I give half of my possessions to the poor, and if I have cheated anybody out of anything, I will pay back four times the amount."
>
> Jesus said to him, "Today salvation has come to this house, because this man, too, is a son of Abraham. For the Son of Man came to seek and to save what was lost."

What a story! Those of us who grew up in certain quarters of the church learned a cheesy—but memorable—song about Zacchaeus being a wee little man, hence his need to climb up in the tree. He invited Jesus to dinner and a bunch of people got pretty ticked off. That's about the sum total of what is taught about Zacchaeus.

Let's take a closer look at the story. I think we'll find that it's a great test case for the things we've been discussing so far.

Zacchaeus was a tax collector for the Romans, which made him persona non grata among his fellow Jews. Tax collectors were considered unclean because they interacted with all sorts of people, and many of the tax collectors were crooked. Thus, they were looked down on as "sinners." As a

Jew, Jesus would have been forbidden from eating with a guy like Zacchaeus, and even just hanging out with him would have been considered a violation of purity laws. So, the first thing Jesus does is break some rules.

The rules that governed who could eat with whom also serve as miniature models for the rules of association and socialization in the society at large. "Once the anthropologist finds out where, when, and with whom the food is eaten, just about everything else can be inferred about the relations among the society's members."[1] By his actions, Jesus was arguing that eating would not be governed by a social hierarchy that created exclusion and marginalization.

When Jesus went to Zacchaeus's house, the tax collector, without explanation, had an epiphany about his business ethics. He had no doubt extorted money from people along the way, because it was how many of the tax collectors lined their pockets. But Zacchaeus stood up and said, "I want to make restitution for all that—and then some. I will go above and beyond the required duty to make amends."

Okay, so why is this controversial? Well, Jesus' response is a bit surprising. He says that salvation has just come to this house and that this man has become a son of Abraham.[†] In other words, Zacchaeus apparently experienced salvation simply on the basis of a business ethics adjustment. Wow! Most of us simply don't have any room in our thinking for that idea.

After my first Sunday message at the church in California, a middle-aged couple grabbed me—well not literally, but they did corner me—and just went to town on me. "If Jesus said this man was saved, then you know he had to have repented and prayed somewhere, that is a given," said Mrs. Certainty.

When I pointed out to her that the text mentioned nothing

[†] One interesting item that we don't have time to explore here is that Jesus, on his own authority, pronounced salvation for Zacchaeus, whereas the Jews would have said that Zacchaeus had to go to Jerusalem and participate in the sacrificial system—or at least have a priest involved—to obtain salvation. Contrary to how the Jews and Pharisees are often portrayed, they were not opposed to love, forgiveness, and grace; they were opposed only to the idea that these were available outside the context of the Temple. For Jesus to make this proclamation on his own authority was scandalous enough.

about prayer or repentance and that Jesus didn't invite Zacchaeus to do anything, her next remarks were priceless.

"I know it doesn't say that, but you know it happened—you *know* it did. Zacchaeus had to say a sinner's prayer somewhere!"

This is precisely why letting go of our cherished ideas and definitions is so hard for us. When I mentioned to this woman that I thought the reorientation of Zacchaeus's life *was exactly* what Jesus was seeking, she responded, "No that can't be. If Zacchaeus was saved by simply righting some business wrongs, then that is 'works righteousness'—exactly what Jesus came to fight against."

I was absolutely dumbfounded. Her understanding of what constituted righteousness at the individual level was so set in stone that she had to add to the text of Scripture things that weren't there so her theology could survive.

Contrast the story of Mrs. Certainty with that of Kate. Kate was from a decidedly conservative background and pretty traditional in all her understandings of the words and concepts we are investigating. In teaching a monthly theology class in her Arizona church, I had come to expect that any push-back on new concepts or ideas was most likely going to come from Kate. The beauty of push-back, of course, is that it reveals passion, and where you have passion you potentially can turn it toward a passion for the true, the good, and the beautiful, instead of a passion to protect "what I have always believed." On the Zacchaeus story and several other gospel narratives, I was getting pretty stiff resistance. But listen to this: At last month's training time, Kate came up to me and said, "You know Ron, I realize I have to be willing to dump out my assumptions if I am going to learn anything new. For the first time, I realize this isn't about what I think of each individual story unit in the Bible; it is about my ability to remain open to even hear the Bible, instead of believing I have already heard the Bible."

I thought her insight was so right on. You can't hear when you think you have already heard.

Thanks, Kate.

10

A Wee Misunderstanding

As we seek to understand the story of Zacchaeus, there are plenty of possible interpretations that don't require us to embellish the text or add material that isn't there. Simply asking a series of reasonable questions based on what the text says should keep us on track just fine. The problem is that when we see a word like *salvation,* or some other theological-sounding word, we think we know what it means so we apply that assumption to the text rather than allowing the text itself to inform our understanding of the word.

What if Jesus meant something different by his use of *salvation* than what we typically think of when we hear the word? What if "business restitution" was really an example of the great commandment to love God with all your heart, mind, soul, and strength, and your neighbor as yourself? Maybe when Jesus looked at Zacchaeus's actions, he saw them as evidence that the tax collector was reorienting his life. Of course, in all fairness, that isn't what the text says. Some scholars on this passage suggest that Zacchaeus's charity and payments of restitution were more about re-integration into his community than they were to prove anything about the seriousness of his commitment. In other words, they were more like Jesus telling the lepers to go and present themselves at the Temple so that the priest could pronounce them clean. Without the priest's word, the lepers would still be considered unclean and unable to mainstream back into society. Without paying restitution, Zacchaeus would not be accepted in the Jewish community.

But if the sum total of our understanding is that Jesus was concerned about getting people to repent so they could get a seat in heaven, we haven't read the stories of his life very carefully, and we certainly have trouble making sense of Zacchaeus's story.

Just by being with Jesus, Zacchaeus apparently came to the conclusion that his own dealings with and treatment of other people were wrong. How he arrived at that conclusion, or his motivation, is quite obviously incidental to the author's concern, because there is nothing in the story about it. What is clear is that Jesus saw in Zacchaeus an example of the precise sort of reorientation to which he was inviting all of Israel. How do we know that it's one and the same thing? Because Jesus calls Zacchaeus a "son of Abraham." What does that mean? (This is huge.) He's claiming that Zacchaeus gets it!

"Zach, you have got it going on, bro. You get it. You understand what it means to be a true son of Abraham."

Two things about this scene deserve mention. First, remember the backdrop of Luke 3, where John the Baptist cautions the Jews against claiming they are sons of Abraham as if their ethnic connection is important. Now here, sixteen chapters into the story, we find Jesus using the same phrase to show us how on-target Zacchaeus is.

Do you see what is happening? John the Baptist had said to the Jews who thought they were "in" because they were descended from Abraham, "Be careful; that doesn't qualify you." And now Jesus says to Zacchaeus, "I know that everyone considers you an outsider to the things of God, but you have come back to God."

The second thing to note is the audience that is watching Jesus and passing judgment on his actions. Verse 7 of Luke 19 is devoted to making sure we realize there was a whole group of people, presumably Jewish, who observed that Jesus was eating with a "sinner" (their word) and breaking commensality rules. Can you imagine the disbelief, the out-and-out sputtering and spray of those people when Jesus said, "And by the way, Zacchaeus is more connected to the true intent I had for Israel through Abraham than a lot of you, who just don't get it and who continue to evaluate everything in terms of who is in and who is out."

One more key observation about this passage: Jesus seems remarkably uninterested in making sure Zacchaeus is going to heaven. Nothing in the narrative would suggest that "going to heaven" is even on Jesus' radar. And this same observation can be made about other prominent narratives in the New Testament. For example, the woman caught in adultery doesn't repent in any way that we can see, or at least not in the way we have traditionally defined repentance. Was she going to heaven after Jesus said, "Go and sin no more"? What about the woman who had been bleeding for more than a dozen years? Again, no indication of any sort of repentance or reorientation, yet Jesus healed her and said she had great faith. And what of the various blind men and paralytics that Jesus healed without so much as a word about repentance or salvation? All these stories, and scores of others, suggest that Jesus wasn't preoccupied with getting people out of this place and into the sweet by-and-by. As a result, I've come to the conclusion that what he meant by repentance is probably quite different from what we think it is. Our word container for *repentance* has been filled from sources different from those in the minds of Jesus and the writers of the New Testament.

When we consider how the stories of Zacchaeus, the woman caught in adultery, the woman at the well, and all the people that Jesus healed fit in with our common understanding of the word *gospel,* that "Jesus died for our sins," I'm not certain we would say that any of these stories are about that gospel. But if the gospel really is a newsflash, a breaking news story announcing that Jesus is King—and King over all—then every one of these stories is about how the King does the sorts of things that compassionate kings do.

Are you starting to see things a bit differently?

I recently had a conversation about these ideas with a number of pastors, including Larry, who was from a rural part of Louisiana. He said, "Ron, this has massive implications for how I help the people I serve understand what we are trying to do. On one hand, I feel overwhelmed; on the other hand, I'm excited to be learning something new that makes Jesus so much more real to me."

I was inundated following a recent meeting by a group of twentysomethings who said, "This *is* something we can share with our friends in those natural moments when the conversations go spiritual." The idea of not having to get everyone to demonstrate repentance through tears or to pray a magical prayer at the altar was a breath of fresh air to them. One young woman named Char said to me, "This really is good news; this is a newsflash. I can tell my friends that this would have been the news ticker running across the bottom of the screen on CNN News if they'd had TV back then. I want to let my friends know this. It isn't about scaring them into heaven; it's about us bringing heaven here and letting them choose which life they prefer."

Char pointed out the passage in Luke 5 where Jesus says he didn't "come to call the righteous, but sinners to repentance" (v. 32), and she said, "You know, I have had only one category in my head for that idea of calling sinners to repentance: get them to an altar so they can say a prayer that someone will lead them in. But now I realize that what Jesus meant by repentance was so very different from that."

Char was having one of those *aha* experiences that I have grown accustomed to seeing as the message becomes clearer for people. Char gets it. She is right on.

Phil and Jess eventually came to a similar understanding. They realized they could simply drop the invitations to repentance from being a primary goal in the spiritual conversations they were having. Jesus didn't invite Nicodemus to repentance—or the woman at the well or the rich young ruler or any of the twelve disciples he called. He invited a reorientation of their lives and a redirection of their thoughts, paradigms, and lifestyles, yet without ever mentioning a seat in the heavenly realm.

With the exception of his conversation with the rich young ruler, Jesus hardly ever talks about how to get to heaven. His desire was to bring the kingdom of heaven *here*. Look at how Jesus taught the disciples to pray: "Your kingdom *come,* your will be done *on earth* as it is in heaven" (Matthew 6:10, emphasis added). Jesus' goal wasn't to create a rescue plan out of here, but to transform our way of living life—here and now.

As a somewhat humorous aside, when we look at what Jesus tells the rich young ruler about heaven—"Sell your possessions and give to the poor, and you will have treasure in heaven" (Matthew 19:21)—we find an answer that few if any Christians in "Bible-believing churches" would give. Either it sounds "too much like works" or they rationalize that "Jesus isn't necessarily saying that we have to sell everything we own." But Jesus has a knack for putting his finger on the obstacles in people's lives that are keeping them from following him.

We've spent some time exploring how our common or traditional understandings of repentance don't necessarily square with key examples in the Bible. But perhaps we haven't yet focused to your satisfaction on what the Bible *does* say about repentance. So, let's turn our attention to a couple of key sections that may help us flesh out our understanding of what repentance means.

> Now there were some present at that time who told Jesus about the Galileans whose blood Pilate had mixed with their sacrifices. Jesus answered, "Do you think that these Galileans were worse sinners than all the other Galileans because they suffered this way? I tell you, no! But unless you repent, you too will all perish. Or those eighteen who died when the tower in Siloam fell on them—do you think they were more guilty than all the others living in Jerusalem? I tell you, no! But unless you repent, you too will all perish." (Luke 13:1-5)

Jesus, in speaking to this group, circles back to the beginning of his ministry and the ministry of John the Baptist in reaffirming a coming event, obviously in the lifetime of his hearers. The only way to avoid it was for Israel as a nation to respond in repentance. His statement about "all the others living in Jerusalem" makes it quite clear that this isn't an invitation to a person or small group to get on their knees for a personal time of confession and conversion. So, what is the issue that Jesus is so worked up about? And what did he intend to do?

Our initial response might be to give a theological answer: "Jesus is concerned about sin, and he came to call the Jews to repent so they wouldn't end up going to hell." Though theologically correct as far as it goes, this response runs the risk of feeding into our modern tendency to treat Jesus' interactions with the Pharisees as abstractions intended only to illustrate some greater philosophical or spiritual truth. But remember, Jesus is talking to real people, in a real historical context, about events he is forecasting to occur in their lifetime. Let's look at the very next verses:

> Then [Jesus] told this parable: "A man had a fig tree, planted in his vineyard, and he went to look for fruit on it, but did not find any. So he said to the man who took care of the vineyard, 'For three years now I've been coming to look for fruit on this fig tree and haven't found any. Cut it down! Why should it use up the soil?'
>
> "'Sir,' the man replied, 'leave it alone for one more year, and I'll dig around it and fertilize it.'" (Luke 13:6-8)

Jesus does here what all the Old Testament prophets had done before him. He uses images and stories to communicate hard truths. But his approach here is particularly arresting. Israel had always assumed that God's return and becoming King in Jerusalem would mean the nation would be vindicated and God would destroy their enemies—in this case, Rome. But instead of vindicating them, Jesus suggests that Israel's *failure to bear fruit* would bring the very judgment on themselves that they were hoping would fall on their enemies. Through an unmistakable allusion to the book of Isaiah,

Jesus strikes right to the heart of the issue—and the Pharisees would have understood this.

In Isaiah 5:1-7, the prophet establishes the image of Israel as the Lord's vineyard, and he addresses a big problem: Israel isn't bearing the right kind of fruit. God was looking for good fruit and finding nothing but bad. "He looked for justice, but saw bloodshed; for righteousness, but heard cries of distress." God says through Isaiah that he will have to remove the protection around the vineyard and it will be trampled down and made a wasteland. Jesus now picks up the same image and identifies the same problem—no fruit. Jesus' words, in turn, echo those of John the Baptist, who exhorted the Pharisees to "produce fruit in keeping with repentance" (Matthew 3:8) rather than relying on their standing as children of Abraham.

So, what can we gather from all this to inform our understanding of repentance? Repentance clearly has to do with a reorientation of life, which is demonstrated by a certain type of fruit and a certain way of being.

11

Assumed Knowledge

After one of our runs where Jess and Phil and I had talked about the Bible, Jess became totally exasperated when I mentioned that the Old Testament backstory would have been assumed knowledge to the hearers and readers of the first century.

"Ron, how in the world are we supposed to know that Jesus is referring to some Old Testament context like Isaiah 5? I'm not an Old Testament scholar, and while I'm sure I've read Isaiah 5 at some point, I do not have a photographic memory. And if I'm someone who goes to church and reads the Bible and *I* don't get it, how in the world are my friends with whom I am trying to communicate about spiritual things ever going to get it, when I need to have all this background?"

"Okay, that's a fair question," I said. "Do we really need all this background? At one level, no. Simple communication should be enough. But you and Phil are really trying to engage all this at a deeper level, and as we go deeper, we find out how intricately woven much of the Bible is. I know it can be frustrating. But it does show how much Jesus was interested in entering into the story of the people he was trying to reach. And this can be instructive for us. When Jesus made allusions to images, metaphors, or even words, he assumed a working knowledge of this background. And for the Pharisees and common Jews, this wasn't an unfair or unfounded assumption; they really did know this stuff."

"But Ron," Jess interjected, "this doesn't help us when we talk to our friends and coworkers about God."

"Sure, I understand that, Jess. But our goal in these spiritual conversations with others isn't to give them a theology or history lesson. Remember, we are trying to use concepts and terms that people can grab instantly so they come to understand what God is doing, what he is inviting us to, and what he is offering. Essentially, we just want to help them hear what is so great about this newsflash that we are supposedly so captivated by. Does that help?"

"Well, yeah, at some level. But it's just overwhelming when I realize that what I thought I knew is probably at best incomplete, and then I have to pause and realize I am not trying to communicate the whole enchilada in one sitting."

Phil, who had been thoughtfully sipping on a bottle of water, now decided to jump into the fray. "Ron, I'm realizing for the first time one of those things you have repeatedly said: 'You have to have knowledge at level seven to communicate well at level five.' I see a lot of what we are talking about right now as being of the 'learn level seven' variety."

"Phil, I think you have the right perspective here. There's no need to be totally overwhelmed, but there is a sense in which you are intentionally trying to engage this at a totally different level from that of the average church attender. And it makes me smile."

"Why's that?" Jess said.

"Because I think you guys are starting to get it. Now let's see if I can pull some of these strings together for you. Ready?"

"Ready," they said in unison.

"Okay, let's start with a question, to get our bearings. From the story of the vineyard, can you see how the kind of repentance that Jesus is inviting the people to isn't a moral turning from some individual sins? That it is very similar to the kind of repentance that Josephus recorded when he was trying to get his revolutionary young bucks to reconsider how they were being revolutionaries? Jesus invited the Pharisees and the people to connect some current events to events from their history by getting Isaiah involved. Jesus was inviting them to consider the story of their exile coming to an end. Repentance to prepare for the end of exile and repentance from a zealous, violent, political overthrow were both present in Jesus' summons. I think he was saying, 'Quit following your political and nationalistic goals, aims, and agendas and, instead, repent and follow me.' Repentance here would mean reorienting their lives around a new center, a new goal, a new way of being Israel.

"This is so important to grasp, because it is exactly this nationalistic pride, which still persists today, that Jesus came to dismantle. Nationalism was the basis for Israel's decided exclusivism. They excluded everyone not like them and enforced Torah living because this is what they thought would prepare them for the end of exile. Jesus was essentially saying they had it all wrong. They were being Israel by fulfilling an agenda of living out the three big law categories: Sabbath keeping, circumcision, and dietary regulations. By keeping everyone "out" who didn't live up to all these rules and regulations, they thought they were keeping Israel pure. Jesus said he wanted to cut to the very root of this tree. In some ways, all the stories of inclusion, whether it was about tax collectors, prostitutes, or people who would have been considered unclean—the lame, the blind, and the paralyzed—point to Jesus' inviting Israel to reconsider what it meant for them to be Israel. His inclusiveness was an invitation to the Jews to repent of their exclusivity as a people, to reconsider and repent of their pride and arrogance.

"Maybe it is clearer now why sinners, tax collectors, the blind, the lame, and all the other people who couldn't or didn't fit the purity mold of Israel were considered outsiders. The Pharisees were convinced this was the way things needed to be in order for them to be a good and proper Israel. But beginning with the promise made to Abraham, the goal for Israel has never been to hoard the blessings of the love of God to themselves. The promise to Abraham was that through him and his seed *all* the families of the earth would be blessed.

"Therein lies the problem. As Israel pursued her path of exclusivity, a long line of prophets throughout the Old

Testament—continuing down to John the Baptist and, eventually, Jesus—came with precisely the same message: 'Bear fruit, Israel. Be a light, Israel. Don't hoard it for yourself, Israel.' Not only did Jesus come in the spirit of the Old Testament prophets, he also came with the same message of judgment. Only now it was 'last call' time, Israel's final shot at changing the type of Israel she had been.

"To be clear about his identity in relationship to the Old Testament prophets, Jesus told yet another story, a subversive and indicting parable that uncovered the pattern engaged in by the Pharisees and their predecessors. Jess, you have your Bible there; why don't you read Luke 20:9-16."

"Luke 20?" Jess riffled through the pages of her Bible. "Okay, got it: 'He went on to tell the people this parable: "A man planted a vineyard, rented it to some farmers and went away for a long time. At harvest time he sent a servant to the tenants so they would give him some of the fruit of the vineyard. But the tenants beat him and sent him away empty-handed. He sent another servant, but that one also they beat and treated shamefully and sent away empty-handed. He sent still a third, and they wounded him and threw him out.

"'"Then the owner of the vineyard said,'What shall I do? I will send my son, whom I love; perhaps they will respect him.'

"'"But when the tenants saw him, they talked the matter over. 'This is the heir,' they said. 'Let's kill him, and the inheritance will be ours.' So they threw him out of the vineyard and killed him.

"'"'What then will the owner of the vineyard do to them? He will come and kill those tenants and give the vineyard to others.' When the people heard this, they said, 'May this never be!'"'"

"Okay, what image does Jesus draw upon?" I asked.

"The vineyard?" Phil said.

"Right, the vineyard again. The story he tells is a story about Israel as a nation. We don't need to look at and comment on every verse, but we should note that many had attempted to come to the vineyard before, and they were spurned, beaten, and rejected. This is clearly the way the prophets of the Old Testament were treated, and Luke records Jesus talking about this, in chapter 11, verses 47-51.

Finally, the owner of the vineyard sends his own son, and the tenants kill him.

"It seems unmistakable that Jesus is telling an autobiographical story here, and his onlookers, the ones listening to this story, are the very ones who are doing the rejecting and killing. Apparently, the Pharisees and the teachers of the law got the point, because a couple of verses later it says—go ahead and read verse 19, Jess."

"'The teachers of the law and the chief priests looked for a way to arrest him immediately, because they knew he had spoken this parable against them. But they were afraid of the people.'"

"Even from these challenging stories of judgment, we can't help but notice that Israel had a sense that they were part of an unfolding story. They were characters in a grand drama. Furthermore, this grand drama was coming to a climax soon, a climax that might have some very strange elements of reversal. Because, you see, Israel assumed she was one of the good guys, which made her feel as if she needed to keep the bad guys out; but Jesus was turning the tables and saying she was in fact one of the bad guys in need of a major national reorientation campaign. The Jews' sense of their climactic story is an important piece to consider in seeking to understand how they thought and lived in the first century."

"So let me get this right," Jess said. "Jesus did die for our sins, but it isn't quite accurate to say that was his mission or what he was really trying to convince Israel of. Is that right?"

"Exactly," I said. "The agenda Jesus brought was the last salvo for Israel to finally respond—because, if not, the judgment predicted by the prophets, and include Jesus in that designation, was going to happen, and happen soon."

Thinking out loud, Phil picked up Jess's train of thought. "Ron, I have never grasped this part of the repentance equation before. But now I see what you have been trying to get us to see for so long—that our little individual experience isn't really Jesus' primary concern in the Gospels."

"Yes, exactly, Phil. You're getting it," I responded. "Now, do you see how quantum the shift is?"

"Ron, so many of the stories now make sense for the first time."

What have we learned so far? How is this practical for us? How does the insight we've gained here help us in the conversations we have with friends and neighbors about spiritual things? Well, for starters, if we are willing to be open to possible new input and adjust our previous understandings to make room for new insights, we can get a fuller picture of what is going on in the New Testament. Then, with our enhanced understanding, we can learn how to talk to people about Jesus without pushing all the wrong buttons before we've even had a chance to get started.

Unfortunately, the words *repent* and *repentance* have become associated in our culture with negative stereotypes and a not-too-friendly view of Christianity. As a result, opening a conversation with someone by mentioning repentance is bound to either shorten the conversation or stop it dead in its tracks. When Phil and Jess discovered that *repentance* could be understood as changing directions or putting one's mind into a different framework, they altered their approach (in a sense, repenting!) to help people think in terms of repentance as a "life shift." Now when Phil and Jess talk to Marty, it isn't so much about repenting as it is about inviting him to consider what might happen if his life were headed in a new direction. They're still talking about repentance; they just aren't using the word. It isn't *compromising;* it's *contextualizing*. It's communicating the full story in a way that considers what the listener can understand. The exciting thing about all this is that many people *are* considering a life change, a life shift, a realignment. Phil and Jess are doing great work. They want to share their faith, but they want it to connect. The language of *reorientation* and *realignment* is helping their conversations in very real ways.

12

Restoring a Shelby Cobra

All I had to do was mention that the "check engine" light had come on in my SUV, and Phil was on his way over to my place like a paramedic answering a 9-1-1 call.

It's one of the things I love about him and Jess. They intuitively grasp that ministry is not just "witnessing"; it's making oneself and one's skills available to others. Knowing that, I felt a little squeamish about accepting Phil's help. At our church, he'd organized a small group of similarly gifted mechanical types, and they spend two weekends a month doing free car clinics for single mothers. They change oil, replace belts, do tune-ups, and even do brakes and complete exhaust systems, all for free. (They raise money for the parts through regular charity motorcycle rides, which exposes our church to yet another set of people.) I didn't want to pull Phil away from that important work, and I said as much when I answered my door.

"Not a problem," he said. He held out his hand and I gave him the keys. "The clinic's next week, so it was either this or mow the lawn. I'll use any excuse in the world to avoid yard work."

I followed him out to the driveway. Something seemed odd, and then I put my finger on it: Jess hadn't come with him. Phil and Jess went everywhere together. Seeing one of them alone was like meeting an old friend and discovering that he was missing a few limbs. I hoped that everything was okay between them, but I didn't say anything. Years of counseling experience had taught me that, with men, you waited until they brought up an issue.

So, instead, I said, "You know, Phil, when I leased this SUV, it came with a service agreement."

He furrowed his eyebrows. Phil was not a believer in leasing automobiles. He thought it demonstrated insufficient mechanical commitment.

"But to use that, you've got to make an appointment, then take it down to the dealership and either get a loaner or wait," he said. "And if you decide to wait, one of the sales guys will show you the new models and talk you into ending the lease early. I know you, Ron. You're a gadget freak."

I didn't respond. What could I say? It was true.

Phil opened the car door and hooked up some sort of analyzer under the dash. He started the engine, looked at the readout for a moment, and then shut the engine off. Next, he pushed the button for the gas tank, walked to the back of the vehicle, and removed and replaced the gas cap. He walked back to the driver's seat, pushed something under the dash, and started the engine again. No "check engine" light came on.

"What'd you do?" I asked.

"Fuel cap was loose. I put it on tight and then reset the warning."

"I'm no automotive genius, but the engine's up there and the fuel cap is back here. What does the fuel cap have to do with the 'check engine' light?"

"Loose cap reads as an emissions fault. What else can we do while I'm here?" Phil glanced at the wheels. "When's the last time you rotated your tires?"

"They rotate every time I drive."

He rolled his eyes.

"I have a service agreement, remember? They get rotated every third oil change."

"All right." He nodded. "Well, let's just take a drive and make sure everything's okay."

Phil drove. I rode in the passenger's seat, waiting. If he was going to tell me something was wrong between him and Jess, now was probably the time.

"So . . ." he began.

Here it comes.

"Tell me about the kingdom."

"Pardon?"

"The kingdom. A few weeks ago, you talked about how Jesus said, 'The kingdom of heaven is at hand,' and you said that meant he was showing people what heaven is like. I'm really not sure how I talk to Marty about the 'kingdom of God.' Remember, this is a guy who watches David Letterman and Jon Stewart ridicule the president every evening. I mean, I've never seen a king or queen or shook a president's hand. What does all this talk about kingdoms mean?"

I started laughing.

"What?" Phil gave me a pointed look.

"That's what this is all about, isn't it? Your coming over without Jess? You've been deputized, haven't you?"

Phil pointed at the dash. "Your 'check engine' light is off."

I was still laughing. "You're right, bro. Tell you what; let's turn this thing around and stop wasting fossil fuels. I've got some iced tea in the fridge, and we can discuss 'kingdom.'"

We were settling into a couple of chairs on my deck when I asked Phil, "Name me a kingdom. Think back, if you have to."

Phil thought for a moment. "Camelot."

"That's a castle. Or actually, a court in a castle. Camelot was the place from which Arthur ruled England."

"Okay, then. England."

"And what's England?"

Phil shrugged. "Rocks. Dirt. Trees. Rivers. Sherwood Forest. The White Cliffs of Dover."

"So England is a place?"

Phil paused. He knew when he was heading into a trick question.

"Yes," he finally declared. "I have a map at home that has England on it. So I am reasonably sure that England is a place."

"And before there were kings, was it a place?"

"Sure."

"And was that place England?"

Phil thought for a moment. "No. But there was the place that we now know as England."

"That's right. In fact, when Rome occupied it, it was a province known as Angle Terre, 'the land of the Angles,' which eventually became anglicized into *England*. But before that it was something else—maybe a place without a name. What was it that made it Angle Terre and later England? What changed?"

"Government. It had to do with who was running it."

"There you go."

Phil looked around. "Where?"

"*Kingdom,*" I told him, "is not a matter of place. It's a matter of rule. These days, true monarchies are rare because *monarchy* literally means 'ruled by one.' England, for instance, is a constitutional monarchy in which the interests of the royals are exercised—several steps removed—by the House of Lords, and that is balanced and tempered by the House of Commons, taking the monarch out of the equation in everything but a ceremonial sense. But in days of old, a king's word was law. All judgment took place in the court of the king, and it truly was a singular vision running the show."

"So where is it?"

"It?"

"The kingdom. Christ's kingdom. I mean . . ." He waved his hand toward the blue sky. "It's up there, somewhere. Right?"

I looked up. "Yes, I suppose you could say that. It's up there, too."

"Too?"

I refilled Phil's glass from the pitcher on the patio table between us.

"What does the word *Christ* mean?" I asked.

"Anointed," Phil answered.

"And who gets anointed?"

"Kings."

"And a king rules a kingdom. We already know two things—that when Jesus said, 'The kingdom of heaven is at hand,' he was referring to his presence, and that the miracles worked in his presence were examples of the status quo of heaven, right?"

Phil nodded slowly.

"Jesus said that whenever two or three are gathered together in his name, then he is there also. I would say, given the nature of this discussion, that you and I are most definitely gathered together in his name, wouldn't you?"

"Sure." Phil cocked his head. "So?"

"So . . ." I opened my arms, taking in the two of us, the patio table, the stone patio, and the yard. "Kingdom."

"No." Phil shook his head emphatically. "That I can't accept."

"Why not?"

"That this is *it*? That we're serving to inherit *this*?"

"It isn't service that gets you the inheritance."

"I know, I know. But . . ." Phil looked down at the table. He appeared genuinely miserable.

"Let me guess," I said. "You're wondering how this could be heaven if it has oil spills and tsunamis and Hitlers and Stalins and people who play their stereos too loud at stoplights and flip you the bird if you look at them, right?"

"Right. And as for this 'two or three' thing, Ron. . . . Christians have been persecuted through the ages, usually in groups considerably larger than two or three. I mean, terrorists still blow up churches in the middle of services, for crying out loud. How is that heaven?"

"Pour me an iced tea," I told him.

Phil poured.

"There," I said. "I didn't make a request. I didn't say 'please' . . ."

"I noticed."

". . . because I didn't want to make it sound optional. I wanted to make it sound like a command. And when you responded as I asked, you placed yourself under my dominion. You obeyed me. But suppose you and Jess had a son, and I told you to kill him. Would you do it?"

"Of course not."

"I hope you wouldn't. I have no business asking you to do that. But that is exactly what God told Abraham to do, and Abraham prepared to do it. He prepared, the author of

Hebrews explains, because he was certain that if he did as God asked and sacrificed his son, God would respond by restoring his son to life. You see, monarchy is a two-part equation. The king rules, but the subjects have to obey. Jesus has always ruled everything he made, which is, quite literally, everything. Earth, moon, sun, stars, outer space, and other dimensions that we're only dimly aware of, if at all. It is *all* his kingdom. But not everyone accepts his dominion. In fact, he has a very powerful adversary who is in revolt."

"Satan."

"Which literally means 'adversary' or 'the enemy.'"

"I remember."

"And until that enemy submits, the kingdom continues in a state of corruption and revolt. Of course, the enemy eventually must submit, not only because it has been prophesied, but also because, as they figured out in Newtonian physics, if there is an irresistible power, which God most certainly is, then there cannot be an immovable object. We have windows of perfection in everything from glorious sunrises to miraculous healings, but we also have reminders of the rebellion that continues at a magnitude that we cannot begin to imagine. Yet it must and will end, and when it does, the rebellious influence will vanish and all that will be left is perfection."

"Still . . ." Phil looked at a small patch of crabgrass in my lawn. "If this is all there is . . ."

I took a sip of tea and set the glass down.

"Do you remember," I asked him, "when we drove down to Indiana last summer to that classic-car auction, and you were trying to convince Jess that the Shelby Cobra they had there was worth buying?"

"Hey, that car was a beaut! Cars like that are . . . they're super rare. Most of the ones you see on the street are knock-offs. This was the real deal, built at the Skunk Works. They're worth a fortune."

"But I looked at that car. It was leaking oil and the seats were torn and there was some weird corrosion thing going on at the fender seam and . . . as I recall, it wouldn't even start, would it?"

"But that's just the way it was *then*. Sure, it would've taken some work, but when I got done with it, it would've been perfect, and it would be . . ." Phil stopped talking, drifting into some four-speed, V-8-powered reverie.

"So," I said, speaking quickly before I lost him entirely to the fantasy. "When you looked at that car, you didn't see it as it was then. You saw it as it would be when it was restored."

Phil nodded.

"Maybe that's a better word than *kingdom,* then. Maybe, to understand which state of the kingdom it is that we are referring to, we should refer to it as 'the restoration.'"

Phil peered at me from under his eyelids. "But what about the streets of gold and the pearly gates?"

"In some dimension, I'm certain heaven is like that, as well. But the physical stuff, the real estate, is not what's going to make it heaven. It's the presence of Jesus. And unlike earthly kingdoms, where you have to enter a court to be in the king's presence, in the kingdom of Christ he is there with you all the time. Right now, even in those moments that we recognize being 'in the Spirit,' where we can really feel God's presence, it's sort of like listening to a distant radio station through hundreds of miles of static and interference on an old radio in a pickup truck. But, to continue that analogy, when the adversary and his influence are removed, all the static will be gone. From a bad AM station to having Eric Clapton in your living room—that's what the difference will be like. Even more so, actually. And trust me, Phil. It will be worth the trip."

13

Four Views of the Kingdom

Is the kingdom of heaven now, or is it something in the future? Is it a real place, or simply a spiritual reality? Is it a combination of these elements, or all of them at the same time? I remember an exercise that my friend Dr. Scot McKnight, the main mentor in my master's program, put us through in a class on the Gospels. We had to go through Matthew, Mark, and Luke, look up every instance of "kingdom of God" or "kingdom of heaven," and ask two questions: "Is it present or future?" and "Is it a place or a presence?" This was the same issue that Phil was grappling with. When we start talking about the kingdom of God, these are the conundrums that naturally arise.

Before we plow headlong into the message itself, let's remind ourselves of the context.

After four hundred years of silence following the end of Malachi's prophetic ministry, the Israelites are hoping and anticipating that sometime soon a messenger, a preparer of the way, will come in fulfillment of Malachi's predictions. The announcement will signal an epochal shift, something that would feel nearly cataclysmic, the coming of God's kingdom.

Several things surrounded this theme of the arrival

of God's kingdom. The messenger would announce the breaking forth of the kingdom, which would signal an end of exile for Israel. Religious autonomy would be ushered in, due to the political autonomy that would attend the new king. This is what the end of exile looked and felt like to the Jews. The Temple would be rebuilt, and its former glory would be realized once again. And all this would be made possible by the defeat of Israel's enemies, which in this case was Rome.

At this particular juncture in history, *how* the kingdom would be ushered in was thought of in widely divergent ways, depending on which school of thought one subscribed to. Because Israel had such a significant sense of playing a role in God's unfolding story, it makes sense that there would be differing views of how to interact and engage with that story.

If you were aligned with Herod or the chief priests, you would have recognized the futility of opposing the immense military power of Rome. Any attempt to hasten the dawning of the kingdom by overthrowing Roman rule was certain suicide. Thus, compromise and acquiescence to the prevailing culture was seen as the only way to go. "If you can't beat 'em, join 'em" may have been the mantra of choice for this group.

In contrast to those on the "make the best of it" bandwagon, the Zealots were a group that would have nothing to do with compromise. They were the fundamentalists of the day, and the only solution they saw to the problem of the Roman Empire in Palestine was to usher the Romans out. In other words, they were in favor of a bloody fight to the bitter end. These were the same revolutionaries referred to in the story recorded by Josephus, where he invited the revolutionaries to "repent." Of course, Herod and Company thought the Zealots were nuts. The Zealots, for their part, thought the chief priests and Herod were big-time liberals who were enamored with keeping everyone happy.

Same reality. Different approaches.

In situations like these, of course, there is always a group that withdraws from the whole thing, not wanting to compromise but also not wanting to go the way of political and military revolution. This third group were the Essenes, who took a "go live in a cave" approach to the conflict. They sought to live faithful and holy lives, untainted by compromise and unruffled by the fury and hostility of others. They lived in caves, in geographical isolation, praying and fasting and studying the Scriptures. The Essenes, who lived in the desert of Qumran, are thought to be responsible for the writings called the Dead Sea Scrolls that were found in the late 1940s. As previously mentioned, some scholars believe that John the Baptist may have been an Essene, based on his desert location and the quotation of Isaiah 40 on his lips. The Essene view of history was something along the lines of "apocalypse now": God returns, righting the world's wrongs, establishing justice in all the earth, and overthrowing his enemies. In the meantime, the Essenes' duty was to live a monastic life in the desert and pray till the cataclysm dawned.

A fourth view prevailed among the group known as the Pharisees. This group of religious leaders and teachers has often been mischaracterized as teaching that one could get to heaven by trying real hard to keep all the laws. What the Pharisees believed, based on their reading of the Scriptures, was that one day God would return to Jerusalem and would rule and reign. Their job, in the meantime, was to keep Israel pure. In other words, their view of how to hasten God's coming and bring about the kingdom was by being ready, pure, and prepared. This meant obeying the full weight of the law, and especially the "big three": Sabbath laws, circumcision laws, and dietary laws. These laws were the way that Israel marked her uniqueness. Sociologists call these boundary markers: highly visible, though relatively superficial, ways of marking who is in and who is out. The Pharisees believed that their job was to keep Israel pure, or else God might not return to Jerusalem. As a result of the boundary markers they established and the fear of being tainted and becoming impure, they marginalized every person who religiously, socially, ethnically, or politically didn't align with them.

Into this matrix of options came John the Baptist as the messenger announcing the arrival of the Coming One, Jesus. When Jesus arrived on the scene, he didn't align himself with any of the four prevailing worldviews, but instead redefined each in unique and inside-out ways. He said the kingdom was coming near, in, and through himself. But we're getting ahead of the story.

"Repent, for the kingdom of heaven is at hand." We have looked at the word *repentance* and spent some time thinking of how our modern understanding needs to be reconsidered in light of a careful reading of the New Testament and a better understanding of the first-century context. But what about the second part of the sentence?

What is the kingdom of heaven?

My friend Phil articulated the most common view I've heard: If you're a Christian, heaven is the place you go when you die. In my experience, this view prevails in 90 percent of the churches I have worked with or visited. Quite simply, if there is a dimension of the kingdom of God that isn't *future,* it is most certainly rather minimal when compared with the great location in the sky where we will play endless golf; enjoy perfect, sunny, seventy-five-degree weather; and live in homes that have been custom designed to fulfill our dreams. Well, that may approximate the image of heaven we've had painted for us by modern-day American preachers, but it's a heaven that didn't exist in the thought world of Jesus' day—not at all.

When people in first-century Palestine heard the word *kingdom,* there was only one immediate point of reference: the kingdom of Caesar. But even knowing that, the implications are hard for us to grasp in the context of our modern American culture. Even a modern-day monarchy such as Great Britain cannot begin to approximate a kingdom where the ruler is called Savior and God and Lord and is bowed to in day-to-day affairs. It's just not the same. Consequently, when we read the birth announcement of Caesar, or even the birth announcement of Jesus recorded in Luke 2, it just doesn't ring with the world-changing significance that the original audience would have grasped and understood.

When we hear the familiar word *Christ,* we are apt to forget that it's a title—a declaration—and not Jesus' last name. The English word *Christ* is derived from the Greek word for "anointed one," which is to say "heir apparent to the throne," or "king." In Hebrew, the word for "anointed one" is *messiah.* Essentially, Christ and Messiah are the same thing. So when the angel announced, "I bring you good news of great joy. . . . Today in the town of David a Savior has been born to you; he is Christ the Lord" (Luke 2:10-11), he wasn't first and foremost making a statement about a king who would come and sit on the throne of our hearts. No, I believe the angelic herald spoke in terms that would deliberately echo the birth announcement of Caesar Augustus, the Roman emperor at the time of Jesus' birth. When the Jews in the first century heard the "gospel of great joy" about the coming of a Savior, Lord, and Anointed One, they could only have whispered in very hushed tones, "Oh my! If this one born in the city of David is Savior, King, and Lord, then that would mean Caesar . . . isn't! Could this be the arrival of the Anointed One spoken of by Isaiah, who will reign in Jerusalem?" One thing we can say with certainty is that when the angel announced the coming of the Savior, those listening weren't thinking about someone they would invite into their lives to save them from a fiery finale called hell.

Now, let's be careful here. Are we saying there is no such place as the kingdom of heaven that we'll go to when we die? No, of course not. There is such a place and Jesus himself talked about it, so no dispute there. However—and this is a big *however*—that isn't primarily what Jesus had in mind when he declared, "The kingdom of heaven is at hand." Nevertheless, when I have informally surveyed people in church congregations, and church leaders at conferences, and have asked one question—"What is the easiest way for you to explain or describe what the kingdom of God (or kingdom of heaven) is?"—unanimously, and I mean without exception, the only response I have ever received, and this includes from church pastors who have a master of divinity degree, is this:

"It is the place all Christians go when they die" or some other nearly identical description. Wow!

Two things seem critically important to point out. First, when we answer the way that 100 percent of respondents did to the question "What is the kingdom of God?" by saying it is a future, invisible, and out-there-somewhere place, we are omitting a very critical—and arguably the most important—component of the definition in the minds of Jesus' listeners. For them, the kingdom was near, at hand; there was a *right now* component to it.[1]

Second, the some-future-place definition of the kingdom of heaven distorts the word out of its historical context. The phrase "kingdom of heaven" deliberately played off the primary historical and political reality of the first century—the kingdom of Caesar. If our only mental template for this phrase is an out-there-somewhere, invisible place with streets of gold, then we will miss all the political, historical, and societal implications that Jesus intended for us to understand.

We have already identified two convergent streams of thought, but we haven't explicitly tied them together. When the Jews in the first century read the Old Testament prophecies of a king coming to Jerusalem to sit on David's throne or the announcement that God would finally reign as King, there wasn't a category in their thinking that would have transported them out of the here and now and the space/time universe to some timeless utopia of the future. The Old Testament backstory just doesn't support an expectation like that. So although the kingdom of heaven clearly has a future dimension, the presentness, the here-and-nowness of the kingdom is clearly what John the Baptist and Jesus had in view when they said the kingdom of heaven is "at hand," or "near."

The second converging stream is found in the first-century cultural context, which we are coming to expect has some influence in shaping the words as they were understood and used back then. Because we live in the twenty-first century, in a democratic society where the idea of kings, tyrants, and dictators is often thought of as ancient or mythical, or at the very least *somewhere else,* the power of comparing the kingdom of God to the kingdom of Caesar is lost on us, for the most part. But the significance of a king being born in the city of David wasn't lost at all on those in power in the actual kingdoms of the day. Remember, it was King Herod who gave an edict to kill every newborn male under the age of two. Why? Why would Herod feel threatened by a little boy two years old or younger? He knew what all the Jews knew, that a king was coming sometime, maybe soon, to sit on the throne of David.

When Jesus came announcing that the kingdom of God was near, if the announcement wasn't primarily about an invisible place out there in the future and apparently wasn't about taking over the literal throne in Rome, what was it actually about? Before digging into that question, we need to be clear on a couple of things. Though Jesus never intended to sit on the throne in Rome, the Romans apparently saw him as something of a political threat. And clearly the Jewish leaders and teachers of the law saw Jesus as a huge threat to their Jewishness—a sort of subversive influence who was out there leading people astray.

Ironically, neither threat was real. In his typical fashion, Jesus redefined for the Jews what Jewishness means and what it means to be a part of his kingdom. And against the prevailing assumptions of Rome, Jesus admitted to being the King of the Jews, but again, not in a way that should have concerned the Roman authorities. It's important that we understand how Jesus redefined these two "threats" before we seek to answer the kingdom question.

14

Redrawing the Lines

Imagine you are part of a club with very exclusive membership requirements that have been set in stone for generations. Let's say it's a club in a beautiful part of Italy, and the primary requirements are that you have to be Italian; you have to be a fabulous cook with unique contributions to those in the club community; and most of all, you have to follow very strict guidelines about the preparation and usage of various olive oils that the club is known for using. These guidelines are complicated and vast, and they require a governing body that oversees careful instruction concerning the regulations. The governing body, Teachers of the Olive Oil Laws (TOTOOL), also has an enforcement arm. Its job is to watch carefully the cooking practices of the members to determine whether they are indeed abiding by the rules and to make sure the members participate in mandatory continuing education to stay abreast of the nearly seven hundred olive-oil laws on the books.

People stay in the club because they are convinced they are creating the best, most healthy, and incredibly unique dishes imaginable. In fact, the recipes for many of their culinary creations have been passed down for generations and are priceless. Members also feel a particular pride that they, and they alone, are the keepers of the oil; and the proper handling of the oil makes them unique, distinct, and you might even say, "God's gift to the rest of the world." Those within the ranks are unquestioning and "law abiding"; after all, it is an honor to be a part of a group with such an amazing history; a group that others cannot be a part of.

But what would happen if someone came on the scene in this area of Italy and decided to start his own club? What if he, though a native of the area and a de facto club member due to his family lineage, began to question the abiding relevance of the ethnic exclusion, and remained entirely unpersuaded that the olive-oil laws really resulted in the best product? What if he began having open conversations about these issues with the TOTOOL leaders? And what if many onlookers became intrigued with the power behind his words? Not only are some French and Swiss observers now interested in these conversations, but some Italian members of the club who have always had some misgivings but no courage to voice them are particularly intrigued and wondering what all this might mean. Does this emerging voice present a viable alternative option?

Over a number of weeks and months of conversations, it becomes clear that the new guy on the block wants to include, not exclude, people. That's right, he wants to cast the net wide to redefine who is in and who is out. For starters, he says the ethnic distinction is unnecessary and unproductive. He thinks anyone who can cook well and contribute delectable recipes to the community should qualify. After all, he says, ethnic exclusivity produces nothing but pride.

Of course, the TOTOOL are outraged and pepper him at every turn with strategic questions about the Olive Oil Regulation Archives (OORA)—the Bible, if you will, of olive-oil laws. Though lots of spirited conversations ensue about the OORA, the man is quite convinced that it can no longer be used as a means of excluding people. Furthermore, he consistently challenges the TOTOOL and their overly strict interpretation of the OORA, which he claims isn't in keeping with the spirit in which it was written. Essentially, he proposes a full-scale redefinition of the club's boundary markers, the rules the club has sworn by for centuries, and he suggests that the proprietary spirit of the club needs to become more open.

Of course, his reputation quickly becomes that of a subversive rabble-rouser and one-man wrecking crew. And the reasons are clear: He isn't just messing with a little club; he's stepping on the toes of societal bigwigs, power brokers, and some of the most sought-after leaders in Italy. His proposals have political implications for the entire region—and economic implications as well. If membership is no longer restricted to the club's elite families of pedigree, then poorer and more marginalized citizens can bring their contributions to the community on an equal footing. His proposal also has global implications. It means that people from all over, not just in this little region, can become part of the community, no matter where they live or what their background.

Are you getting the connections? When Jesus came on the scene, he essentially redefined Israel's identity. He redescribed the boundary markers that determined who was in and who was out. Israel was proudly exclusive along ethnic lines. Jesus came and demolished that. He chose twelve disciples, echoing the twelve tribes of Israel, and then said point blank that in the end the twelve disciples would sit on twelve thrones and judge the twelve tribes of Israel. The symbolism is obvious. The twelve disciples have superseded the older version of the twelve tribes (see Matthew 19:28).

On another occasion, when it was mentioned to Jesus that his mother and brothers had arrived to see him, he responded by asking, "Who are my mother and my brothers? . . . Whoever does God's will is my brother and sister and mother" (Mark 3:33, 35). In other words, race is out, ethnicity is out, bloodline is no longer a boundary line. A heart connected to God is the only requirement. There is no room for ethnic exclusivity.

We already saw this approach in John the Baptist's chiding of the Pharisees and teachers of the law who tried to act as if their connection to Abraham allowed them an exemption from connecting their hearts to God. The Gospels include many other instances where Jesus essentially redefines what it means to be a part of his tribe. He flips the lens from one of exclusion to one of inclusion.

When Matthew wrote his account of the life of Christ, he set it up in an interesting way. After detailing Jesus' genealogy through his earthly father, Joseph, and recounting the stories of Jesus' birth and childhood, the coming of John the Baptist, Jesus' baptism and temptation in the desert, and the calling of the first few disciples, Matthew opens the next section with a summary statement: "Jesus went throughout Galilee, teaching in their synagogues, preaching the good news of the kingdom, and healing every disease and sickness among the people" (Matthew 4:23).

A careful reader might ask why Matthew is telling us this when Jesus hasn't done anything yet? Why does the writer include a broad, sweeping, far-reaching summary statement when the narrative up to this point makes it clear that Jesus is barely getting started? That's a good question. It turns out that Matthew is telegraphing what he's about to show us over the next several chapters. He wants to draw our attention to the focus of Jesus' life and work: traveling, teaching, preaching, and healing.

What follows in chapters 5–7 of Matthew is an exposition of the most famous sermon in human history, known as the Sermon on the Mount (Jesus preaching and teaching), followed by an account in chapters 8 and 9 of Jesus' travels and the variety of illnesses and infirmities that he healed (Jesus traveling and healing). Then, in Matthew 9:35, he echoes almost verbatim the summary statement he made at the beginning of the section: "Jesus went through all the towns and villages, teaching in their synagogues, preaching the good news of the kingdom and healing every disease and sickness."

Why does Matthew deliberately set his account of Jesus' work between these two almost identical bookends? Because he doesn't want us to overlook the importance of what Jesus was doing—namely, reframing Israel's relationship to the law (the central piece of their identity) and redefining who was in and who was out (the central piece of their relationship to the world).

In chapter 8, Matthew opens his account of Jesus' healing ministry with a short but important story about a leper. Let's try to get to the heart of this story to see what it teaches us about Jesus' efforts to redefine Israel's boundaries.

When Jesus came down from the mountainside after his momentous sermon, he encountered a leper who knelt before him and said, "Lord, if you are willing, you can make me clean" (Matthew 8:2). If you're like I was for many years, you don't quite grasp the importance of this statement. I used to look at Jesus healing this guy and think that was the primary point of the story. But I'm no longer certain that healing as we usually define it—the eradication of disease—is really the main point at all.

I've had the opportunity to travel to India many times, and I've been to several leper colonies there. Leper colonies exist for one purpose: to keep the lepers segregated from the rest of the population. The fear is that the rest of the world would be infected if it weren't for this segregation. The sad and very isolated existence of these people deemed unclean just breaks one's heart.

So when the leper in Matthew 8 encounters Jesus, I think he sees in him far more than someone who can heal his leprous condition. I think he sees Jesus as a means to social restoration, to relational reconnection to the rest of the world. While the leper certainly wanted healing from his disfiguring and numbing disease, I think he was looking for something deeper. And Jesus heard that deeper request. Not only did he heal him of his disease, but he also opened the pathway to wholeness, or what we might call societal mainstream living, by telling him to go and show himself to the priest.

This instruction to go to the priest is a key turning point in the story. Why? Because the priest had the authority to pronounce things clean and unclean, and thereby determine who would be socially acceptable, who could or couldn't come to the Temple for worship, and who could come to dinner with you. Jesus didn't just make a disease disappear and physically fix something that was broken. He restored the man socially, placing him in a position to return to the fullness of life and to social reconnection. In short, he brought the leper out of exile and restored him to multidimensional wholeness. I think this is why Matthew chose this very short, four-verse story as the first example of healing.

The opening story of Matthew 9 also seems to be a signature event. Some friends bring a paralyzed man to Jesus, and Jesus perceives this as a great act of faith. Interestingly, what the friends were hoping for is not specifically mentioned, though we can surmise they were seeking the eradication of disease. But what if Jesus' initial response reveals the real thing they were after—healing of a spiritual kind? What if the physical absence of disease was again more of a by-product than a goal? The rest of the story seems to hint in this direction.

The first thing Jesus says to the man is, "Take heart, son; your sins are forgiven" (v. 2). Does it strike you as odd that a statement about forgiveness would be the first thing out of Jesus' mouth? If the man had come repenting of some sort of evil, maybe Jesus' response would seem predictable and natural, but this guy didn't even come of his own accord. He was carried there by some friends. It would seem rather obvious that his physical condition was the primary concern. Not only that, but according to the "rules of the game" at the time, only a priest could offer forgiveness through the sacrificial system in the Temple. When the Pharisees heard Jesus offering forgiveness, they were incensed. But Jesus is again giving us strong clues as to the kind of empire he is ushering in.

Notice what happens next. Jesus asks a question that in our modern context seems easy to answer, but apparently the right answer is the opposite one in the world in which Jesus is living and operating.

"Which is easier: to say, 'Your sins are forgiven,' or to say, 'Get up and walk'?" (v. 5). Well, that's actually a very tough question if you reflect on it at all, because it totally hinges on the meaning of *easier*, doesn't it? If by *easier* we mean there is no verification necessary, then "your sins are forgiven" is much easier to say. There's no way to prove or disprove it. At least superficially, "your sins are forgiven" is a much easier statement.

If you're like me, you're running this question through a modern, Newtonian, scientific worldview. According to the scientific mind-set, "get up and walk" is instantly verifiable and will provide onlookers with "proof" as to whether the healer is legitimate or a fraud.

On the other hand, if by *easier* you mean what can a mere man do and what can only God do, then saying "your sins are forgiven" is far more difficult, because only God can do that. Any magician or healer can say "get up and walk," but few people in their right mind would think they had the authority to forgive sin; that is obviously God's exclusive domain.

Jesus takes all the guesswork out of it. He looks at the paralyzed man, a social outcast because paralytics were assumed to be cursed by God, and he says, "Let me prove to you I can forgive sins." He then pronounces the man's sins forgiven and heals his paralysis.

As an aside to our previous discussion, isn't it interesting that Jesus doesn't seek any statement or sign of repentance from the paralytic? There is also no evidence to suggest he talked to the man about his heart, his eternal destiny, or whether or not he was going to heaven. Instead, Jesus was as concerned about the man's relational and social brokenness as he was about the diseased condition itself.

Immediately following the story of the healing of the paralyzed man, we come to a story that at first glance seems out of place: the calling of Matthew to follow Jesus. What's going on here? Matthew has already given an account of the calling of the disciples, prior to the first summary statement about teaching, preaching, and healing, and prior to the Sermon on the Mount. Why wouldn't the calling of Matthew be positioned in chapter 4, where the flow of the narrative would make more sense to our chronological sensibilities? Also, based on the structure of Matthew's narrative thus far, we would expect to find another story of physical healing here. So, what gives?

The first thing we're told is that Matthew is a tax collector. We've already looked at the story of Zacchaeus, so we know that tax collectors were social outcasts and considered unclean. Once again, we have an example of the boundary markers erected by the Pharisees and teachers of the law. Jesus, as a supposedly good Jew, was in violation of the cleanliness laws because he was eating with the wrong type of people, associating with *that* kind. When the Pharisees see Jesus eating at Matthew's house, they want to know why he is consorting with "sinners."

"On hearing this, Jesus said, 'It is not the healthy who need a doctor, but the sick. But go and learn what this means: "I desire mercy, not sacrifice." For I have not come to call the righteous, but sinners'" (Matthew 9:12-13). It's interesting that in this story that is not about physical healing but is set in the midst of other stories about physical healing, Jesus opts to use a medical metaphor for removing a social stigma.

The weight of Jesus' statement about those who need a physician provides a scathing rebuke as well. The Pharisees are branded as those who think they have it all together and have no need for anyone to help them. In essence, Jesus says to them, "I am not here for you." Ouch! The implications of that statement will only fully sink in as we progress deeper into the story.

Jesus is redefining who is in and who is out. And his redefinition is one that doesn't fly well with current convention. In many of the stories recorded in the Gospels, Jesus heals people and doesn't even invite them to become his followers. We may choose to assume they did, but it would only be an assumption. Numerous times he heals people or talks with them and never brings up the issue of following him, unlike his invitations to the twelve disciples. He simply loves these other people in ways that deeply and permanently etch their lives. Anyone can be in who wants to be in; the playing field for the formerly marginalized is identical to the playing field for the trained scribe and the teacher of the law.

In the stories we've looked at or mentioned, there seems to be a common theme emerging. With Zacchaeus and Matthew, the woman caught in adultery, and certainly with all the people who were physically healed, the idea of restoration seems central. What if the kingdom of heaven is essentially about the restoration of things to the way God intended them to be?

I want to suggest something here that maybe you've never heard or considered. What if we can't understand Jesus bringing the kingdom of heaven until we understand God's original intent in creating the world in the first place? What if we have to understand the story from the very beginning in order to come to grips with Jesus' intervention into human history and why he did what he did and said what he said? By doing a "back to the future" thing, we can see that when Jesus came and announced the dawning of a new kingdom, he was essentially reestablishing God's original intention for his creation. Think of it this way: What if the coming of Jesus was the arrival of God's future in the present? What if he was trying to show how this new kingdom, this new empire, was dramatically different from any empire in history, in part because it was built upon inclusion and acceptance of an unprecedented sort?

If what I'm suggesting is true, it *would be* an important newsflash. It would be *tremendously* good news, as important in Rwanda as in Rochester, and as powerful in Uzbekistan as in Utah. Are you beginning to see why having a fuller and broader definition of the kingdom of heaven is so powerful? Now, instead of selling tickets for a seat in some far-off heaven, we are inviting people into something far deeper, more immediate, and life changing. We are inviting them into a way of love and life they have not yet experienced. But it is a love and life that can be experienced here and now, not just at some unspecified time in the future. The kingdom of heaven is at hand. Restoration is possible. A new way of living is available to everyone.

15
False Starts and Waffles

One Friday, Phil called me with a note of desperation in his voice.

"It's Jess's weekend." He let out a huge sigh. "She chose Saugatuck again." There was dead silence on the line.

I knew what that meant. Jess and Phil had an agreement that every weekend one of them would choose the "fun" activity for the weekend. Phil's weekends were filled with mountain biking, rock climbing, and stuff like that. Jess chose long car trips to her favorite breakfast nooks, antique shops, and art galleries. Saugatuck was one of her favorite places to visit. Phil was looking for company for when the "browsing" became too much.

I glanced at my calendar. "You're in luck, Phil. This weekend is free. But you owe me one."

"Okay, we'll pick you up at nine." The line went dead.

I had a feeling we would be continuing our discussion about the kingdom—and I was right. Jess brought it up after brunch had been served.

"Ron, you've been telling us that the kingdom of God isn't simply a ticket into heaven—that it's really about 'restoration.' But what does that *really* mean to Marty? He's more interested in throwing away his old Sony Vaio and getting a Mac Pro than 'restoring'anything."

"Marty sounds like my type of guy. I'd much rather own the latest gadget for my iPod than restore anything. I am not the antique sort of person. Nothing in me appreciates the old, musty, and broken."

Jess rolled her eyes.

"I know, call me callous and uncultured. I wasn't exactly excited about the stop we had to make at the antique store fifteen minutes ago, Jess. Maybe I was wrecked that summer in high school, between my sophomore and junior years, when my summer job was stripping paint from an old staircase in a very large and old estate home in our town. It was mahogany wood, imported from Africa, and some 'uncultured' soul had had the audacity to paint it with multiple coats of paint. The new owner of the estate, disgusted by what he called 'such uncultured disrespect,' decided he would undertake the monumental task of stripping all the paint off this precious wood. Or to say it another way, he decided to hire some gullible high schooler to 'have the honor' of spending most of the summer stripping years of paint from the huge staircase and the door frames and window sills. What else I did that summer, I don't quite remember; I was too high from paint-stripper fumes to remember."

"I would love to have seen that staircase." Jess stared into space. I could tell she was envisioning the pristine finished product.

"Well, let's put it this way," I said. "Whenever I walk into an antique shop, the distinct smell of peeling paint comes back to me. Maybe that's why I don't like those places."

Jess looked at me with a mixture of pity and disdain. "You should have felt pride in what you were doing, Ron. There aren't many homes around that still have genuine, imported, mahogany staircases."

"Okay, I know, I know. I'm uncultured. I realize the point of the whole summer project was to restore this gorgeous wood to its original beauty—to recapture, if you will, the original intent of the first owners when they paid exorbitant amounts of money to import the wood over a century ago.

True restoration has to have some vision of what the original looked like or else it isn't true restoration; it's just paint stripping. That's true whether you are restoring imported wood or a 1968 Camaro."

"Oh, yeah. Marty shares Phil's love of classic cars," Jess interjected.

"Well, my point is, Marty couldn't possibly be interested in 'restoration' until he falls in love with what Jesus came to restore. That's the allure of restoration."

"So, what did Jesus restore?" Phil asked.

"Well, one of the challenges we face, in the evangelical church in particular, is that we've been telling the same story for a long time, but we've never stopped to ask whether the story we're telling is the whole story. There's Fall and Redemption, we've got that part down. But, what is Jesus redeeming? What's he restoring?"

Phil and Jess looked at each other and then back at me.

"Do you realize what is at stake here?" I continued. "If we are telling a shortened or incomplete version of the story, we are in some serious danger of distorting the message, and misleading all the Martys of this world."

"What do you mean, Ron?" Jess asked with a puzzled look on her face.

"I went to seminary," I said. "I've been around 'the system' for more than two decades. And I know we have shorthand for the story we tell. It might best be summarized by what a seminary professor once said: 'The story we are here to tell is one of Fall and Redemption.' His point was well taken and understood by all in the class. Adam and Eve screwed up; they needed a fix, and God provided it by sending his Son to die for us and redeem us from our sins so we can spend eternity with him. Make that issue global and the church now has a mission. Humanity is fallen, and God sent his Son to redeem fallen humanity so that we can have a seat in heaven with him forever. That may sound a bit reductionistic, but it isn't far off the mark for what many of our seminaries and churches teach. But is it the whole story? Is it even the main part of the story? I'm not convinced." I paused to sip my coffee and take in the view of Lake Michigan.

"But where else would you start? The story of Adam and Eve

and the apple is the first story of the Bible," Jess said in a "here we go again" tone that she seemed to reserve only for me.

"Is it, really?"

"Well, it's the first story our Sunday school class would always go over," Phil interjected.

"What about 'On the first day, God created . . .'"

"Oh, yeah. The story of God creating night and day—and all the animals."

". . . and creating Adam and Eve," I added, finishing Phil's sentence. "Not that many years ago, I would have done the same thing you just did. I would have started with Adam and Eve and the apple. According to my view of the world, Creation was forgettable. Why? Because what was important was Fall and Redemption. But the biggest problem with the Fall and Redemption summary is that it starts the story in chapter 3 of the book. What about the groundwork of the first two chapters? What about the creation story that Phil and I always forget? We can never fully understand any story if we start by skipping the first couple of chapters. Usually the opening chapters in a book are critical for the story line and development of where the author is heading. If you start in chapter 3 of Genesis, then of course you are entering the story at the point of a problem. But there is little room there to talk about restoration because you've skipped over what the original looked like that you are trying to restore. It seems clear, then, that we need to really look at the first couple of chapters in Genesis before we sign off on the idea that a good summary of the biblical message is Fall and Redemption."

"Well, I usually don't bring a Bible with me," Jess said as she reached for her purse, "but I thought we might be talking about this." She pulled out a small blue-leather Bible and quickly leafed past the table of contents to the first page of Genesis.

"All right, let's take a look at this," I said, taking a bite of fruit salad from my plate. "When we look at the first two chapters of Genesis, a couple of things become evident. God created a beautiful place called the Garden. It was lush, plush, and full of all kinds of fruit. He also created human beings—human beings made in his image. The word for 'image' in the Greek Old Testament is *eikon,* or in English, *icon.* If you do a quick look at any dictionary, an icon is an image, a picture, or a representation; it is a sign or likeness that stands for an object by representing it. God wanted some 'icons' in his Garden—some representations of himself, some objects that had similarities so they could be stand-ins for him. Important in all this is that God made male and female together, so they both reflected his image." Phil and Jess glanced at each other and touched hands on the tabletop.

"In other words, the reflection of God's image in humanity is complete only with both masculine and feminine. God said it was not good for Adam to be alone, so Eve was introduced. Furthermore, Adam and Eve were given a purpose, a reason for being. Not only were they to walk around the Garden and enjoy it, they were to be full-time gardeners."

I looked at Jess. "Jess, you'd love their job. At this stage in the story, the Garden doesn't have thorns, thistles, or weeds."

"What a deal." Her eyes brightened as she reached out to run her finger along the edge of a daisy petal in the table's centerpiece.

"One of the ways to state neatly what God's original intent was in the Garden is to use the Latin word that first appeared in English in 1617—the word *cult.*" I paused to take a bite of my spinach and avocado omelet.

"Ron, are you going a bit wacko on us here?" Phil snorted. "You're saying God intended to start a cult? Like that guy from Waco?"

"Yeah, that's what the word *cult* means now. But the English word is derived from the French word *culte,* which means 'worship.' And the French word came from the Latin *cultus,* which means 'care,' 'cultivation,' or 'worship.' The infinitive form of the verb means 'to till.'"

"So-o-o, what's the point of this little linguistics lesson?" Phil and Jess exchanged their "he's doing it again" look.

"Yeah, I know, I know. I talk about history and language too much. But, trust me, this all relates to your conversations with Marty. Anyway, the word *cultus* summarizes what God was doing in the Garden. *Cultus,* or worship, or connection to God, is fundamental to God's intention for the Garden and for humanity. So, listen to this: *Culture,* or relationship with others, is also key to the original design of the Garden. *Cultivation*—our relationship to the land, or dirt, if you will—brings a sense of purpose and connection to creation. In fact, I've thought about writing a book to show that the primary reason for the creation of the Garden was a sense of relationship in three directions: 'Godward,' 'otherward,' and 'dirtward.' That's a pretty cool summary of what God was up to. In this garden setting, men and women could be complete; or, to use the language of the Bible, it was all good, very good."

"Like this banana-nut waffle," Phil joked as he stuffed another big bite into his mouth.

"Uh-h-h, yeah. Connection to God, to each other, and to creation—banana-nut waffles, in your case, Phil—are the primary reasons for the Garden. Interestingly, when Adam and Eve sinned, they were kicked out of that perfect place, which was lush, plush, and full of awesome waffles." I grinned at Phil, who was nodding in agreement as he cut another bite of waffle with the edge of his fork. "In the Garden, there were harmony, health, balance, and wholeness. Garden living, especially without any thorns, thistles, and weeds, is pretty nice. We'd probably call it utopia."

"Like this place." Jess gestured toward the picture window overlooking Lake Michigan where a dozen or more white sailboats dotted the horizon. "You have to admit this is a near-perfect day."

"It is, indeed," I said, pausing for a moment to watch as one of the sailboats hoisted a particularly colorful spinnaker. "Now, not to rain on your parade, Jess, but as you know, Adam and Eve disrupted the Garden plan by disobeying. They disrupted things with God, themselves, each other, and the created order. I hope you can see how by jumping to chapter three and starting with the problem, we miss something. It's as if we knew only a cloudy, rainy Saugatuck instead of the bright Saugatuck we're enjoying today. When we jump to chapter three, we miss God's purpose. He designed us as *eikons* with Garden cravings—longings for beauty, yearnings for wholeness, a magnetic pull to connect with the divine, and a deep connection to the dirt from which we were taken. Is it possible that every time you see this"—I gestured out the window—"you're quietly, but unmistakably reentering Garden moments?"

Jess stared out at a passing boat and nodded. Phil rolled his eyes.

"And, Phil, is it possible that every time you go rock climbing and enjoy the view at the top, you're reentering a Garden moment?"

"No, Ron, I'm enjoying my Garden moment right now with this waffle." Phil winked at me and reached for more syrup.

"Is it possible we are reentering the Garden every time we enjoy a sunset from the back porch, view the vast desert out West, pan a mountain range in the Colorado Rockies, watch the first snowfall, or stand on one of those islands around Miami that you visit every year and soak in the natural beauty? Is it possible these deep consciousness connections to the world around us only prove the vast, and yet deeply connected, world God has created? Isn't this why God created the Garden in the first place?"

I paused to sip a freshly refilled cup of coffee. Phil was busy finishing his waffle, and Jess was still staring out the window at a couple who were walking their dog on the waterfront.

"When we really reflect on what God created in the Garden and why he created it, we realize that what we see in our contemporary culture is nothing but an effort to experience the Garden—misguided efforts to be sure, but Garden-directed efforts nonetheless. Our cultural obsession with money, sex, power, prestige, cosmetic surgery, agelessness are all dim reflections of how we yearn for the Garden."

"I've got to keep bringing up the question, though, Ron," Jess interrupted. "You can talk eloquently all day long about this great Garden. But what does it have to do with Marty?"

"Why, I'm glad you asked, Jess," I said with a smile. "It brings me to my point, which was about to get away from me. What if, instead of hitting Marty with statements about repentance, we tapped into his natural yearning for the Garden? What if you started spiritual conversations around Marty's experience of the Garden? Does he enjoy rock climbing? Does he bike? Does he enjoy traveling? Start there in your conversation about God with Marty."

"Well, Marty does go biking with me sometimes," Phil said thoughtfully.

"That's right. It's much better to start with Marty's glimpse of the divine than with the problem. Why? Because most people in our culture don't know the full story line. For them, it can never be reduced to just the Fall and Redemption. At the very least, it has to start with Creation. For in the Creation narratives we come to grips with God's purposes, his hopes, his heart, his intention for the whole project. The problem should follow the purpose. The problem is obviously not the main point of God's creativity. His purpose was not the Fall. His purpose wasn't to have Adam and Eve sin. His intentions were to have them in open and harmonious relationship with him and with each other and to enjoy a meaningful destiny and existence, a destiny rooted in connection to the earth. Marty's glimpse of the divine is his connection to God's original intention for creation."

"So, we need to discover where Marty has glimpsed God in his life already. Is that right?" Jess pointed her fork at me.

"Sure, that's the starting point." I paused to take another sip of coffee. "But the conversation doesn't stop there. The story we tell certainly begins with Creation, Fall, and Redemption. But there's still another part to the story. Can you guess what it is? Creation, Fall, Redemption, and—"

"I got it. Restoration," Jess said.

"Yes. Jesus came for the purpose of *restoring*. What if the story we need to tell is the story of Creation, Fall, Redemption, and Restoration? We have made a portion of the story all there is to the story. But what if Fall and Redemption, as important as they are, aren't really the whole story, but simply a major section in the middle of a larger story? What if the real story is the Garden, what it means to live in the Garden here and now, how to get back to the Garden, and the sort of pitfalls that exist in our experience of Garden life now? What if Jesus came to hand out free samples of the Garden? What if when Jesus says the kingdom of God is at hand, he is saying that Garden living is now possible, here and now? The restoration of the Garden is near. It is at hand. You can experience it now—not all of it, but a bunch of it. Jesus stated his mission: I have come to bring them life, a richer, fuller, more incredible life than they ever imagined. What if the story we have been telling is a thin-sliced version of the truth, rather than a thick, full, juicy slab?"

16

All Riled Up

Maybe some clarity is now dawning about what Jesus meant when he used the word *kingdom*. Earlier we said that Jesus redefined a couple of big ideas for the people in the first century. First, he redrew the boundary markers. He redefined what it meant to be in or out. He essentially leveled the playing field. He challenged the ethnic exclusivity of the Pharisees and teachers of the law and told them he was including in his kingdom the very people they were excluding. And the kingdom of inclusion he was bringing was a kingdom of restoration. Jesus could easily have said the restoration of God is near, just as he said the kingdom of God is near.

We haven't yet fully examined the second redefinition, but we have tasted it. Jesus redefined *kingdom,* as in *empire,* for the power brokers and rulers of the first century. He redefined not only who would be included in the empire but also how that empire would operate. In talking about "kingdom," Jesus was automatically talking about the power structures and systems of the political/historical empire of his day.

Rabbis of the first century—and long before that, of course—were trained to recognize that at some future time, God would right all wrongs, fix all brokenness, eliminate sickness, and make the lions lie down with the lambs, to use the picturesque images of the Old

Testament prophets. The picture is one of harmony and balance, much like the Garden (and not by coincidence, I'm sure). So as the rabbis and religious leaders of the day read passages out of the prophet Isaiah, for instance, they would read about these great reversals to happen some time in the distant future. We can read passages such as Isaiah 29, 35, 42, 52–53, and 61 and see that they have numerous common features, the biggest being the grand reversal that is to eventually come.

Lame people would walk, blind people would see, the deaf would hear. These would be obvious and clear indications of what? Of God's arrival to finally set the world straight, to right wrongs, to even out the playing field. It would be nearly impossible to conceive of these great reversals happening in any other way than at the end of time, at the end of the space/time universe, at the end of it all.

So think about what happened when Jesus stood in the synagogue in Nazareth as a Torah reader one day, reading one of these passages from the book of Isaiah. Luke records in the fourth chapter of his Gospel that Jesus stood and read from the Isaiah scroll, the first verse and a half of chapter 61. The passage mentions the coming of someone who will be anointed to preach good news, someone who will bring a newsflash and will bring freedom to prisoners, help the blind to see, help the oppressed to experience freedom.

Jesus was probably assigned this particular reading for the day. So for him to stand and read this text was nothing special. But what he did following the reading was particularly dramatic. He claimed that the prophecy was being fulfilled right there and then—in him. Based on what we have just discussed, how do you think the Pharisees responded?

What the Jewish religious leaders and teachers of the law always thought would happen at the end of time for all Israel, Jesus was now saying was happening right there and then for all the world. What Israel thought was a statement of *future* unprecedented blessing for *them,* Jesus said was a *present* state of unprecedented blessing for *the world*. What Israel thought would happen through her, Jesus said was happening through him as a representative of Israel. "God so loved the *world* that he gave his one and only Son."[1]

As an aside, note that Jesus stopped quoting verse 2 of Isaiah 61 in the middle of a sentence. He omitted the phrase "the day of vengeance of our God." Why? The day of vengeance wasn't being introduced in and through Jesus' ministry, but as we will soon see, that day was being announced in his ministry and he was giving them an alert that such a day was just around the corner.

Now try to put yourself in the minds of the rabbis who were present in the synagogue on that day. They are doing a quick mental scan and remembering that this is a passage of hope for the end of time; a hope to be realized when God returns to Zion and sets the record straight. And now this peasant from Nazareth is claiming that the promise is being fulfilled right here, right now, in him? What do they do? They are angered by his arrogance and run him out of town.

The picture is relatively clear, then, why the Pharisees and religious leaders didn't like Jesus. He simply wasn't a good Jew. He ate and mingled with the wrong people, and he broke dietary and Sabbath laws. But what was the big deal that got Rome so worked up? If what Jesus was talking about was primarily spiritual, what was the issue about his pronouncement of a new empire that got everyone so riled up? This question takes us to the very heart of why Jesus was crucified.

If you do an informal survey of Christians in Sunday school or in the church lobby, simply asking them why Jesus died, they will almost universally state that he died for our sins. It might very well be the answer that came to your mind when I asked the question. As true as that may be theologically, it is not a historical answer. The authorities did not crucify Jesus so he could die for the sins of the world. So the question must be framed differently. What did the authorities see as so threatening that they would kill Jesus? If, as we've seen, a good alternative word for *kingdom* is *restoration,* then what was the big threat? If some blind people had their sight restored, isn't that fine? If a few crippled folks got to walk again, isn't that good? What were the authorities getting all torqued out about?

We have already noted that Jesus was called, on numerous occasions, the Christ, or the Messiah. Because we tend to think of *Christ* as Jesus' last name, rather than as a title or a declaration of his identity, we miss the historical significance of this title. Remember what we saw before, that *Messiah* (Hebrew word) and *Christ* (Greek word) mean exactly the same thing: "anointed one," which is to say, "heir apparent to the throne," or "king." Now add to the mix that the high priest and other religious leaders have decided that compromise with Rome is the best way for them to exist side by side, since the Jews can't overthrow Rome, and the picture becomes a bit clearer. Jesus is being hailed as Messiah, the Anointed One. He is traveling around performing the types of miracles the Messiah will do when he comes, according to the prophecies of Isaiah. He has the religious leaders worked up and the Roman authorities suspicious. So what gets him killed? Let's look at the events that brought together the two strands of antagonism and sealed his fate.

When I was growing up, in the late 1960s, I remember heading to church every Sunday. We put on our Sunday clothes, we experienced all the church calendar events per the lectionary cycle, and we went to the same restaurant every Sunday after church. We were regulars. In my family, we actually got a double dose. In the morning, we went to the Presbyterian church service, and at noon, we trooped off to the twelve o'clock Catholic Mass. We had our bases covered.

Without a doubt, the most memorable church services for me as a kid were on Palm Sunday. No, not Christmas and not Easter. Those two big highlights of the Christian year just didn't register with the same weight as Palm Sunday. I'm pretty sure I know why. At both churches, we were handed palm branches, these long reedlike things that my two brothers and I would either bend in half to make loud snapping noises or, when out of earshot where yelps couldn't be heard, would use to whip each other. Okay, I know this is not the memory anchor the church was hoping for in my adolescent spiritual development, but Palm Sunday nevertheless sticks out in my mind.

The story of the original Palm Sunday, and what is known as the Triumphal Entry, can be found in Luke 19:28-44.

> After Jesus had said this, he went on ahead, going up to Jerusalem. As he approached Bethphage and Bethany at the hill called the Mount of Olives, he sent two of his disciples, saying to them, "Go to the village ahead of you, and as you enter it, you will find a colt tied there, which no one has ever ridden. Untie it and bring it here. If anyone asks you, 'Why are you untying it?' tell him, 'The Lord needs it.'"
>
> Those who were sent ahead went and found it just as he had told them. As they were untying the colt, its owners asked them, "Why are you untying the colt?"
>
> They replied, "The Lord needs it."
>
> They brought it to Jesus, threw their cloaks on the colt and put Jesus on it. As he went along, people spread their cloaks on the road.
>
> When he came near the place where the road goes down the Mount of Olives, the whole crowd of disciples began joyfully to praise God in loud voices for all the miracles they had seen:
>
> "Blessed is the king who comes in the name of the Lord!"
>
> "Peace in heaven and glory in the highest!"
>
> Some of the Pharisees in the crowd said to Jesus, "Teacher, rebuke your disciples!"
>
> "I tell you," he replied, "if they keep quiet, the stones will cry out."
>
> As he approached Jerusalem and saw the city, he wept over it and said, "If you, even you, had only known on this day what would bring you peace—but now it is hidden from your eyes. The days will come upon you when your enemies will build an embankment against you and encircle you and hem you in on every side. They will dash you to the ground, you and the children within your walls. They will not leave one stone on another, because you did not recognize the time of God's coming to you."

Several things about this story are noteworthy and really bring us to the crux of Jesus' perceived threat to the Roman authorities. For starters, this was not the first time a triumphal entry like this had taken place. Other would-be messiahs had entered Jerusalem on horseback before. That's right; this was not a unique event. I can remember the first time I heard, and then read, accounts of other people entering the city to the waving of branches, the placing of cloaks on the ground, and the hailing of a new would-be messiah. It was confusing to think that this seemingly signature event in the life of Jesus was not a one-of-a-kind thing.

In the past, of course, the would-be messiahs had eventually been defeated and killed, their attempted revolution or overthrow vanquished, and their followers disbanded—until another, better possibility emerged. You may be aware that one of the teachers of the law, a rabbi named Gamaliel, summarized the fact of these occasional uprisings when the Jewish Council was debating what to do with Peter and John after the two apostles refused to stop teaching outside the Temple (see Acts 5:28-39). When asked how he thought this new group, the followers of Jesus, should be handled, Gamaliel mentioned two previous would-be messiahs whose followers disbanded when their leader was killed. He argued that the same would happen with the followers of Jesus unless their movement was from God.

The most telling portion of this particular passage in Luke 19 comes as Jesus approaches Jerusalem. He weeps. While the people are lauding him as king, Jesus is weeping because they really don't understand what kind of king he is. They want to see Rome overthrown. But Jesus is saying, "If you had only known what would bring you peace. But you have no idea, Israel. You are thickheaded and dense; you don't get it."

What is their penalty for missing all the warnings—warnings that go all the way back to prophets such as Isaiah; warnings that continued in the mouths of John the Baptist and Jesus? The very enemies they want to conquer will be used as an instrument of punishment against them. The very Romans they want to overthrow will, in the words of Jesus, "build an embankment against you and encircle you and hem you in on every side. They will dash you to the ground, you and the children within your walls. They will not leave one stone on another, because you did not recognize the time of God's coming to you" (Luke 19:43-44).

Obviously, Jesus isn't winning many new friends at this stage. His message is one of judgment on the very ones who thought they were the special chosen people of God. Yet, at the same time, he poses a threat to Rome because, by being hailed as king, he is at least tacitly declaring that the emperor in Rome is not the rightful king. What comes next, however, when Jesus stirs things up in the Temple, is the event that really gets him into serious trouble.

17

Pink-Spoon Samples

Immediately following the account of the Triumphal Entry, we encounter a little two-verse story that is often referred to as "the cleansing of the Temple." In fact, in many Bibles, the editors have used that title as the header for this section. Let's take a look at what it says: "Then [Jesus] entered the temple area and began driving out those who were selling. 'It is written,' he said to them, '"My house will be a house of prayer"; but you have made it "a den of robbers"'" (Luke 19:45-46).

Calling this story "the cleansing of the Temple" makes it sound as if Jesus was trying to reform the Temple and get it back on the right track. In fact, some churches cite this story as proof that God is against anything being sold on church property. Wow, there's a crazy jump. But that doesn't seem to be the main point at all. Instead, Jesus is forecasting the destruction of the Temple and the temple system. How do I know that? The clues are subtle but unmistakable.

Throughout the New Testament, characters in the narratives and the authors of the letters quote Old Testament texts for the express purpose of giving us clues and hints to broader story lines. The line in Luke 19:46 is actually a partial quotation from two Old Testament passages that are vitally important for understanding what Jesus is actually doing in the Temple. In fact, his actions here are so symbolic that some New Testament scholars have resorted to calling events like this *enacted parables*. Rather than speaking a parable, Jesus is acting one out. Let's look at the Old Testament quotes before we tie it all together.

When Jesus uses half a sentence from one author and book and combines it with half a sentence from another author and book, he is obviously trying to communicate something very intentional. When you finally see what Jesus is doing here, it becomes unmistakable. Each half sentence highlights a particular issue that Jesus has been pursuing throughout his ministry.

The first phrase, "my house will be a house of prayer," comes from Isaiah 56:7. At first glance, it might appear to say, "Don't sell stuff in church because it's a place where we are supposed to be praying," but as we've mentioned, we mustn't rush to application before we try to understand what the passage would have meant to readers in the first century. When Jesus quotes a phrase that is embedded in the middle of an Old Testament passage, it's fair to assume that he expected his listeners to make the connection to the full story from which the phrase came. Isaiah 56 is a passage about how foreigners and social outcasts who "bind themselves to the LORD" (v. 6) will not be excluded from temple worship. Isaiah goes to great pains to show that God's love and acceptance extends to those who are considered outcasts and foreigners. And the Lord says, "I will give them an everlasting name that will not be cut off" (v. 5). The only requirement? Serve God and love and worship him. Does this sound strangely similar to the other stories we've been looking at?

In Luke 19:46, Jesus is repeating a very old message that God had communicated through the prophets for hundreds of years. But Israel still doesn't get it. Likewise, just as Ezekiel and Isaiah said that God would use foreigners to come in and discipline Israel and take her into captivity, Jesus says the same thing about Rome, only this time it won't be a temporary captivity, it will be wholesale destruction—a destruction that Jesus predicted would happen within the generation of his listeners; a destruction that actually happened in AD 70. This is why the paragraph heading found in so many Bibles—"the cleansing of the Temple"—is so misleading. This isn't a passage about cleansing, reforming, and refocusing the Temple. Not at all. It is an announcement of impending destruction.

Here's another clue: The phrase "my house will be called a house of prayer" in Isaiah 56 concludes with the phrase "for all nations." Jesus quoted Isaiah 56 to help the Pharisees and the people realize that their exclusionary, exclusive, and elitist attitudes toward foreigners and outsiders was not what God intended. Jesus was simply echoing the historical voices that Israel should have been heeding all along. He reiterates the same concerns voiced by God through Isaiah.

When we read Isaiah 56 in its entirety, the similarities being addressed are as striking as they are intentional. As Jesus is overturning the tables in the Temple, he is unmistakably telling the people, "You have become far too narrow. Foreigners, outcasts, and those in need are being excluded, and that just will not work. You are using your power and position in oppressive ways. This Temple, therefore, is being superseded. It will be destroyed and the new Temple, the new location of God's presence, the place where heaven and earth meet, will no longer be in a place but in a person. That person is me. I am the new Temple, the location of forgiveness, the source of love and acceptance. I am the place where the invisible and the visible merge. What you thought would happen at the end of time, through you, is happening in the middle of time, through me as a representative of the true Israel. I am the arrival of God's future in the present."

God intended for the Temple to be a house of prayer for all nations, "but you have made it a den of robbers," Jesus said. Again, this phrase is often understood as support for the "don't sell stuff in church" thesis. But again we need to understand the original context in order to properly understand the quote. The phrase "a den of robbers" comes from Jeremiah 7, a crucial passage in the Old Testament prophets. The chapter starts out talking about the need for those in the

Temple to reform their murderous, adulterous, and idolatrous ways and not to trust in the simple fact of their temple worship to make them right before God. Furthermore, the prophet highlights the need to care for the marginalized and the excluded.

Read the first fifteen verses of Jeremiah 7. God, through the prophet, reminds the children of Israel of an earlier destruction of the Temple due to disobedience and the wickedness of the people. Jeremiah makes it clear that the earlier destruction was the anger of God coming down on his people—and what God has done in the past he will do again in the future, if necessary.

So, is it a coincidence that Jesus quotes a half sentence embedded in the middle of a historical illustration about the destruction of the Temple hundreds of years earlier? I don't think so.

This brings to light an important study tool: Whenever we see a New Testament character or writer quoting a passage from the Old Testament, that should be our clue to read the chapter and surrounding context where the quote is originally found. If we do that kind of homework, the full context behind the "sound bite" of the quote will become clear—or at least clearer. When Jesus quoted Isaiah and Jeremiah, he knew that the Pharisees and teachers of the law would recall entire chapters of Scripture and the original context, and they would know precisely what he was referring to and would make the connection to the current context. When the issues that Jesus addresses in the Temple echo the context in Jeremiah in uncanny ways, and when Jeremiah uses a historical illustration of temple destruction, the point is pretty clear. Most of us today simply don't have that kind of background, but we can study and learn based on the clues we're given in the Bible text.

Far from bringing some sort of "cleansing" to the Temple, Jesus seems to be enacting the destruction of the center of Jewish life, the very locus of their identity, the icon that demonstrates their uniqueness before the rest of the world. When Jesus enters the Temple, he flips over the tables, symbolically disrupting the temple activities for those moments. Further, he announces that the coming destruction will be the consequence of Israel's failure to include foreigners, outsiders, and the underprivileged in the temple system, and the failure on the part of Israel's religious leaders to lead the people into being a blessing to the whole world. He does all this through a one-sentence statement that appears to be relatively innocuous until the sentence is examined. When we carefully read Isaiah 56 and Jeremiah 7, we find both contexts charged with indictment against Israel's religious leaders and against the temple system.

We might miss the significance of Jesus' words, but you can bet the Pharisees didn't. How did they respond when they heard and saw Jesus do this? They sought a way to kill him! What Jesus did in this temple narrative, which comprises only a few lines in the entire New Testament story, was not at all vague or unclear to the religious leaders. They understood the message completely, and the message wasn't that selling Jesus junk in the church bookstore is sacrilegious.

Most New Testament scholars, I think, would agree that this incident in the Temple, along with Jesus' quotation from Isaiah and Jeremiah, was ultimately the reason Jesus was executed. In many respects, it was the final straw. From this narrative alone, we can conclude quite clearly that the authorities of the day considered Jesus to be a subversive and a potential political revolutionary.

According to Luke 23:32-43, Jesus was crucified between two criminals. One of these men attacked Jesus verbally while on the cross, but the other man asked Jesus to "remember me when you come into your kingdom." Although none of the major English translations of the Bible refer to these men as "thieves," it's not uncommon to hear the second man referred to as "the thief on the cross." But these two men were not petty thieves or shoplifters. More likely (based on the Greek word *lestes* used to describe them) they were political revolutionaries who were trying to fund their revolution by whatever means they could. That Jesus was crucified between these two men clearly indicates that he, too, was perceived as a political and religious threat.

No one in the first century would have been crucified simply for claiming to be God—which is often cited as the reason Jesus was crucified. Such a claim may have been blasphemy, but it was not a capital crime worthy of the death penalty. In many ways, the claim to be God would have been treated no differently than it is today. If I were to go around claiming to be God, some people in white coats might come and carry me away for treatment, but no one would suggest that I be put to death. However, if I were wandering up and down Pennsylvania Avenue in front of the White House claiming to be the next leader of the United States; and I started sawing on a bar of the steel fence around the White House announcing that a foreign power was going to come in and destroy the White House so that not one stone would be left unturned or standing; and I was bringing in a new movement that would leave the current system passé and dead—yep, the Secret Service would be out there grabbing me and taking me to an interrogation room. Claim to be God, you're loony; claim to be a revolutionary, and you'll be in it up to your earlobes.

Jesus was crucified between two *lestes* because he was perceived as a *lestes,* a political revolutionary.[1] Remember the story of Barabbas? Pilate wanted to let Jesus go and allow Barabbas, a political insurrectionist and murderer, to be crucified. Jesus couldn't be officially charged with anything. Neither Herod nor Pilate could find anything about Jesus that was genuinely worthy of crucifixion, but the religious and political leaders wanted him dead. No doubt it was because he brought a kingdom, an authority, a restoration that no one had ever seen before.

Now that we've looked more closely at the historical context, I think we're in a much better place to understand what Jesus meant when he said, "The kingdom of heaven is at hand." Like all words and concepts in the New Testament, the backdrop for this kingdom announcement is twofold. First, although Jesus' announcement of a new kingdom was perceived as a threat to Rome, the kind of kingdom he was announcing wasn't one that would displace Caesar from the throne—at least not literally and not yet. Second, the Old Testament backdrop, the restoration of the Garden, provides the goal toward which God's history is moving. The final book of the Bible, Revelation, pictures the new heavens and new earth in Edenic terms. When Jesus came announcing the kingdom, he came announcing restoration of God's created order. When we look at miracle stories, they seem to be indicators, or foretastes, of restoration—a free sample of the Garden.

How does all this affect the conversations we have with people like Phil and Jess and the conversations they have with people like Marty? In my experience, most people, both inside and outside the Christian faith community, don't have any point of reference for the phrases "kingdom of heaven" or "kingdom of God." In fact, we've had to spend a number of pages here to explore what these phrases mean. We've found that the kingdom of heaven really doesn't have much to do with some invisible destination we're transported to at death if we have the right ticket for the ride. But is it any wonder some of these concepts are perceived so wrongly by people outside our communities of faith, when we don't even understand them ourselves?

Jesus came, announcing the kingdom of God, to invite people back into an experience of the Garden right there and then. In a sense, he was handing out free samples of the Garden. When I think of free samples, I instantly think of going to Baskin-Robbins for ice cream when I was a kid. They had those little pink spoons for samples. The spoon itself couldn't have been bigger than a dime, but you could get a free sample of any flavor of ice cream you wanted. It was barely a taste, but enough to get you really hungry for more.

When Jesus came preaching and teaching and healing the sick, he was handing out pink-spoon samples of a restored creation. He wasn't saying, "If you follow me, you will eventually get to heaven." No. He was saying, "You can experience much of what the Garden has to offer right here and right now." His goal was to transform the world, not to help people escape from it. This is one of the fundamental differences between Christianity and many of the other religions in the world. Jesus came to earth to transform it through love. He taught the disciples to pray, "Your kingdom come, your will be done *on earth* as it is in heaven" (Matthew 6:10, emphasis added). The direction here is important. The kingdom is coming *here,* invading *this space,* transforming *this place.*

We have to help people fill their word containers with appropriate pink-spoon samples when they hear "kingdom of God." Of course, a future inheritance is part of the package, but it is simply the culmination of our life with Jesus here and now. When we say, "Let's talk about heaven," people assume we mean a future out there somewhere. But that is only a part of the story and not the part Jesus seemed to be most focused on. Heaven, as we often think about it in Christianity, isn't a place we are trying to get people to go to; it is the by-product of living the kingdom of God here and now. Relationship with Jesus *now* means relationship with Jesus *then.* At this moment, the relationship is here on earth; then, it will be on a *new* earth, a *restored* earth.

So what is our role in this restoration project known as the kingdom of God? We are windows to the Garden. We are pink-spoon sample givers. I think this is why, when Jesus was asked about the most important commandments, he said simply, "Love God and love people." That's what the Garden is like. That's what people are craving. That's what people need here and now. Jesus came to say, "Your 'now' can be different. The kingdom is among you, the kingdom is within you" (see Luke 17:21). We can live in the Garden now, and get the Garden then too!

18

Breaking It Down to Brokenness

I got into the back of Phil and Jess's car with a gift-wrapped iPod in my hand. One of our closest friends had a daughter graduating from high school, and parking was limited, so they'd asked us to carpool to the ceremony. As for the iPod, I figured she'd be up to her ears in watches and pen sets, and I use my iPod so much that I swear my ears have conformed to the shapes of those little white earbuds.

But I don't listen to my iPod around friends. I don't need a soundtrack running beneath our conversations. As I got into the car, a conversation was already in progress.

"He is, and you know he is," Jess was saying, "and you need to tell him."

"But Ron was right," Phil replied. "That would be a real turnoff."

My ears pricked up.

"Well, I don't see how you get started if you don't," Jess concluded.

"Excuse me." I leaned forward from the backseat. "I don't mean to intrude, but I think I just heard my name taken in vain here. Can I ask what this is about?"

Jess looked back. "Phil's friend at work. Marty. He needs to know that he's a sinner. And I know what you said before, but let's face it; if he doesn't realize that, there's no place to start with him."

"A sinner?" I asked.

She nodded.

"Okay," I said. "Let's examine that. What's sin?"

Jess's eyes narrowed. "Don't you go getting all philosophy-professor on me, Ron. I'm not in the mood for a 'why is there air' conversation."

"No. Seriously. There's a point to my question. What is sin?"

Jess glowered back, clearly not playing. Phil turned and said, "Sin is . . . you know, *evil.*"

"Evil as in mean spirited and despicable?"

"Well, sure."

I turned to Jess. "Don't you and I have the same dentist?"

"Dr. Sharif."

"That's the one. Amin Sharif. Tell me something. Are you absolutely certain that Amin is going to heaven?"

Her face softened. "No. And that's never struck me as fair."

"Huh?" Phil looked my way.

"Dr. Sharif is a Muslim, Phil. He doesn't believe in absolution of sin through Jesus. He accepts Jesus as a great prophet, but nothing more."

"But he's a good man," Jess said. "He's active in the community, he helped start that community center for kids, he's always raising money for juvenile diabetes, and—well, he takes time and really talks with me when I go to his office."

"Me, too," I agreed. "And I've talked to him about his faith. He believes in the Virgin Birth, and he has the same basic Old Testament background as we do, and he even agrees with 90 percent of what the New Testament says about Jesus. All except for the parts about his deity, the Crucifixion, and the Resurrection. The Koran says that a substitute was crucified in Jesus' place, and that's what he believes. And he thinks that the very concept of God taking human form is blasphemous. He respects us; he calls us 'people of the Book,' because we have some of the same Scriptures. But his faith is based on the Five Pillars of Sunni Islam, not the redemptive sacrifice of Jesus Christ."

"But he believes in the same God."

"Does he? The God you and I believe in became human and walked among us. Did Amin's God do that?"

Jess sighed.

"And I understand your distress, Jess, because you see Amin as good."

She nodded.

"So do I. And if we see him as good, we do not see him as evil. Yet, if he is not going to heaven, something is stopping that, and the only thing that can stop that is sin."

"Whoa." Phil held up his hand. "Sin's not evil?"

"In the classic definition of perceived mean-spiritedness, or expressed hatred? No. Sin is not evil."

They both started talking at once. When they realized what they were doing, they stopped. I took advantage of the silence to ask, "Do you remember sets and subsets from school?"

Phil nodded. "As in 'all numbers divisible by two are even'? That makes even numbers a set. They have something in common."

"Exactly. And that's a perfect set. All numbers divisible by two are even, and all even numbers are divisible by two. It works both ways. But if I say, 'All broccoli is green,' even though that's true, I cannot turn it around and say, 'All green things are broccoli.'"

"Because 'broccoli' is a subset of 'green things.'"

"You've got it. And the same thing is true of sin. All things that we perceive as evil are sinful—all the ones related to people, at least. Murder, theft, hatred, racial slurs—those are all evil things and they are all sin. But not all sin is perceived by us as evil. Trusting in the Five Pillars of Islam is not evil—not to us. It's just incorrect; or maybe a better way of saying it is that it's incomplete. Yet if someone trusts in the Five Pillars instead of accepting Christ, Christianity has traditionally labeled that a sin."

"A sin of omission," Jess half muttered.

"Sometimes it's called that. Yes."

In the silence that followed, I could hear the low sound of the car engine, the air conditioning, even the springs in Phil's seat as he shifted position. I figured that as long as I'd half unpacked the bag, I might as well do it all the way.

"That becomes an issue," I said, "because we have been taught to treat sin symptomatically—we tell people that they can recognize their sinful state by the sense of shame they feel . . ."

"That's it," Phil interjected. "My guy at work? He's on live-in girlfriend number three over the last two years. But he sees absolutely nothing wrong with that. In fact, he thinks he's doing the right thing, trying the situation out before committing to marriage."

"So he sees no symptoms," I agreed. "And because he doesn't, offering him a cure doesn't make sense. It would be like one of your coworkers offering you cough syrup and cough drops, even though you weren't coughing. You'd think he was some kind of kook. To your friend—and to Dr. Sharif—sin is like water: colorless, odorless, and tasteless. That's because the classic definitions—evilness, nastiness—don't include the state of sin that the great majority of people today find themselves in."

More silence.

"So," Phil asked. "What exactly is sin?"

"It's a barrier," I told him. "It's the thing that keeps a person from connection with God. I can be the nicest person in the world, yet if my beliefs lead me to pour honey on a stone altar every morning and believe that, and nothing else, is going to make me acceptable to God, then I'm wrong. My belief is a barrier between me and God because he has already said that belief in the redemptive sacrifice of Christ is the only thing that works. Yet, over the years, we've browbeaten people with sin, and now that backfires because they think, 'Sinners are nasty people, but I'm a pretty nice guy, so how can I be a sinner?' They don't see the wrong in telling God, 'Well, you said the way to heaven is through Christ, but I don't believe that, so I'm going to do it my way.' They don't realize that, in doing that, they are calling God a liar. It just doesn't dawn on them."

Phil nodded.

"But Jess is also right. You do need a starting point."

"So what is it?" Phil said.

"If you can do it without making him squirm, ask your friend if he loves God. If he says yes, then ask if there's anything standing between him and God. Or better yet, talk about how you thought things were fine between you and God until you discovered this barrier that was keeping you apart. Don't even call it sin. Call it a barrier. People understand barriers, and that word doesn't come with all the baggage of the word *sin*. I actually think the best word, though, may be *brokenness*. Most people I know recognize brokenness in their lives. Suggesting that their brokenness is a barrier between them and God can be a powerful starting place for a conversation."

Phil and Jess both nodded.

"And Phil?"

"Yeah, Ron?"

I tapped on the gift-wrapped iPod. "If we don't get out of my driveway, we're going to be late for the ceremony."

19
Freedom, Favor, and Fake IDs

In our twenty-first-century world, few words are as apt to leave a bad taste in one's mouth as the word *sin*. There's no way we can even begin to convince our friends that they are sinners who sin all the time and who, therefore, need God in their lives to fix their sin problem. Sin simply isn't a category they kick around in their heads. Most people I know don't go around feeling guilty about anything they've done. My guess is the same would be true of the people you know. Guilt and the need to resolve it don't make the top-ten list of priorities in life, if they're even thought of at all.

Is it possible that all the jargon about sin has created static that obscures the reasons why people need Jesus? Is it possible we have filled the word container of *sin* with such dark, evil, heinous, and demonic descriptors that the average person in our postmodern world simply can't relate? Is it really any wonder that it seems so hard to get the conversation tuned to a frequency where two parties can hear each other?

I'm convinced that part of the reason we don't see more people choosing to follow Jesus is because we have presented the message in terms they are quite convinced don't apply. Unless they recognize and acknowledge sin in their lives, our version of the story doesn't connect very well.

I can already hear the concern—in fact, I've heard it directly from some people who are very close to me.

"When you start redefining sin, Ron, you are messing with the very reason Jesus came and died."

So goes the argument, but I am not convinced I agree with the underlying premise, at least not entirely. Is *sin* the reason Jesus came? There is no doubt that his death atoned for sin, but is it the primary reason he came?

This is one of those interesting conversations I love to have with people. Because although we may find some indication that dealing with sin is what Jesus thought his life and ministry were all about, it seems like pretty scant evidence. For one thing, Jesus didn't spend a lot of time talking about sin, and he certainly didn't initiate conversations with people by telling them they were sinners. Calling people "sinners" was the stock-in-trade of the Pharisees, as we've seen in the stories of Zacchaeus and Matthew the tax collector.

In what is perhaps the signature story in which Jesus "confronts" sin, the story of the woman caught in adultery (John 8:1-11), his approach is rather indirect. He simply says to the scribes and Pharisees who have brought the "obviously sinful" woman to him, "If your conscience acquits you, go ahead and throw a rock at her." When the men, instead, slink away, Jesus doesn't then take it upon himself to confront the woman's sin. In fact, he says, "Neither do I condemn you. . . . Go now and leave your life of sin" (v. 11).

If Jesus' primary mission wasn't to confront sin, what was it? What did he say it was?

At the outset of his ministry, immediately after his temptation in the desert, Jesus went to his hometown of Nazareth. While he was there, "on the Sabbath day he went into the synagogue, as was his custom. And he stood up to read. The scroll of the prophet Isaiah was handed to him. Unrolling it, he found the place where it is written: 'The Spirit of the Lord is on me, because he has anointed me to preach good news to the poor. He has sent me to proclaim freedom for the prisoners and recovery of sight for the blind, to release the oppressed, to proclaim the year of the Lord's favor.' Then he rolled up the scroll, gave it back to the attendant and sat down. The eyes of everyone in the synagogue were fastened on him, and he began by saying to them, 'Today this scripture is fulfilled in your hearing'" (Luke 4:16-21).

When I read this passage in Luke, what I see is that Jesus came to *set people free* and *proclaim the Lord's favor* (not the Lord's condemnation). Think about it. If delivering a message about sin was what it was all about, God could have hung a gigantic plasma screen in the heavens and piped in a live global feed. He could have miraculously implanted an MP3 download in the head of every person on the night they turned the magical age of thirteen. He could have airmailed a personal invitation to every household on the planet, inviting everyone to come and follow his ways. But he didn't. Instead he came to establish personal, unmistakable, intimate interactions with people. God in his wisdom decided that human-to-human interaction and relationship was the only way the message could be unmistakably communicated.

While we're on the topic of Jesus coming as a human, we may want to note a few things. First, when he came into first-century Galilee, he wasn't wearing a two-piece, hand-tailored, Armani suit. He didn't arrive on the scene speaking refined Cantonese. When he appeared, he wasn't driving a gray 2001 Dodge Dakota pickup and drinking a Jones green-apple soda. I know it seems ridiculous to mention all this, but it seems the point is often lost on many followers of Jesus who attempt to carry on spiritual conversations. Jesus was 100 percent tuned in to the culture of his day—speaking, looking, dressing, and interacting with it at nearly every conceivable level. At the same time, he was antagonistic toward the religious establishment of the day, taking on the pastors, teachers, and church institutions and challenging the religious "requirements" necessary to "belong." In other words, Jesus was in sync with the culture and noticeably out of sync with the prevailing religious environment. In fact, he called the church leaders of the day vipers and dogs and said they were pompous and arrogant.

What would he say in our day?

In order for us to see our own culture the way Jesus saw his, we may need to reread the New Testament and identify ourselves with different characters than perhaps we're accustomed to doing. Experience tells me that when most of us read the New Testament stories, myself included, we read them as if when Jesus reaches out to heal, feed, and comfort, he is reaching out to us. In other words, we typically identify ourselves with the people Jesus came to help. I have yet to meet a Christian—including pastors, church leaders, and veteran church attenders—who doesn't identify with the ones Jesus came to save. And, of course, there is an element of truth to that.

But let's be very careful here. Are we among the marginalized of our culture? Are we carrying a disease that puts us on the fringe of the social circle? Are we among the disadvantaged that the "system" takes advantage of? Are we the socially, economically, and intellectually challenged souls that Jesus seemed to reach out to constantly?

What I have learned is that I may be identifying with the wrong people in a story. Believe me, I get very, very uncomfortable when I start taking a closer look. And I know I'm not alone. Everyone I know gets equally uncomfortable when these topics come up in conversation.

Even though I have been a pastor for almost twenty years, if I'm honest I find that the characters in the New Testament who are much closer to who I am (and who the contemporary church has been) are the Pharisees, the religious leaders of the day. Inside the church, we'd like to think we have been Jesus to a hurting world. But the antagonism toward the church felt by many in our society suggests that the world has experienced us more as the Pharisees than as Jesus. There are, of course, exceptions, but the American church, by and large, hasn't been forgiving, open, or willing to embrace the messiness of those who are gay or pierced or addicted or poor or stinky or uncouth or [you fill in the blank]. We aren't interested in those issues, because they aren't the real reason Jesus came (or so we say). We say that Jesus was interested in making sure that people got to heaven, and *those* people are going to hell unless they repent and become more like us. Be honest now. Am I overstating it?

When I'm honest with myself, I have to admit I am more like the Pharisees than I am the blind man at the pool of Siloam. And I would fit right in at more churches than I can count. How many congregations have you seen that are judgmental, narrow, controlling—and all in the name of either holiness or pure doctrine, neither of which Jesus seemed to give a hoot about. In fact, on the holiness issue, I think Jesus would just shake his head if he were to read the sort of lifestyle statements some of our churches have people sign before they can become a part of the church. We need to rethink our definition of holiness.

Faithfulness to what God has called us to do requires more than our own understanding of the basic message he has for the world. We also have to translate the message into a "language" other people will understand. Effective translation is often quite a bit more complicated than many of us are willing to pause and consider.

I went on my first missions trip to Asia when I was seventeen. Since then, I have been to Asia, Eastern Europe, and the Middle East more than a dozen times. And every time I've gone into a new location, I've had to learn how to communicate effectively by translating the *biblical text* into the local *context.* I couldn't speak English in Novosibirsk or Irkutstk and expect the Russians there to have a clue what I was saying. And it goes deeper than simple, spoken language. We must also pay attention to metaphors, idioms, slang, colloquialisms, and humor.

I remember one American pastor—this is a true story—who in a remote context in India used an illustration about Dunkin' Donuts to explain baptism by immersion. Come on, are you kidding me? Can you imagine the gyrations the interpreter went through trying to translate that one?

I know that at one level all this seems obvious and clear, but is it really? Do we not, in effect, do the very same thing as that hapless American pastor when we use religious jargon and examples from our own culture that make as much sense to people here as Dunkin' Donuts does in remote India? When we talk about international communication, it seems obvious there is a bunch of homework to be done before we can communicate with the nuance necessary to make the message clear. Why is the same point any less obvious in our own society? When it comes to clearly communicating the message that God has entrusted to us, we can't simply mouth the message with no attention to the language, location, age group, social context, and so on.

One author put it this way: "Metaphors work within cultures where a shared encyclopedia can be assumed. Crossing cultures requires the creation of new metaphors, new ways of conceptualizing and communicating."[1] What we need to understand is that communicating within our own context is increasingly becoming a cross-cultural experience. As such, maybe we need to rethink what being faithful in communicating our message *really* means.

Do people understand and engage with what we are saying? That's the real litmus test of the effectiveness of our communication. Notice I didn't ask if they *agree* with what we're saying, but do they understand? For all the people who have supposedly "heard the message of Jesus," I can't think of one person I have ever met, outside of the church, who actually had heard and really understood it. Most of these people have heard various characterizations, distortions, Americanized versions, or modern, Westernized embellishments; but as far as I can tell, they haven't heard of the Jesus of the first-century Gospels.

So, back to the issue that started us on this short excursion. The central focus of this book isn't to say that familiar words and concepts such as *gospel, repentance,* and *kingdom* aren't valid or potentially useful. The point is that we must probe past the common modern definitions of these words to discover the more nuanced backstory of the Old Testament, Jewish, and first-century contexts from which they emerge. Once we've done our homework on the backstory, then we can begin the hard work of translating these stories and concepts into words that our contemporary listeners will understand.

When we have done this sort of work, we have typically found that real faithfulness to the message means we must set aside well-worn words in favor of words that better and more fully communicate the concepts of the first-century world to our twenty-first-century context. In short, faithfulness to the message means we *must* change; not to change would be unfaithful. And if we carefully read the Gospels, this challenge is precisely the same one Jesus offered to the Pharisees.

Unfortunately, the Pharisees were stuck in concrete, unwilling and unable to let go of the way they had always done things, always said things, and always required things to be. Know any churches like that? I don't need to look too far, because for years *I* was like that. Again, if you're at all like me, you can identify with the Pharisees more often than you'd care to admit. Reading the New Testament through the lens of the Pharisees provokes fascinating discussions inside the church. I invite you to try it sometime.

20
Hungarian Goulash

There's a trail near my home that runs through a field of prairie grass and around a small lake. The best part about this trail is that it's exactly six miles long. If I hike it fast, I can have a refreshing hour-long walk and return—invigorated—to my standing desk, where I do most of my writing and brainstorming. I usually enjoy my hour in unspoiled nature alone, but recently, Phil, Jess, and their black Lab, Gator, joined me. When the four of us got around the bend, and my house and our two SUVs had disappeared from view, we all breathed easier. The world of stress and bustle was gone.

Jess picked a yellow flower from the five-foot-tall prairie grass near the trail. "Wow, imagine yourself as a settler seeing this prairie grass for the first time ever."

Phil threw a tennis ball far down the trail, and Gator bolted after it. "Well, Ron, I did what you said and asked Marty whether he loved God and whether he felt there was a barrier between him and God."

"How did it go?"

"Uh-h-h . . ." At that moment, Gator returned with the slimy tennis ball in his mouth, and Phil paused to wrestle it away from him. "Well-l-l, he said that with all the pain in the world, he wasn't sure if God loved anyone enough to break down any barriers if there were any. He wasn't sure God deserved his love."

"So, what did you say next?"

"Tell him, Phil," Jess chided. By now, she had put the yellow flower behind her ear. "No, I'll tell you, Ron." She smiled at Phil, who grimaced back at her. "All he did was order a nacho-and-cheese appetizer. . . . Phil dropped the subject completely."

"Well, what am I supposed to say to that, Ron?" Phil shot the tennis ball down the trail once again, and a barking Gator ran past me. "I didn't even get close to the idea of the barrier being *sin.*"

I looked past Phil to the horizon. It was a picture-perfect day. The bright blue sky contrasted nicely with the greens and yellows of the prairie grass.

"Well, let's start from the beginning," I said. "We always need to remind ourselves that we're 'translators' of God's message to our neighbors, like Marty. And there are always three texts to examine: the biblical text, the context, and the human text. Remember, too, that according to the standard model of Fall and Redemption, Jesus came to earth for the express purpose of fixing the sin problem."

"Yeah, yeah, we're sinners . . . and Jesus died to pay for our sins. I know," Phil said as he picked up a stray stick on the trail.

"So, the 'biblical text' question is this: 'Is that the best way to describe why Jesus came to earth?'" I paused and bent down to tie a bootlace that had become loose.

"Why else would Jesus come to earth?" Jess was incredulous.

"Okay, I know that is the typical answer. But,think about it while I ask you the second question, the 'human text' question: 'Do people inside and outside the church really resonate with the sin issue?'"

"That's an easy answer," Phil said. "Definitely no."

"What do people usually wrestle with? What do people usually perceive as the problem? What are the stories that people usually tell themselves in their heads? That's the human-text question. What issue is Marty wrestling with?"

"Well, he did seem to be angry and depressed about something that day," Phil replied. "He snapped at me when I brought up the subject at lunch."

"Maybe he felt shame about something." A strong wind hit me, and I slowed down to zip up my jacket.

"H-m-m-m," Phil mused.

"What are you saying, Ron?" Jess interjected. "Are you saying that we're to ignore what the Bible says in order to solve the problems and issues of the Martys of the world?"

"Hold on, Jess. I am not suggesting that we let people define the parameters of the playing field or allow them to bend the rules of the game, but I am suggesting that if we can't answer their legitimate questions about life, we will *never* translate the message Jesus brought to this world. *Never.*"

I paused as Gator ran by me once again down the trail. "My sense is that it's difficult for many of us to answer the question of what type of problems and issues people are wrestling with today. What is Marty wrestling with deep down, Jess? Do we really know? Our lack of understanding illustrates that we aren't quite as interested in translating God's message as we often say we are."

We walked in silence for a while, and within a few minutes we saw the calm blue lake for the first time. We soaked in the sight and then followed the galloping black Lab down toward the water's edge.

"Ron, come on. Does it really matter that people don't resonate with the sin message? Don't we all need to hear it anyway? Marty needs to hear it." Jess sounded annoyed this time. She had pulled the flower out of her hair and dropped it on the ground by now.

"Yes." I paused. "And, no."

"What?!?" Now she was clearly exasperated.

"Hear me out, Jess. . . . I do believe sin exists. I do believe we have all been exposed to its nasty effects. We are all virally infected, if you will. The fact that no one is perfect is pretty good proof sin exists. But come on. Aren't we stating the obvious when we focus on sin? I don't know anyone personally, and I mean *anyone,* who has ever claimed to be perfect. But, bottom line, that isn't the question I'm addressing here. Do you know Sallie McFague's book *Speaking in Parables*? It's a great book. In it she says, 'The purpose of theology is to make it possible for the gospel to be heard in our time.'[1] That's the question I'm asking here. Bottom line, is the newsflash Jesus brought to this world the message people are actually hearing today?"

"Okay, Ron. Marty doesn't understand what we're talking about. We get it." Jess picked up a pebble and started tossing it up in the air and catching it. "But what does that have to do with *sin*? Can't we just explain what *sin* is to Marty? Isn't that what sermon podcasts are for?"

"Well, Jess, remember when we discussed the words *gospel, repentance,* and *kingdom*? Remember discovering that our understanding of these words has been culturally informed? Sometimes the information comes from misunderstandings by well-meaning Christians, and sometimes it comes from media characterization or completely false information about Christianity. Whatever the case, we have learned that these words were not communicating the ideas of the Bible. Bottom line, we weren't using words and concepts that could connect with anyone today—including Marty."

"Yeah, I remember. That's why we talked about using words like *newsflash, reorientation,* and *empire.*" By this time, all of us were sitting beside the lake, watching the honking geese settle and rise on the water's surface.

"If I were to teach this to a seminary class, I would say that our context had overshadowed the biblical text, thereby obscuring the message the biblical text was trying to communicate. So, instead of abandoning words like *repentance,* we drilled deeply into the biblical world in which those words were used and discovered their true meaning. We found better and different English words to reflect their original meaning. We were simply making sure the biblical text was accurately translated into our context. What I'm suggesting is that we need to do the same thing for the word *sin.* Is it possible there might be a better way of communicating this issue that Jesus came to address? Is it possible there is a better way to describe to Marty why he needs God in his life?"

"Wow, that's a mouthful!" Phil threw a stick in the water, and Gator dove in to get it.

"Okay, let me illustrate what I'm saying. What if you turned on CNN, Phil, and you saw a news ticker break into the bottom of the screen saying, 'Very important newsflash'? What if the words then shifted into a language script and alphabet you have never seen before? The newsflash is apparently important, but you can't read it."

“I sometimes felt that way when I was in Russia,” Jess said as she stretched out on the grass. “I could recognize Russian script when I saw it. But I didn’t have a clue what it was saying.”

“Yeah, I wonder if we are using words the same way. We claim to have a very important message to communicate. Then we proceed to use words that are either unintelligible or push negative buttons and disconnect people from the dialogue, rather than engage them in deeper reflection about what’s important. If it’s our job to make the newsflash understandable in our day and age, maybe we haven’t done a very good job.”

“Wow, Ron. You’re really indicting us today. If I had known I was going on trial here, I might not have joined you for this hike.” Phil lobbed a stone into the water, and Gator circled hopelessly in the water trying to find it.

“Okay, let me give you another illustration. If a Hungarian came to the United States and claimed to have made a medical breakthrough, a breakthrough that may well be chronicled as one of the most important in all of human history, and then spoke Hungarian, with no translator, throughout his tour of the United States, we would be scratching our heads as to the wisdom of all the press conferences and interviews. And what if his attitude was, ‘If you want to hear about this incredible thing, learn Hungarian and then come back and talk to me. I am just getting the message out. I really can’t worry about the results. My job is to research and then tell you what I find. I can’t spend time trying to break through barriers to understanding. That’s up to you. Take it or leave it.’”

Just at that moment, Gator splashed out of the water and shook himself next to Phil. Phil grimaced and threw another stick in the water to get the sopping wet Lab away from him.

“Think about it. Wouldn’t we consider the attitude of the Hungarian scientist cavalier, uncharitable, selfish, and disingenuous? If this really is that important, if this really is a breakthrough in human history, if this really can affect countless lives, then isn’t he under some moral obligation to share the knowledge in a way that other people can understand it? We would be incensed if the Hungarian government said, ‘We will only release this breakthrough information to those who can prove their fluency in Hungarian.’”

Jess giggled. "I'd love to see that happen. Countless Americans struggling to learn Hungarian?"

"But, do you see what I'm saying here? We, who call ourselves Christ followers, don't seem to understand our own newsflash very well. Is it really any wonder, then, that those who don't take the name of Jesus seriously, people like Marty, are a bit confused, if not completely turned off, by what we have to say? We're speaking Hungarian and telling people that once they learn the language they can hear this incredible, life-altering message."

Phil's stomach growled loudly. "I think I hear another life-altering message that only I can decipher . . . and I think it's calling me this way." He scrambled to his feet and whistled for Gator.

Jess and I looked at each other, smiled, and followed Phil and Gator back toward the house. "I have first dibs on the last Jones soda," Jess yelled.

21

Soaking in a Sin Solution

Sin language dominates the contemporary Christian landscape. From preaching to evangelism, it often sits front row and center. Further, it is not just the Christian imagination that has been steeped in this marinade. The public characterization of Christians, and especially of the evangelists who most often get airtime or are parodied, is that these people are, shall we say, sin obsessed.

I grew up in two mainline church contexts where this sort of sin focus was woven into every service. I got it not only within the Catholic liturgy but also during the weekly prayer of confession in the Presbyterian order of service. The idea that we are sinners full of sin, who need to confess our sins, and who need forgiveness from sins is central to many Christian worship experiences. The "sin problem" is the reason given for the incarnation, death, and resurrection of Jesus. But is talking about *sin* the best way to communicate the central human problem, or sickness, or issue? Is sin the best framework for connecting with the people we are trying to communicate with concerning Jesus? I'm afraid that when we reduce the newsflash of the gospel down to the thin-sliced, lo-cal version of "Jesus came to die for your sins," we flatten out the rich landscape and mute the variegated colors to gray.

So what are we to do? Well, in the case of *sin,* as with the other words we have examined, we need to ask ourselves if this word, as it is commonly used and understood in our society, presents an accurate view of what the Bible depicts as the central reason for Jesus showing up on the scene. And, if not, is there perhaps a better way of getting at the story of Jesus so that more people can connect to it and understand it?[1]

Simply changing words or redefining sin will probably not work. Although reframing and rephrasing has proved a fruitful strategy with the other words we've explored, in the case of sin, I think we need to realize there is something we must address first. I think you will see what I mean.

Simply stated, the word *sin* (from the Greek *hamartia*) means "to miss the mark." In Aristotle's famous *Poetics,* the word *hamartia* is usually translated as "tragic flaw" or "tragic mistake." Usually, the tragic flaw is hubris, or what we commonly refer to as pride. In the writings of Homer, *hamartes* refers to a warrior, an archer, or a spear thrower missing the target. More recently, some scholars have suggested that interpreting *hamartia* as "a fatal flaw is itself flawed, and that the word more properly means any disproportion in the character's makeup that leads to downfall; thus an excess of a valuable or virtuous quality can in some circumstances be seen as *hamartia.*"[2]

Clearly, a variety of nuances are swirling around the word *hamartia,* or *sin.* Actually, this is a helpful first step into our discussion. But regardless of the definition we use, if *sin* is the primary story line that we share with people who we think need to find faith in God, then the antidote, so to speak, is *forgiveness.* It will always be forgiveness. If the issue is always sin, the solution will always be forgiveness. So what do we need to do first?

Is forgiveness the primary thing that people need?

"Of course," we might say, "*everyone* needs forgiveness," and thus forgiveness becomes the one-size-fits-all remedy, regardless of a person's perceived needs, because—or so the argument goes—everyone is a sinner. That's true at one level, but totally unhelpful at another.

How many people have you engaged in spiritual conversations who were just chafing to figure out how to alleviate the guilt they feel? How many people were just craving to be forgiven and have their sins washed clean? The point is that it doesn't matter how correctly we articulate a biblical doctrine (the *biblical text*); if it doesn't intersect the *human text* (the stories we tell ourselves), then the biblical text will never be translated into our *context* (the current world we live in) and thus touch human lives.

Richard Rohr notes that the church's doctrine of sin has been used as a tool of intimidation.[3] He's not the first person to have suggested that Christians are misguided in using the idea of original sin as one of the major categories for understanding and expressing the church's mission. But Rohr argues for a return to the idea of sin as "missing the target." He writes, "Sins are fixations that prevent the energy of life, God's love, from flowing freely."[4] Rohr says that he views sin as self-erected barriers that cut us off from God and therefore from our own authentic potential. If you read Rohr carefully, you'll see that he isn't referring to the human-potential movement's idea of potential. He is arguing for genuine hearts and lives, lived in the service of God, as we serve those around us, especially those in need.

The reason for entering into some of the discussion in these pages is to help you recognize that this is a topic of concern in the church at large today. Perhaps you have had these very thoughts, questions, and misgivings. I want to invite you to continue to think, to continue the journey, to continue down the path of risky reflection about how the words we use can bring static or clarity to the conversations we are having about spiritual issues.

Whatever definition for sin you adopt, the bigger issue is the current condition that people find themselves in—their state, or situation. Or to say it another way, what consequences or implications of sin are they experiencing? It may not even be sin they themselves have committed; it may be someone else's sin, but they are feeling the effects of it.[5] Sin always has implications for those around us and for the culture in which we live. In other words, sin has large-group or corporate implications. When we call someone a "sinner," what we are really saying is there is estrangement, distance, or alienation from God. "Sin is the proclivity to act as though things created, including ourselves, were the Creator. To sin, then, is to turn away from authentic human existence by turning away from God."[6] Jesus came to address this estrangement, this distance, this alienation.

Sin certainly creates a distance between us and God, but it's not the only thing that causes this alienation and estrangement. I'm not saying that everyone isn't in need of God's grace and forgiveness. Sin has nasty implications for every human on the planet, and Jesus wants to address it in every person's life. But the implications of sin, the victim side of the sin someone else commits that affects me, the cultural implications of living in a global environment of sin, these are the things people *feel*; these are the things that make people realize sin exists in the world. And in public conversations with friends and coworkers, this is where we must begin. If we want our conversations to flourish and bear fruit, we must start with the real-life issues that are most immediate for the person to whom we're speaking, not with our theological definitions. This is absolutely essential.

Let me start by suggesting that even though everyone needs forgiveness, not everyone senses that need. And all the preaching in the world won't make the need clear. If it did, the world would already be well on its way to conversion. Jesus himself, when he read the Isaiah scroll in the synagogue in Nazareth (Luke 4:16-21), didn't launch into a sermon on sin management. Instead, he said he had come to bind up the brokenhearted, to bring deliverance to captives, and to bring a newsflash to the poor. None of these objectives has sin management as its focus. Do you find that intriguing? We have already noted that Jesus repeatedly performed miracles and healed people without so much as a glance in the direction of sin or guilt management. What gives?

Before we get too far ahead of ourselves, we need to look to the vast Old Testament background that provides the grounding necessary to understand the various strands that come together in the New Testament. What I want to suggest for your consideration is that Jesus took his cue from the Old Testament backstory. What I mean by this is that Jesus did not simply read Isaiah 61 and then say "this Scripture is fulfilled"; rather, the overarching stories of the Old Testament, the meta-stories, if you will, were the primary impetus to his ministry actions. In theology, we call this phenomenology: What can we understand about Jesus' thoughts, self-perception, and ministry based on his activities and actions?

We could spend a tremendous amount of time on this exploration, but to stay within the scope of our present discussion, we simply must cut to the chase. When we survey what theologians have told us for the past hundred years or so, a number of stories have vied to be the central story under which everything else fits.[7] Old Testament scholars have proposed various programs, based on how well their overarching story or schema makes sense of the rest of the Old Testament. We have had everything from the glory of God to the Torah, to the Covenant, to God's loving-kindness proposed as the central story line. By the end of the twentieth century, many scholars had concluded that there probably isn't a center but rather several overarching stories that weave together into a larger whole that highlights several primary themes. These several themes then serve as the umbrella under which everything else in the Old Testament neatly fits. What follows is a brief summary of the findings you might assemble if you did this homework yourself.

The first and most obvious story is Israel's bondage in Egypt, which culminated in the events of the plagues, the Exodus, and the parting of the Red Sea. There is no sense in this story that the slavery in which the Israelites found themselves was somehow their fault. It is simply a given. They are in slavery and need to be set free. God's clear concern in calling Moses was to have him go to Pharaoh to negotiate the release of God's people. This event is known to us as the *Exodus*, a word that derives from two Greek words meaning "out" (*ex*) and "way" (*odos*). Exodus is the story of Israel's way out. In the New Testament story of Jesus' meeting with Moses and Elijah on the Mount of Transfiguration, Luke, referring to Jesus' death, writes, "They spoke about his departure [*exodus*]" (Luke 9:31). Jesus' death was a new exodus, a new way out.

Have you ever seen the connection between the story of Exodus in the Old Testament and Jesus' claim in John 14:6 that he is "the Way"? How might these intersecting images help us to reconsider and redraw the ways we communicate about why Jesus came? These connections would have been unmistakable to first-century listeners and readers. But in translation across the centuries into our culture and language, we lose the obvious play on words. When Jesus claims he is the *odos* (way) and his death is referred to as an *ex-odos,* the intentionality is hard to miss.

There's more.

Israel's release from bondage in Egypt is symbolic of God's desire that all people would be free and would know him. And just as with Israel's coming out of Egypt, God has made a way for everyone to be liberated, to be set free. But how do you think Israel would have responded if God had sent Moses into Egypt with this message: "Israel, rejoice, you are forgiven! God this day pronounces you a forgiven people. Now enlist others in the cause by pronouncing to those around you the 'good news' of forgiveness." I think you can see the point.

Did Israel need forgiveness? Well, yes and no. Do all of us need forgiveness? Sure. But was forgiveness what Israel needed to fix her immediate situation? Was forgiveness enough to show Israel that God had redeemed her and entered into a relationship with her? Clearly, no. Those in slavery or bondage need liberation; they need freedom. Forgiveness is quite beside the point. Forgiveness does nothing to liberate; it simply says the offended party is letting you off the hook. You can be forgiven and still be in bondage.

Israel was not praying, "Lord please forgive our slavery. We repent of being in bondage to Pharaoh, and we pray for your forgiveness as we continue to labor under impossible conditions. Please forgive us, O God." The whole idea is quite crazy. Slavery and bondage beg for liberation and freedom. So although missing the mark can create separation from God, sometimes I wonder whether separation from God is through no fault of the person who is separated.

Here's the concern I hear expressed all the time: "But Ron, God's goal isn't to 'fix' Israel's problem; his goal is to receive the glory due his name. That's what the creeds tell us—that this is all for God's glory, not some utilitarian 'What's in it for me?'"

I hear the objection, but I think it misses the point. We are not trying to look at the biblical narrative through the window of historic Christian creeds, or what is for God's glory. No one disputes any of that. The real issue is how do we connect people *today* with the message of God's love and restoration of relationship? I think the only way to do this is to look at Old and New Testament stories and see the various ways God connects with those in the world he created. And though we'll never read any text completely objectively, we can at least be aware of the some of the biases we bring to the reading task. I'm not trying to read our current situation in the church and our culture through the creeds. I am trying to read them through the multiplicity of narratives the Old and New Testaments give us for making sense of the larger, overarching story.

I went to school with a guy named Darren, who grew up in an urban ghetto. His mother was a drug user and small-time dealer. His father, whoever he was, was nowhere to be found. From the day Darren was born, drug dealing and drug addiction were the environment of his life. He witnessed shootings, death, overdoses, and the life of drug-running as the primary, if not only, frame of his existence. Because of the dysfunction in his home, cousins and other family members helped to raise him. But they, too, were caught up in a world of addiction, fear, and control from the drug suppliers who literally manipulated their lives.

Question: Was Darren in need of forgiveness? Sure. We all are. But is forgiveness from sin an announcement, a newsflash, that would find any mooring in Darren's heart? The answer is no. Lots of people tried that, and Darren didn't respond. Why? Not because Darren thought he was perfect and didn't need to be forgiven, but because sin wasn't his issue, so to speak. His self-conversation had nothing to do with feelings of guilt over sin, or wrongdoing, even though he had plenty of wrongdoing to feel guilty about. Sin wasn't his issue; slavery was, bondage was. The pharaoh controlling Darren's life made bondage and slavery the only world he had ever known. Total freedom from fear, from control, from having no choice—those were things Darren craved. For Darren, what was enticing was a genuine, workable, practical alternative to the current life he was living. That was a newsflash he could hear, a newsflash that would indeed be good news.

To be honest, early in my Christian experience I was very harsh, judgmental, and compassionless toward guys like Darren. And yet, with some mature reflection, I wonder if I wouldn't have done exactly the same things Darren did if I had been born into his family instead of into my own family seven miles down the road. I have come to see Darren as no more responsible for his situation in life than were the children of Israel under the domination of Pharaoh, or than I was for my birthplace and upbringing.

When I heard things like what I just said in the last sentence, my response used to be, "Yeah, but at some point Darren had to choose for himself to adopt that sort of lifestyle as his own." True enough. But let's be honest. How many other options do guys like Darren have? We might just as easily say that, at some point, every Israelite had to *choose* the life of slavery under Pharaoh's regime. But realistically, Darren could have walked away from his bondage and slavery about as easily as the Israelites could have walked away from Pharaoh. After living their entire lives in bondage, where were they going to go?

Some might say that Darren is an extreme example and an unfair illustration. But the truth is, Darren is only one example among many I could cite. Here's another one.

When my son Skyler was fourteen, he and I had a conversation one afternoon when I picked him up from school. He had some questions about the world religions unit in his social studies class. As it turned out, his questions were not the sort I expected. Skyler had been to India with me, to some very remote contexts where tribal people live, including a trip to the state of Assam, located on the other side of Bangladesh. He had also been to Nepal and had seen a lot of people in religious, as well as nonreligious, contexts there. The connection he made to his social studies class was that he realized he had friends in junior high who didn't know any more about Jesus than the people we had met in India and Nepal. He realized that his friends were in a very interesting place because they didn't go to church and they didn't really understand anything about Jesus. Simply telling them they were forgiven didn't connect to any point of reference with them, their parents, or their friends.

Both situations, Darren's and Skyler's, illustrate a point we will soon discuss in some depth: What is the dominant self-conversation people are having when it comes to the topics of God, sin, and life?

22 A Garden-Variety Longing

A major portion of the Old Testament is devoted to the issues of exile and alienation from God, followed by restoration. In some ways, the exile story begins in the Garden when Adam and Eve are exiled from Eden. When they are uprooted from the Garden and sent packing, there is a sense that nothing will ever be quite the same until they and all humanity can return.

In the Garden, Adam and Eve had an open and loving relationship with God, a harmonious relationship with each other, and a close relationship with the earth, which was also vested with a sense of purpose and destiny. Getting kicked out of Eden created a sense of alienation, grief, aloneness, anger, shame, and despair. In this context, it might be said, "Well, Adam and Eve got what they deserved. After all, they did sin." And of course that is true. But what about their kids and their grandkids? Though none of them would be classified as perfect (and for the record, Adam and Eve were never called perfect), certainly they were the victims of Adam and Eve's wrongdoing. Their circumstances might be quite analogous to Darren's. He wouldn't have chosen the life he was born into if he'd been given any options. If he could have grown up in the suburbs, playing Little League and soccer, taking music lessons, and having two parents around who loved him, he probably would have opted for it. When you compare that to drugs, shootings, overdoses, and murders, the choice isn't all that hard. But that's the point: These are not choices most people get to make.

When we look at the stories of exile in the Bible, we see the children of Israel separated from their homeland and living with a deep longing, a longing that can only be satisfied by a return to the Garden, the location for which they were originally created.

With exile comes a whole host of emotions—anger, depression, and grief, just for starters. All of Adam and Eve's offspring, born in exile outside the Garden, wished for a return to the plush, provisioned surroundings that still lived in their hearts, even though they had never been there. In many ways, all our pursuit of satisfaction, joy, peace, love, and community stem from an effort to experience Garden living in non-Garden ways and in non-Garden locations. When we look at human sin, most of it swirls around our efforts to produce Garden-type benefits and satisfactions that just can't be duplicated outside that context. We could say that sin is a fundamental effort to experience something the Garden had for us in its original setting, but through brokenness we attempt to experience it in inappropriate ways. When we end up alienated from God and need restoration, we are seeking a return to the Garden that is available only when we are in relationship with the God of the Garden. We are in exile, seeking a return to our homeland.

I wonder how many people view their lives in terms of exile and restoration, instead of sin and guilt. Are the two related? Naturally. But the category of exile and restoration is about a journey—a journey back. A journey that has complexities and nuances that a simple "You are a sinner and need to be forgiven" doesn't cover. What would it mean if we were to initiate spiritual conversations based on one of two frameworks: slavery and freedom, or exile and restoration? It seems clear to me that so much of what Jesus did was rooted more in a restoration from exile than it was in managing the guilt that people feel from sin.

A third primary story in the Old Testament, referred to by scholars as the sacrificial cult of Israel or the priestly story of cleanness and purity, is about the vast and elaborate system of sacrifices that Israel practiced to maintain her uniqueness, purity, and separation from the rest of the world. Unlike the unfolding stories of Exodus and of Exile and Restoration, the priestly sacrifice story is constant and repetitive. It is about a transaction, not a journey. It is about fulfilling a legal obligation, not about transforming from one thing to something else.

Most of the stories in the Old Testament fit under one of the three overarching frameworks: bondage and liberation, exile and restoration, or sacrifice and purity. Are all three of these stories important? Yes. Are all three part of the big picture in Scripture? Absolutely. But is the church telling all three of these stories? I don't think so.

It seems silly to state the obvious, but if any one of the three overarching stories has been capitalized on in our day, it is the priestly story of sacrifice and purity. The church, in its most recent and prevalent narration of God's story, has opted to place front and center a story that puts the sacrificial cult at the heart of the Christian message for the world. Many would say, "Well, Jesus did come for that reason." But that is exactly what we are investigating.

Let's return for a moment to the statements that Jesus made about his own mission, and look at his actions that illustrate it.

> The Spirit of the Lord is on me,
> because he has anointed me
> to preach good news to the poor.
> He has sent me to proclaim freedom for the prisoners
> and recovery of sight for the blind,
> to release the oppressed. (Luke 4:18)

Look carefully at each statement. Is Jesus predominantly focusing on exodus, exile, or sacrifice? Is he talking about freedom, restoration, or forgiveness of sin? Jesus makes his primary focus so clear that we are almost embarrassed to ask the questions. The issues of exodus and freedom, exile and restoration seem to be at the very forefront of Jesus' ministry and self-understanding. And when we look at his actual ministry (what he went about doing), this is only further confirmed.

How many of Jesus' miracles are either about moving from slavery to freedom or from exile to restoration? Without looking at actual texts, just run through some of the ones you might be able to remember. Weren't the lepers in exile, living on the fringe, relegated to the margins? Wasn't the woman with the issue of blood in exile, unable to enter the Temple to worship and perceived by some as cursed by God? Weren't the blind, the paralyzed, the tax collectors, and the prostitutes in slavery or exile and seeking a pathway back into relationship?

Therein lies the beauty of the slavery-to-freedom and exile-to-restoration stories in the Old Testament: They are about a journey, a path, the human trek through life. These two story lines summarize everything about the human condition; thus, they have instant resonance with everyone. Do all the characters in these stories need forgiveness? Of course. But in their current condition, Jesus does not pursue that particular conversation. Perhaps you find this as troubling as I did when I first started looking at it. Where does it say that Jesus finally got these people to admit their sin so he could forgive them? Jesus never tells the blind man, the prostitute, the lepers, the woman with the hemorrhage, and others "to repent and receive the good news of the gospel." If the priestly story is the *primary* or *main reason* why Jesus came, then he missed some tremendous opportunities to make that clear to a vast number of people with whom he interacted. Think about it. The feeding of the five thousand was a great captive audience, but he didn't say a word about the priestly sacrificial story.

There may be a fairly straightforward explanation as to why the sacrifice and purity story appears less prominent in the Gospels than perhaps you've been taught or led to expect.

What if in their very healing the people received the good news of the gospel? What if in their healing they received what Jesus came to bring: a release from slavery, a restoration from exile, a cleanness and wholeness that affected them right there and then? What if in their healing they experienced a real-life example of "*Thy kingdom come . . . on earth as it is in heaven*"?

I want to tread cautiously here, but I also want to challenge an approach to talking about Jesus that currently prevails in the church. Although Jesus came and gave his life for the world and although he was the final and ultimate sacrifice for us (see the book of Hebrews, for example), why does it seem as if this priestly story of sacrifice is the *primary* (and perhaps only) story the church has to share with the world? This is not to minimize the story or the profound compassion that fuels it. But when we also have available to us a complex and varied story of the journey from slavery to liberation in the Exodus narrative and a story of the journey from alienation to restoration in the Exile narratives, isn't it a bit odd that we have capitalized on the only story of the three that reads like a business deal, a point-of-sale transaction?

You are a sinner and here is the sacrifice for it.

Most people simply don't connect with a story that feels like a sales call. And I think that's why they're not buying it.

There's no doubt that the sacrificial system and the priestly roles of presiding over the rituals of sacrifice were important in the Old Testament. It was the primary means by which Israel identified and maintained her uniqueness as the people of God. But as we move into the New Testament and the story of Jesus' mission to the world, does the sacrificial system continue to play a primary role? What role does it play? And what roles do the Exodus and Exile stories play in Jesus' sense of mission and how he interacted with people day to day?

There's no way we can comprehensively answer these questions within the scope of our present discussion, but the complexity of the questions should be more than enough reason for us to consider a far more nuanced understanding of why Jesus came to earth, and the various ways his message to us took shape in and around him.

The conversation I am attempting to foster in this section is one that has been going on in blogs and books for the past several years, with writers such as Scot McKnight, Alan Mann, Steven Chalke, Ted Peters, and Mark Biddle, among numerous others.[1] I'm trying to open the conversation to a broader audience, because I've observed that believers everywhere are struggling with how to communicate their faith to their friends and neighbors. I'm trying to show how the way we understand ideas like *repentance, gospel, kingdom,* and *sin* has profound and far-reaching implications for how we tell the world about Jesus.

Is this a lot of fuss about nothing? I don't think so. It's about tuning out the static and opening our ears—possibly for the first time—to the nuanced symphony of the Scriptures, and what *all* of it (not just *some* of it) has to say about our lives. It's about refusing to focus on only one melody, played on a single, brassy instrument, and instead allowing ourselves to be blown away by the entire orchestra—the complete and multifaceted story told in God's Word.

What is at stake is the possibility of not engaging most people in the conversation. In the past when it seemed people weren't listening, we simply turned up the volume on the message: "*You are a sinner in need of a Savior who can remove your guilt and give you a seat in eternity.*" But there is seemingly an inverse relationship between the volume of the message and the number of people who will hear it: The louder it gets, the fewer who listen.

Authors such as Richard Rohr, Steven Chalke, and Anthony Thistleton have suggested that most people in our postmodern Western society simply find no connection to the idea that they are sinners in need of a savior. That doesn't mean they are accurate in their self-assessment, but it does explain why they have moved on to other conversations.[2]

When I was growing up, and going to two separate church services every Sunday morning, all my friends were going to church as well. There were a few who didn't, but they were the exception, not the rule. In the late '60s and early '70s, at least in the American Midwest, where I lived, there was a perceived obligation about church attendance. In fact, the generation of baby boomers and the generation before them, called the builders, still live with a built-in sense of obligation to support the institution of the church. Some have suggested that this same ethic of obligation and commitment is what kept people in those generations working at the same company for thirty-plus years before retirement.

The modern era had a certain story line, an overarching, all-encompassing story (sometimes called a metanarrative) that made sense of life and how life was to be lived. Writers such as Alan Mann have suggested that moderns carry on internal self-conversations that include a sense of what Mann calls "the Other." What is the Other? A sense of the divine; a sense there is a God, whether it is a god or God. In the modern mind-set, where there is a sense of the Other, there is also an internal dialogue about our relationship to that Other and what is expected and assumed in that relationship.

Mann and others further argue that this sense of relationship to the Other is fueled by the same thing that fuels many things in modernity—namely, obligation. And when we have a relationship with the world or organizations in the world or the Other that rules the world, we are going to deal with guilt when we fail to meet our obligations.

Notice what I said about the Other: He *rules* the world. That is a crucial view of God in the modern mind-set. He is a rule maker and rule enforcer, as well as judge and jury when the rules are broken. When we have obligation-based relationships, we will inevitably feel guilty when we have "fallen down on the job" or "haven't come through" the way we should have or when we haven't "paid our dues" as expected. There is no doubt that this ethos of obligation is what drove my family not only to attend church but to attend two services every week.

Many family relationships in the modern era functioned on the same guilt and obligation basis. How often did your parents say something like this: “We need to stop by and see Uncle John.” “We need to at least go in for a few minutes and say hi.” “We won’t stay long, but we need to at least go have a quick bite with them and then we can go.” The underlying message to the kids was, “We don’t want to do this any more than you do, but we have to.” Of course, nobody ever said that out loud.

I’m not the only one whose life experience conformed to the obligation/guilt story line. In the church I served for almost two decades, the number of people I ran into who told me their guilt stories was quite staggering and dramatic. We jokingly referred to these mainline migrations into our church as “recovering ________.” Sometimes the blank was filled in with Catholic, Lutheran, or Presbyterian, and because I was two out of three of those, it was pretty easy to resonate with their stories. Obligation and guilt were simply part of the fabric of the modern God equation.

Many Christians I know become defensive when they hear a statement like that. They are quick to point out that Christianity is about relationship, not rules. And I agree. But go around and listen to some sermons. Go around and talk to the people who hear those sermons. Talk to people who in their mode of seeking have visited a Christian church. The results are conclusive and damning. We claim it is all about relationship, but in our weekend messages and our membership requirements, the rules stand supreme. So not only do moderns have a sense of obligation and guilt due to a number of cultural factors, the church is quick to jump on the bandwagon and affirm the same sense of obligation and guilt in our experience of God, religion, and spirituality.

What is the point of all this? It seems as if times have changed. Those who have come of age in a more postmodern society don’t seem to have the same sense of guilt and obligation that moderns have in their self-understanding or self-conversations. They also don’t seem to have the same sense of the Other. When we talk to postmoderns, we find they refer to themselves as deeply spiritual but definitely not religious. They want to connect with invisible spiritual power, but there is little or no sense of a personal relational element in that connection. There is no obligation; there is no guilt. Think about it. How many people do you know today who go around with feelings of guilt over their sin, over missed obligations, over offending God? We talk about our cultural values having shifted, and this is part of the reason why—the sense of the Other has mystically evaporated, along with the guilt associated with that sense of the Other. The metaphor is intentional. There is still spirituality in culture—in fact, it's stronger than ever—but it has undergone a change of state. The solids of the modern world have become ethereal vapors in the postmodern world. Guilt and obligation are categories from a bygone era, not among most people in their twenties, thirties, or even forties. But what are the implications of this lack of obligation and its attending lack of guilt?

As much as we would like to think that the message of the Bible as we presently understand it is *the* accurate view, maybe we don't have the final understanding quite yet. Instead, we're discovering that our understanding is immensely conditioned by our cultural context and location on the timeline of history, and we've been blind to just how significant this conditioning has been.

23 Recentering Our Storytelling

What if we were to reconsider the dominant biblical story line we tell? What if, knowing the three primary stories in the Old Testament and looking at the actual ministry of Jesus, we were to think twice about whether the message of "you are a guilty sinner in need of a savior" is our best frontline story.

I know the danger here. We don't want to throw out the baby with the bathwater by letting the audience write the script on what they want to hear. That, however, is not what I'm suggesting. What if, instead, we came to embrace a larger purpose for the death of Jesus, a purpose we already affirm in principle but that hasn't made it into the story we tell as we attempt to connect with people? There are probably dozens of ways of getting at this issue. I don't think there is "one new right way" and forget all the rest. But the fact that a good deal of both the Old and New Testaments is written in the creative genre of story indicates to me that we are well within our bounds to creatively tell, retell, and recast the story. I didn't say *distort* the story, or prostitute the story; I said retell it, recast it, recontextualize it.

First, when we're talking to people who have an ill-formed or nonexistent concept of the Other, and thus have little or no sense of obligation and guilt, is there a better way to connect with them than the old sin-and-repentance model? What would be a good alternative? Let me suggest a possible alternative—and let me emphasize that it is a *possibility.* I think we need to come up with a number of ways to effectively communicate the message of Jesus to the new, emerging culture.

When we enter the story of humanity in Genesis 1, we find Adam and Eve, who were made as *eikons* of God. In the Septuagint, the Greek version of the Jewish Old Testament, in use at the time of Jesus, *eikon* is the word for "image," as in "let us make man in our image, in our likeness" (Genesis 1:26). God created and placed in the Garden a man and a woman, who were made as reflections or representatives of his image. God saw that all of it was good. But something happened. Eve's encounter with the serpent led her and Adam to disobey a directive that God had given them. The result is interesting to note. In the story we typically tell about the Garden, we tend to capitalize on the fact that Adam and Eve sinned. As a fact, that is true. But the results of the sin are equally fundamental, though sometimes overlooked. Immediately after Adam and Eve ate the fruit, they recognized they were naked and sought a way to cover themselves.

Bible scholars and psychologists agree as to why Adam and Eve wanted to cover themselves: They were ashamed. When God came to walk in the Garden with Adam and Eve, they were hiding—a further indication that shame is at least part of their self-understanding. Look at what Stephen Pattison says in his perceptive treatment of the topic of shame: "One of the main features of the experience of shame is a sense of uncontrollable exposure."[1] It is this exposure that leads Adam and Eve to the strong desire to be covered, not only in their nakedness but also in their hiding physically from God. Is it possible shame is part of the new verbal currency that better describes the self in our postmodern world? And if so, is it possible to retell the story of Jesus' death in such a way that addresses the issue of shame? Isn't that just as much a part of the Genesis story as sin? Aren't we well within biblical bounds to focus on *shame* as a connective element into people's lives?

Some will no doubt object, saying we need to stick true to what Scripture says. But that is to miss the point. Scripture records a story of what God did in and through Jesus in a particular culture at a particular time. The question isn't Does that story still have relevance and significance? The questions are *How* does it have significance? and How can it be told in such a way as to be relevant?

Joel Green recounts an interesting story about Norman Kraus, a missionary to Japan. In the Japanese culture, the idea of Jesus paying the price by dying for the sins of the people simply didn't connect. Why? The culture wasn't based on guilt and the need to have guilt removed. The culture was based on shame and the need to have shame addressed. This led Kraus to reframe the message of the Cross in a way that addressed shame and paid little attention to guilt.[2]

Kraus concluded that shame was associated with concepts like defilement and uncleanness, whereas guilt tended to be associated with specific acts of wrongdoing for which the individual must bear responsibility. Kraus argued that retelling the story of the Cross in such a way that it addressed the issue of shame wasn't a distortion of the biblical text, but in fact was much more a part of the biblical text than most Westerners understood.[3]

When we read a story set in an overseas context such as Japan, we don't have a problem with reframing the biblical story because we conclude that that's what we have to do in foreign missions. So why wouldn't the same principles apply in our own context, such as when Jess and Phil are talking to Marty? Why wouldn't we make the same sorts of adjustments when we take the story of Jesus into our neighborhood or workplace and attempt to authentically connect people to the story? How much of what we usually say is open to being changed because it is culturally conditioned rather than biblically imperative?

Stephen Pattison did an informal, nonscientific survey of what came to people's minds when they heard the word *shame*. The list is quite predictable: feelings of being dirty or defiled, having something hidden come to the surface, being demeaned and put "on view," unworthiness, being diminished, exposure, not measuring up, not being good enough, feeling wrong but not knowing why. These are just a start. But they are the kinds of things you would expect.

Now ask yourself the same question. What comes to mind when you hear the word *shame*? Find any resonance? How many people do you know who are not connected to God in any formal way and who claim no "personal relationship" with God, but for whom the category of shame at some level would be deeply connective? Is it possible that *shame* is a better entry point than *sin* in a conversation about spiritual needs?

The postmodern world in which we live amply reinforces the message that we are deficient and diminished. In the experimental learning community I'm a part of, a group called Vortex, we had a conversation about the messages the media send our way every day. Don, one of those in our community, said, "It's amazing how often we're bombarded with messages telling us we're not pretty enough, young enough, strong enough, sexy enough, hip enough, thin enough—and that's just for starters." Lori, a college professor, chimed in, "Even when we don't believe those messages consciously, they get embedded in our unconscious minds and we begin to act and behave as if they were true. And then we realize we really do believe these things that are pummeling our minds."

Shame, which in part is a deep inner sense of being defective and insufficient as a person, is another way of saying *self-judgment*. Shame involves a sense of uncontrollable exposure, in which we have a sense of being viewed and seen in all our ugliness and defectiveness.[4]

It's interesting to note the differences between shame and sin/guilt/obligation. Shame is an inside issue, connected to a faulty self-understanding (we've lost touch with *who we are* as *eikons* of God); whereas, the sin/guilt/obligation complex is centered outside ourselves, in *what we have done*.

In my present capacity, I have the opportunity to host learning conversations all over the country. These are groups of fifteen to thirty-five people who come to engage in peer-to-peer learning and make application in their own contexts of the things we are talking about here. Shortly after one of our conversations, one of the participants posted the following recap on his blog:

> The conversation we had about the gospel going beyond the cold, legal language of "you suck—you're forgiven—welcome to heaven" to the more relational language of shame really hit me during our time together. A light went on this week as I was reflecting on that: Forgiveness is really based on behavior (what I do), but shame is really about identity (who I am), and thus, strikes deeper than "forgiveness" language.
>
> To say to a student, "You're forgiven," that's no big deal. I get a few shrugs and a lot of cold shoulders. "Besides, who are you to tell me I'm so bad!" But to say that, in Christ, you are free from shame—that's just huge! It cuts deep into who they are as humans—broken, lonely, and alone—without a place to belong.
>
> So . . . how do we share God's story of salvation, not as mere forgiveness, but as freedom (and more) in the 21C context? I liked Ron's illustration of the disconnect that would have happened if Moses had gone to Pharaoh and said, "Your sins are forgiven," instead of "Let my people go!" What does that look like in our emerging context?
>
> Any thoughts?

I have no intention of providing a comprehensive justification for *shame* as "the new category." I simply want to note it as one possibility, to get us thinking about others. If you think we're going easy on sin here, I think you might be missing the point of what I'm trying to say. Let me try a slightly different track. If God wants to be in relationship with us (and I hope we can agree that he does), the central issue is not one of right versus wrong; it is about brokenness versus wholeness. In other words, we were created for wholeness, and anything that prevents or impedes relationship with God is brokenness. Brokenness comes in all sorts of packages. Murder is brokenness, adultery is brokenness, addiction is brokenness, and so is shame. All these are issues that prevent relationship with God and undermine the abundant life that Jesus came to provide. It simply doesn't seem helpful to reduce all brokenness to one simple issue: You're a sinner. It may be true, but if it doesn't reconnect people to God, it accomplishes nothing.

Please understand that I am not *excluding* the sacrificial priestly story (sin/guilt/obligation) from our conversations. I'm simply trying to suggest that as our primary story line, or as a means of initiating conversations with people in our postmodern context, it is not the best choice of the three dominant stories in the Old Testament. The story line of shame—which we've seen has currency in our contemporary American culture—seems to fit better with the story of Exodus, which is about slavery to freedom, and the story of Exile, which is about alienation and restoration. If we start there, our conversation might eventually come around to the sacrificial priestly story.

For some followers of Christ, of course, this will not be enough. For them, all shame traces back to the issue of sin, and thus, the story of Jesus' death on the cross should still be the primary story we tell. Perhaps another way of saying it is that shame is not an expansive enough description of the condition that Jesus came to address. But therein lies the rub. Jesus' death and resurrection were for the reconciliation and healing of the world. In the case of the woman with the issue of blood, it was healing and restoration from her marginal and desperate situation. In the case of Zacchaeus, it was a business ethics epiphany that led to his acceptance back into community. In the case of the lepers, it was their ability to be free and mainstreamed back into the culture, no longer disenfranchised. All these examples, and lots more, all of which have shame as a central component, point to the Exodus and Exile stories as fundamental backstories to Jesus' message.

However, these sorts of stories don't fit into the typical evangelical framework for what it means to be saved. If the gospel for us is a newsflash that is limited to "your sins are forgiven" and "now you get to go to heaven," these stories are nice examples of Jesus' healing power, but they don't get to the main point. On the other hand, if shame and other sorts of brokenness *are* addressed by Jesus' life, death, and resurrection, then these stories are valuable windows on Exodus and Exile.

Narrating the story of the Cross according to the needs of the current culture has always been, and always will be, the job of the Christian church. But we need to make sure we're telling the full story. One contemporary theologian has argued that the current understanding that Jesus came to pay the price for the sin of the world not only was highly contextual when it was developed nearly one thousand years ago but is one of a cluster of five images from the Mediterranean world that round out a more complete picture of the purpose of Jesus' death.[5] Maybe we haven't been multifaceted enough in our storying of the Cross. Maybe we need to refamiliarize ourselves with the other ways the story of Jesus' death and resurrection can be told. We might just find that we are moving into new areas in people's lives where the message will more easily, quickly, and transparently find a home.

Shame comes from a completely different ecosystem of metaphors than sin does. Shame is tied up with issues of defilement, pollution, and stain. This is where leprosy, bleeding, blindness, paralysis, and other such maladies fit. The answer to these issues is found primarily in Exodus and Exile. Sin and guilt, on the other hand, are tied up with issues such as debt, judgment, punishment, and right and wrong. These issues are addressed in the sacrificial system established in the book of Leviticus.

Can the story of Jesus' death encompass such a broad brushstroke? The answer seems obvious. He came to do all this, and much more we haven't even mentioned. Though our usual articulation of Jesus' death has focused on his death for sin, we do have in our biblical narrative and Christian history ample examples of understanding Jesus' death as setting people free from the dark powers of shame, slavery, and bondage.[6]

Do we start with the message of the Bible and move toward the context in which we are telling the story, or do we start with the context and move back to the biblical text? I think we need to begin reading the cultural signposts *at the same time* we are reading the biblical text, because the text and our lives are already in a give-and-take rhythm, sometimes called a symbiotic relationship.

When you and I read the Bible, we do not approach it objectively. That would be impossible. Instead, we come with a particular set of social norms and customs that are so ingrained that we are unaware of most of them. We become more aware of inbred perspectives and biases (what we think is normal) when we travel internationally. In every situation, we come with certain presuppositions that we have inherited wholesale from our family upbringing, schooling experiences, life-shaping events, and circumstances. All those factors, and many more, influence how we approach this message of the Bible. And all the same factors affect the story we tell ourselves about ourselves.

We all make sense of our lives and our experiences by telling ourselves certain things about the world we live in. For instance, when someone mistreats us by looking at us with disgust or disdain, the impact of their actions depends on the story line running in our heads. If our predominant story line, which has been molded and shaped by all sorts of influences since the day we were born, is that we have a healthy self-image and are well adjusted and liked by most people, then we will likely consider a look of disgust from someone as inconsequential. If we have what psychologists call a hardy temperament, we might think, *That person is having a bad day*, or, *That person doesn't like me, but who cares anyway?*

We would be unlikely to take it personally. A healthy self-understanding translates into healthy self-talk that interprets challenges and challenging people in a positive way.

On the other hand, the same look of disgust or disdain directed toward a person with a helplessness temperament might cause an internal emotional hiccup or maybe even a meltdown: *Why don't people like me? No one ever does. What did I do to them? I guess my mom was right; I'm just a screwup.* People with this type of self-understanding are often described as glass-half-empty people. No doubt you know both types.

If people have such widely divergent self-stories playing in their heads, often without their conscious awareness, how do we help them grab the story that Jesus brings?

A new field of therapy called narrative therapy can be a huge help in this regard. If we discern that a person's dominant story line is not about guilt but is instead about shame or the prison of addiction or slavery or an abusive marriage or whatever, we will have to intersect that narrative with the message of Jesus if the person is ever to see the value of following Jesus and living the abundant life he offers. Narrative therapy is a deep well, but it illustrates the importance of the stories we tell ourselves and how understanding a person's dominant story line should greatly influence the way we tell God's story.[7]

Though shifting our primary story line from sin to shame, or something else, is potentially challenging, I believe it is critical for clearing up some of the static that has clogged the communication lines for so long. Not only has our story been stagnant for the past two hundred years, but we have also had all sorts of frequency interference that has confused people as to what the real message is. I hope this discussion has opened up some creative new possibilities for more fruitful future conversations.

24 Not There Yet

Winston Churchill once defined golf as "a game in which the object is to place a small ball into an even smaller hole, with implements ill-suited to the task."[1] That goes along with Mark Twain's characterization of golf as "a pleasant walk spoiled."

Both definitions make golf sound like a kind of torture. And on those days when each stroke requires a mantra of knees-slightly-bent-left-eye-on-the-back-of-the-ball-smooth-backswing-don't-overrotate-the-wrists-remember-it's-headspeed-not-strength-don't-look-up-and-above-all-relax, golf *is* a sort of torture. But some days, everything clicks, you have your drives and your short irons both working at the same time, the greens run the way you read them, and life is good.

This particular Saturday had been one of those days.

I'd had a beautiful morning. I'd played eighteen holes with my favorite playing partner—my father—and I'd gone out and come in with nine-hole scores that started with a three. Life was good. My plan was to get out the yoga mat when I got home and stretch a bit (I'm still working on the "and above all, relax" part of my game) and then maybe spend a little time in a vegetative state on the sofa with a DVD.

So I was more than a little surprised to see Phil and Jess's Lexus in my driveway.

"Hey, guys," I said as we all got out of our cars. "What's up?"

My mind was racing. Had we scheduled something for this morning? I didn't think so. On Saturday mornings when I'm not on the road, the only thing I usually have scheduled is my tee time.

"We just had brunch with my guy from work," Phil said. "We decided to do the full-court press . . ."

"*I* decided," Jess said glumly.

"I didn't want to say that," Phil said. "But yeah—Jess decided to do a full-court press. She talked to Marty about getting saved, and he asked what 'saved' meant, and we—"

"I," Jess said.

"Okay, Jess told him that salvation was entry into a life with Christ," Phil continued. "To which my guy replied that he knew lots of people who said that they were saved, and they seemed to keep right on cheating on their taxes, having trouble with their marriages, fighting with their kids, gossiping about other folks in the office, and so on. And he said they also seemed to get catastrophic illnesses and suffer hardship at about the same rate as everybody else. So life with Christ to him seems like just about every other life, and he doesn't see a compelling reason to make the switch."

I nodded. It didn't seem as if I'd be hitting the yoga mat anytime soon.

"'The Same,'" I said. "That's what a friend of mine said Christians should have printed on their T-shirts because we divorce, argue, backbite, become serial killers, and get incarcerated at about the same rate as the general population. Statistically, we're indistinguishable." I got my clubs out of the back of the SUV and nodded at the house. "Want some iced tea?"

They did. We were moving out onto the patio when Jess said, "I've always heard that salvation keeps us from suffering the consequences of our sins. Yet one of the consequences of our sins is that we sometimes behave in ways that are less than admirable. So does that mean we aren't saved after all?"

"There are some pulpits where you'd hear that message," I agreed.

"What do you think, Ron?" Phil asked.

"Before I answer that, let me ask you something. When, exactly, are we 'saved'?"

“As soon as we accept Christ,” Jess answered.

“Yet if we go by your definition of salvation as removal from the consequences of our sins, then obviously we are not saved at that point, because we continue to act like sinful creatures.”

“But we still *are*,” Jess insisted.

“And that’s a further complication. To say that we are saved and then to say that we are sinners, in the same breath, seems like a contradiction. And it is. What is Jesus’ admonition in the Gospels when he forgives sins? It’s ‘go, and sin no more.’ Yet who actually does that? So, to the world around us, when we say, ‘You’ve got a problem and I’ve got the cure’ . . . well, that seems to them to be pretentious or just plain stupid, because obviously we don’t have a cure; otherwise, we wouldn’t be showing the same symptoms that they are. We don’t behave like a saved people. In fact, we can’t, because we continue to live in a sinful environment, a world that exhibits its distance from God.”

I went into the house to get the pitcher of tea, and when I came back, Jess said, “All right. I’ll bite. When are we saved? As soon as we accept Christ, or at some time in the future?”

“Yes,” I replied.

“Don’t you get all ‘Yoda’ on me, mister.”

“Well, honestly, everything depends on what you mean by ‘saved.’ But I think I know what you’re talking about; you want to know about *saved* as in ‘going to heaven,’ right?”

She nodded.

“Okay, I’m going to go with you on this one, Jess, but we need to start by looking at the definition we’re using. We might find it a bit incomplete. From God’s perspective, we’re saved right away. That’s because, to God, the concept of future is immaterial. The future is that time in which we do not have a clear idea of what will happen. But, for God, who is prescient—he knows the future as well as or better than we know the present—there simply is no such time. God has only one tense—*now.* When we come to Jesus, God sees the eternal consequences of that decision, and we are saved immediately. But from our perspective, we keep on muddling through. So, if you define *saved* as ‘without consequences of sin,’ then for us, that is definitely a future event. We’re not there yet.”

Jess frowned. "That seems wrong."

I nodded. "Probably because our definition of *saved* is wrong. I think you're coming around to what I mentioned earlier. In the Genesis story about Adam and Eve, we always dwell on the serpent and the apple and sin; and because we place the emphasis on sin, we see the overarching theme of the Bible as 'remission of sin.' But what's the worst thing that happens to Adam and Eve in Genesis?"

"They get kicked out of the Garden," Phil said.

"Exactly. They lose Eden. And even though Eden has some very cool features, such as beauty and comfort and bounty that grows with very little work on the part of its inhabitants, the central thing about Eden is that it is a place where human beings are in relationship—close and beautiful relationship—with God, with themselves, with each other, and with the earth. It is the only environment we were ever designed for. Without it, we are fish out of water, creatures in an environment for which we were never designed. Every fiber of our being yearns to be restored to a state in which we can reenter the Garden."

"And Jesus allows us to come back in?" Jess half-whispered.

"Bingo."

"But we're not there yet," Phil said.

"Bingo again." I sipped my tea. "Remember when we talked about the word *gospel* and about giving out pink-spoon samples of heaven? After we have accepted Christ, God asks us to be agents of change in other people's lives, so they can head toward Eden as well. That's what we do between the time we are first saved in God's eyes and the time when we enter eternity in our own eyes. *Saved* probably isn't the best word for what happens to us. *Restored* is better. Restored to communion with God *now,* and restored to Eden . . . in due time."

25

The Quintessential Question

One afternoon, after teaching a class in an adjunct capacity at a university in Virginia, I decided to head over to a local mall and hit the Ben and Jerry's joint I'd been told about, which was conveniently located next to the movie theater I thought I would also investigate. I enjoy going into local places when I travel; it gives me a real feel for the local vibe and allows me to people-watch.

As I found the mall entrance closest to the cinema, I noticed a group of people who appeared to be taking a survey. Several people with clipboards were asking shoppers if they had a few moments, and when someone was kind and gullible enough to say yes, the clipboard carrier would begin a battery of questions. Know where I'm going with this? This is a true story!

I admit to eavesdropping and knowing exactly where this was headed, so when I was approached, I consented to the "interview."

I'll give you one guess at the opening question.

That's right. "Sir, if you were to die tonight, do you know where you would go?"

As the thirtyish young man asked the question, he glanced down at his clipboard, as if to prepare for question two. Playing along, I told him I hadn't a clue where I would go. (I had a hankering to say, "I don't know where the hell I would go," but I thought that might be a bit much for this guy, who really was hoping to have a conversation about hell.) The rest of the questions were all quite predictable:

"Would you like to be sure where you are going?"

"Do you believe that Jesus is Lord and do you believe God raised him from the dead?"

"Would you be willing to say this prayer after me so you, too, can be saved?"

I know what I did was pretty unfair. This poor guy was just out at the mall with his church evangelism class, accosting people with the good news of the gospel. He had no way of knowing that the guy he picked to "interview" was a part-time professor at a local Christian university and a full-time pastor in the Midwest. But that's also part of the point. He was taking a one-size-fits-all solution and applying it wherever he could, regardless.

The story may make you smile, but it reminds us that this approach is indeed what a swatch of the Christian population thinks about when it comes to salvation. They expect that by mentally assenting to a couple of propositions about Jesus and saying a particular prayer, a person will be able to answer the quintessential question in the affirmative: "Yes, I know where I'm going when I die." In their minds, this is what constitutes "getting saved." The challenge as I see it isn't simply that some people have this particular view. There are all sorts of views about all sorts of things that I feel no compulsion to address. But this issue is different because—if for no other reason—it provides a substantial basis for broad and negative characterizations of Christianity.

"Getting saved" and "being born again" have become shorthand for the biblical doctrine of salvation. I can't tell you how many times over the years that people who know what I do have asked me, "Are you one of those 'born-agains'?" "You born-agains" refers to a whole host of traits and characteristics. My experience at the Virginia mall is a relatively fair example of how many "born-agains" think. To be born again, or saved, means you have decided to enter into a relationship with Jesus. That relationship is entered by assenting to some propositions about Jesus and ratifying your mental assent by saying a rote prayer, usually repeated after the person who is "leading you to the Lord." The postprayer condition of the praying person is now presumably different from his or her preprayer condition. Whereas before the prayer, the person was going to hell, now he or she is saved and bound for heaven.

I'm concerned that the terms *born again* and *saved* are two more terms that put people on the defensive when they come up in conversation. I try to avoid using them with other people because they have nothing but negative connotations.

When we look at the Old Testament, we find the word *salvation* used quite extensively, but the concepts of "getting saved" or "being born again" do not appear at all. So what is *salvation* in the Old Testament? The first several instances set the tempo: Salvation is deliverance, deliverance from enemies, prosperity. Most references will have one of those definitions in mind, but none support the idea that salvation is a rescue from sin that then enables one to have a seat in eternity.

Israel's defining experience—where salvation is first articulated as "deliverance"—is the story of the Exodus. As we've seen, this narrative is also central in establishing the overarching biblical story line of the movement from slavery and bondage to freedom. Right here, then, is the first definition in the Hebrew Bible of what salvation is: deliverance from slavery into freedom and an established relationship with God.

The story of the Exodus starts in the first chapter of the book of Exodus. No surprise there. The careful reader will note that the first fourteen chapters of Exodus are written in narrative prose, which is simply a fancy way of saying the author is telling a story. In the fifteenth chapter, something very interesting happens. The author shifts from prose to poetry, which signals the reader that something profoundly theological is about to be said. This pattern of narrative followed by a section of poetry is found throughout the first five books of the Old Testament. We see it in chapter units such as Genesis 2, 3, and 4. We see it at the book level, such as where Genesis 1–48 is primarily narrative but chapter 49 is primarily poetry. And we see it here in Exodus, where fourteen chapters of prose storytelling are followed by a big unit of poetry. But what's the point?

When we speak, we can change our volume, tone, and inflection to make a point. When a speaker changes any one of these things, or a combination of them, the listener knows to pay special attention or look for a particular emphasis. Writers do not have volume, tone, and inflection at their disposal. So what do they do? They change writing styles. When we see a shift from prose to poetry, the author is telling us to get ready for something important. Typically, in the Old Testament, what follows is a theological summary of the story the writer just told. In the examples I've listed from Genesis and Exodus, you might be surprised by what you find. (As an aside, the same technique is used in reverse in the book of Job. That book has narrative prose at the beginning and end that provides the punch line and interpretive framework for the thirty-eight chapters of poetry in between that tell the story of Job and his friends.)

In Exodus 15, after what is arguably one of the most defining events in Israel's history, the shift from narrative prose to poetry is indeed highly theological; it records the celebration in dance and song of the parting of the Red Sea and the destruction of Pharaoh's chariots and horsemen. In one smashing blow, Israel has been delivered from destruction and set free from the bondage of slavery.

> Then Moses and the Israelites sang this song to the LORD:
>
> "I will sing to the LORD,
> for he is highly exalted.
> The horse and its rider
> he has hurled into the sea.
> The LORD is my strength and my song;
> he has become my salvation.
> He is my God, and I will praise him,
> my father's God, and I will exalt him. (Exodus 15:1-2)

This passage goes on to develop the most comprehensive theological statement, thus far in the Bible, about who God is. And it also provides our first definition of *salvation.* If we look at other instances of the word *salvation,* we will often find the same elements found here—namely, release, restoration, protection, or victory.

Another word that helps us get our bearings on the Old Testament concept of salvation is *shalom.* No doubt you've at least heard the word and probably know it is Hebrew for "peace." But the word is even richer than that. When we hear *peace,* we usually think of either inner tranquility or the absence of war. Both of these definitions reflect the Hebrew word, but *shalom* also encompasses the ideas of *wellness, completeness,* and *wholeness.* When Israel was rescued from slavery under Pharaoh, she experienced a return to wholeness, wellness, health, and freedom. *Shalom.*

Salvation, then, is a re-establishment of *shalom,* or essentially a return to the fundamental state of the Garden of Eden. *Shalom* was what Adam and Eve had from the beginning. The Garden was all about provision, fullness of relationship, wellness, a general and overall sense of wholeness and completeness. *Shalom* encompasses the full gambit of human existence—relationship with God, each other, ourselves, and creation. The Garden was the ultimate three-dimensional picture of *shalom.*

Salvation in the context of the Exodus story line is a return to the provision of safety and of being under God's dominion instead of Pharaoh's control. There is no reason to develop this idea any further, except to say that it is the rough backdrop against which Jesus entered the first century. When we look to see where the word *salvation* is used most often in Scripture, we find it is in the Psalms and Isaiah. In both books, the definitions center around the idea of restoring *shalom*. It is interesting that Isaiah is one of the main locations of the word *salvation,* given all we have seen about how Isaiah provides so much backstory for Jesus' ministry.

In the Old Testament, the concept of salvation isn't framed around an escape from this space/time universe, or isn't about securing a location in the afterlife. In fact, some scholars believe there isn't much of a concept of the afterlife in the Old Testament. At least until the period of the Exile and a passage such as Daniel 12:2, we have no evidence of the idea at all. Salvation, then, was more about *restoration,* and how that restoration affected the people's relationship with God, with themselves, with each other, and with creation.

Though there are many passages we could look at in the Old Testament, one specific text warrants mention because of its importance to a previous discussion. Remember looking at Isaiah 52 when we were uncovering the Old Testament background for the word *gospel*? Take a look again at Isaiah 52:7.

> How beautiful on the mountains
> are the feet of those who bring good news,
> who proclaim peace,
> who bring good tidings,
> who proclaim salvation,
> who say to Zion,
> "Your God reigns!"

When we read this passage and the next several chapters of Isaiah, we find that the proclamations of salvation are surprisingly Edenic in description. God wants his people free from enemies, free from infirmities, and free from struggles with a broken creation. Isaiah 52:7 says that the newsflash Jesus brought was "God reigns." And wherever God reigns, there are at least whispers of Eden.

To summarize: Salvation is actually about God's rule and reign. Whenever and wherever God reigns, there is a return to the original intention he had for all of creation. That is why in these passages we so often see reversals—from desert to streams of water, from thistles (another reference to the curse of the Garden) to myrtle, from blindness to sight, and from lameness to leaping for joy. In short, salvation isn't an escape from this place to some invisible somewhere out there; it is the transformation of this world as a result of God's invasion of it.

What did Jesus actually bring when he came to earth? How does salvation factor into that equation? And what is the nature of the salvation he brought? We've already made reference to Jesus' statement about why he came, spoken in the synagogue in Nazareth after he read from Isaiah 61. In John 10:10, Jesus makes another signature statement about his purpose: "I have come that they may have life, and that they may have it more abundantly."[1] The curious thing about this saying is not what Jesus says, but also what he doesn't say. When you think about the modern Christian obsession with securing a seat in heaven, don't you think that if Jesus shared that obsession, he would have said something about it? He could have said, "I have come that they may get to heaven, and that they may get there by reciting a sinner's prayer." Jesus could have used any number of phrases to highlight the main reason he came. But if we think he came primarily to get people to heaven, it seems we have the compass pointing in the wrong direction. If Jesus, by his own proclamation and teaching, came to invade this world and transform it; to bring abundant life *here;* to set free the captives *here;* to bind up the brokenhearted *here;* to see that God's will is done *here on earth,* as it (already) is in heaven, why are we trying to get people to disconnect themselves from this world and escape it? Is it possible we're directionally challenged?

We have already noted that Luke, the writer of one Gospel narrative, uses the word departure (meaning "exodus") in reference to Jesus' death (Luke 9:31). It is a new exodus, so to speak, a new way out. But why do we assume, as some have, that the way out is a way out of this world? Is that what Jesus taught in his ministry as the content of salvation—finding a way off the planet, a sort of precursor to the old *Star Trek* "beam me up, Scottie"? Let's take a look at the hints and clues that Jesus gives us.

In Luke 1, Jesus is identified as a "horn of salvation" for Israel, coming from the house of David (v. 69); one who would provide salvation from their enemies (v. 71); and the one who will "give his people the knowledge of salvation" (v. 77). And in Luke 2:30, a devout old man named Simeon, having seen the baby Jesus, says he can now die in peace, "for my eyes have seen your salvation," the salvation of God. These usages of *salvation,* the word *soterias* in Greek, establish Luke's understanding of what salvation means. It is quite clear that salvation, as pictured in the early part of Luke's narrative, is geared more toward *wholeness* than heavenly seat assignments.

In the inscription from the birth of Caesar Augustus that we looked at in a previous chapter, the emperor was called "a savior for us and those who come after us, to make war cease, to create peace everywhere." The word for "savior" in this inscription is *soter,* which is the root word for *soterias,* the word translated as "salvation" in the New Testament. So, not only is Caesar called the "salvation bringer," but it also says he will make wars to cease and will bring peace. As we've also seen, the idea of "bringing peace" can be expressed as "restoring shalom." In a sense, Caesar was being billed as savior and shalom restorer.

It's against this backdrop that Luke writes the birth announcement of Jesus:

> And there were shepherds living out in the fields nearby, keeping watch over their flocks at night. An angel of the Lord appeared to them, and the glory of the Lord shone around them, and they were terrified. But the angel said to them, "Do not be afraid. I bring you good news of great joy that will be for all the people. Today in

> the town of David a Savior has been born to you; he is Christ the Lord. This will be a sign to you: You will find a baby wrapped in cloths and lying in a manger."
>
> Suddenly a great company of the heavenly host appeared with the angel, praising God and saying, "Glory to God in the highest, and on earth peace to men on whom his favor rests."[2]

We are finally seeing the various strands come together as the words *gospel, salvation* (savior), *peace,* and *kingdom* converge. In this setting, it becomes clear why Jesus' reading of the Isaiah scroll was such a dramatic trump card, even in the empire of Caesar. Jesus said that he was bringing salvation, a release from oppression of all sorts: physical, economic, and spiritual. Unfortunately, our English Bible translations don't always help us make that connection.

In most English Bibles, the word *sozo,* which is the verbal form of *soterias,* is translated as both "heal" and "save." When someone came to Jesus with a physical ailment, Jesus would often respond and heal them; in our English translations, it would say, "You are healed," which is a correct translation. But the word *sozo* is also sometimes translated "saved." The point is that there are numerous cases where Jesus heals people and the text says either "You are saved" or "You are healed." To apply the language of restoration to these same stories, we might say that when Jesus healed people, he was saying, "Here, experience a foretaste of the Garden. This is what the empire of God is like. You are being invited back to the restoration of shalom in your life."

Salvation in the New Testament looks and feels like the shalom we looked at in the Old Testament. Is it possible that the newsflash of the gospel—the good news being given to the poor, the announcement to prisoners that there is freedom, the restoration of sight to the blind—is simply this: "Shalom is yours"? In other words, the invitation to follow Jesus is an invitation back to the Garden, where shalom presides; where wholeness is one's companion; where wellness and completeness are the average, run-of-the-mill experience. And though there is a sense in which there's no way we will fully experience this until the full and final restoration of God's rule and reign, that in no way eclipses the very real sample of it we can experience here and now. Salvation and shalom have very real, present, and tangible effects that serve as pink-spoon samples of the larger and fuller expression yet to come.

Looking at salvation this way may seem strange to those of us who are used to thinking of it more as a way to ensure a place in heaven at the end of our lives. But what if salvation is actually much richer, fuller, and deeper than just a seat in heaven? What if heaven is included, but as a by-product, an assumption, a fitting conclusion and obvious part of what it means to belong to Jesus and follow him in relationship?

What if?

26
Everything

"Starbucks, up on West Avenue. Sure. See you there in twelve minutes."

It was a Wednesday evening. I was in the middle of running a few errands around Jackson, but Phil called so I carved out some time for Jess and him. Wednesdays used to be *our night*. That's why Phil knew I'd be available. He and Jess had been a part of a discussion group I led regularly on Wednesday evenings. But then Jim, another member of the small group, was transferred to DC, and Deb got married and moved away. Soon, our regular Wednesday group disbanded, but thankfully my friendship with Phil and Jess survived. That's why meeting them on a Wednesday felt so right.

I knew they both wanted to continue our ongoing conversation, so after I got my latte and settled into one of the comfy chairs near the gas fireplace, I dove in immediately.

"Why would Jesus perform a miracle, like feeding the five thousand, and yet not give an altar-call appeal?" I paused to take a sip of my hot latte. "Why did Jesus heal people and yet not make them say *the prayer* to get into heaven?"

"Well, Jesus probably did give an altar call," Jess said. "The Bible doesn't record everything Jesus did, you know."

"Isn't that called 'reading into the text'?"

"Well, yes . . . but—" Jess stammered.

I pulled out my BlackBerry and clicked on the Bible I had loaded into it. "Let's look at Luke 8, the story of the woman touching Jesus. Go ahead and read it." I handed the PDA to Jess as I continued talking. "Crowds are swirling all around Jesus. People are brushing up against him on all sides . . . and then a woman touches Jesus, and he senses something special has happened."

"It says here that Jesus asked, 'Who touched me?'" Jess was reading along.

"Okay, does it say who this woman is?"

"Well, it says that the woman had experienced bleeding for twelve long years and had spent a ton of money on doctors."

"So, here's my point," I said, leaning forward a bit in my chair. "This woman had a physical condition that had tapped her dry—and she thinks, *If only I can touch the robe of Jesus, I will be healed.* That's what psychologists today call 'magical' thinking. 'If I say or do the right thing, then I can make miracles happen.'" I stared at the fire in the gas fireplace. "And . . . what does Jesus say to this woman?"

Phil had the BlackBerry now and scrolled down to find his place. "Daughter, your faith has healed you. Go in peace."

"Anything else?"

"No."

"Are you sure? Nothing about heaven?"

"No."

"How about prayer? Anything about praying a prayer?"

"No."

Jess grabbed the BlackBerry, "But, Ron, it says that while Jesus was speaking, he was interrupted by a messenger from Jairus's house. . . . Maybe a disciple followed up with the woman."

"That's what I would have said a couple of years ago. You know, 'They must have left out some of the details that everyone at that time would have just known.' But I started to realize that I was reading my theology into the Bible text, instead of letting the Bible stand for itself and speak for itself. So, if we read the passage straightforwardly, what are we to make of this?" I looked intently at Phil and Jess.

"Well, maybe the woman wasn't saved." Jess waved her paper cup in my direction.

"But the Greek word *sozo,* which means both 'save' and 'heal,' is in the passage. And Jesus says to her, 'Go in *eirene* (or peace).' That's the Greek translation of the Hebrew word *shalom.* That's the word I've been saying is intricately linked to salvation in the Bible. Shalom equates to wellness, health, wholeness, salvation. Okay, so in the story now, what happens? Instead of becoming unclean by his contact with this unclean woman, Jesus cleanses her. He overcomes fracture, brokenness, alienation, and uncleanness with one touch. The woman was brought out of exile and restored. Saved? You bet. Seat in heaven? Well, the passage doesn't say anything about that."

"But, Jesus *had* to be concerned about that," Phil interjected after scrolling up and down the passage on my Black-Berry.

"I'm just challenging us to read what the Bible actually says, not what our theologies dictate." I leaned over and pointed at verse 47 on the screen. "Luke, inspired by God, clearly uses salvation language in this passage. The Greek words *sozo,* meaning saved, and *eirene,* meaning peace or wholeness, are both in the passage. But nowhere does Luke discuss the woman's heavenly state. Those are the facts from the Bible."

"So, is the woman saved?" Jess leaned over, pleading.

"Well, Luke says she's both healed and saved," I said. "See the word *healed* in verse 47? It's *sozo,* which means both healed and saved."

This time Jess was busy scrolling through the Bible text. "But what about her soul?"

"Read the passage. Does it say anything about that?"

"I can't find it anywhere," Jess said after a minute.

"That's my point. For some reason, Jesus wasn't as concerned about eternity here as our theologies would like him to be."

"Well, you can't build your case on just one passage," Phil said.

"This isn't the only passage like that. Read the story of Jairus in Luke 8 as well. The synagogue ruler comes to Jesus, pleading with him to come because his daughter is dying." I stole a look out the picture window. The wet streets reflected the lights of the oncoming traffic.

"Yeah, I see that passage," Jess said as she stared at the backlit scene. "Once Jesus finally makes his way to the house where the little girl has died, he says she really isn't dead but merely asleep."

"And the people laughed at Jesus for thinking the girl was asleep," Phil chimed in, "but then Jesus went into the house and brought the little girl back to life." It was nice to know he was still listening. For the last few minutes, he had been leisurely flipping through a discarded newspaper.

"Look carefully at that passage, Jess. The English word translated 'heal' is *sozo,* the Greek word that means both 'healed' and 'saved.'"

"Yeah, I see that. Jesus asked Jairus to believe and then he healed the little girl." Jess placed the BlackBerry on the coffee table, and Phil reached for it.

"Okay, let's think about this," I said. "Jesus has just resurrected a little girl from death. What would almost every preacher we know today talk about at a time like that?" I reached for the newspaper, flipped to the obituaries, and pointed.

"Oh, I get it," Phil said. "The people gathering around the girl were preparing for her funeral. At every funeral I've been to, the preacher talks about how this life will end for all of us, but we have hope. There's another life. A heaven, and a hell."

"And, what we should do about it . . ." Jess said.

"Exactly. This would be a perfect time to talk about death, heaven, hell, and what 'a personal relationship with Jesus' could do. But do you see any of that in the Bible passage?"

"Not exactly." Phil looked up and shook his head.

"Does the Bible assure us that Jesus 'closed the deal' with Jairus or the little girl, so that the healing became merely a superficial opportunity to talk about eternity?"

"Well . . . I'm not sure," Phil mumbled.

"All right . . . I'd better take my BlackBerry before it runs out of juice." I reached for the gadget. "Think about it some more. Ask yourself whether Jesus is concerned about the issues that so much of our teachings and our theologies focus on."

“And, if Jesus isn’t as concerned . . . ?” Jess threw her empty cup toward the trash can.

“Then, we need to question our teachings and our theologies, don’t we?” I opened the door so we could jog to our cars through the drizzle.

I’ve had a number of conversations with people like the one I described with Phil and Jess. And Luke 8 isn’t the only passage that challenges the focus of our theology. Another well-known story is found in Luke 17:11-19.

> Now on his way to Jerusalem, Jesus traveled along the border between Samaria and Galilee. As he was going into a village, ten men who had leprosy met him. They stood at a distance and called out in a loud voice, “Jesus, Master, have pity on us!”
>
> When he saw them, he said, “Go, show yourselves to the priests.” And as they went, they were cleansed.
>
> One of them, when he saw he was healed, came back, praising God in a loud voice. He threw himself at Jesus’ feet and thanked him—and he was a Samaritan.
>
> Jesus asked, “Were not all ten cleansed? Where are the other nine? Was no one found to return and give praise to God except this foreigner?” Then he said to him, “Rise and go; your faith has made you well.”

All ten of these lepers are healed. But only one returns to give thanks, and to him Jesus says, “Your faith has saved/healed you.” Clearly, the point of this narrative is not about who goes to heaven and who doesn’t. Or what the formula is for getting to heaven. Salvation, wholeness, wellness, shalom are apparently broader than the idea of heaven and the afterlife.

People often say to me that these passages were obviously not included to show how to get to heaven. Precisely my point. Which prompts the question: Why, then, are we so obsessed with the idea of getting to heaven? Jesus had tons of opportunities to make it an emphasis in his ministry, but he didn't.

And let's not forget Zacchaeus, whose willingness to right wrongs in his business dealings prompted Jesus to tell him that salvation had visited his house. Most people in the modern church would never use that as an example of evangelism.

What about the rich young man who comes to Jesus in one of the few instances where the conversation is actually about how to get to heaven (Matthew 19:16-22). After telling the man to keep all the commandments and the young man's response that he has already done that, Jesus says, "Sell everything you have and give it to the poor." A lot can be said about this passage, but do we have enough room in our understanding of salvation to allow what Jesus says to stand on its own merits? When the disciples hear Jesus' response, they are upset and ask, "Who then can be saved?" (v. 25). Jesus now has a premier opportunity to make the "gospel of getting to heaven" absolutely clear. His response? "With man this is impossible, but with God all things are possible" (v. 26).

When Peter says to Jesus, "We have left everything to follow you! What then will there be for us?" (v. 27), Jesus affirms that in leaving everything they would inherit eternal life.

I'm afraid this is yet another example of a passage that doesn't fit conveniently into our typical modern, church-in-the-West theology of salvation. These stories seem to gloss over situations where the message of getting to heaven could have been explained. But maybe the issue just isn't as important or central to the gospel as we have tried to make it.

Everything. Thinking about that word in the context of the stories we just looked at in Matthew, I was reminded that Jesus said there were a couple things that stood head and shoulders above everything else: Love God and love other people (Matthew 22:37-40). *Everything,* he said, in the law and the prophets was summed up in those two mandates. Yet nothing about getting people to heaven. Is it possible that in really loving God, and in really loving people, heaven is simply included? Is it possible that when someone really engages with God and really shows compassion to other people, he or she inherits eternal life and gets to spend forever with God—that heaven is simply a by-product of obeying the two great commands he gave? For many of us, this seems a bit too simplistic. We can't control it. It seems a bit squishy and soft. But doesn't it seem to be in line with what Jesus taught?

If it rocked your boat when Jesus told the wealthy young man to sell everything to gain eternal life, what about this next story?

> Then he turned toward the woman and said to Simon, "Do you see this woman? I came into your house. You did not give me any water for my feet, but she wet my feet with her tears and wiped them with her hair. You did not give me a kiss, but this woman, from the time I entered, has not stopped kissing my feet. You did not put oil on my head, but she has poured perfume on my feet. Therefore, I tell you, her many sins have been forgiven—for she loved much. But he who has been forgiven little loves little."
>
> Then Jesus said to her, "Your sins are forgiven."[1]

Here is another story that doesn't fit very well into our understanding of salvation. A woman, characterized as one "who had lived a sinful life" (Luke 7:37), is granted forgiveness based on her expression of love for Jesus. Not your typical altar call. No declaration of repentance according to any of the modes we typically require. And yet Jesus says, "Your sins are forgiven." We could again ask the question, Does her being forgiven mean she is heaven bound? Or is Jesus recognizing deep shame in her brokenness and telling her that she is whole again, that shalom is hers?

Do we know?

The goal here is not to be vague but to recognize that the Bible establishes a much larger framework for understanding salvation and how it comes about than has typically been taught in the church.

You know what always tripped me up? For years, I read passages like this but couldn't let them speak on their own. I always read my preconceived theological notions into the stories so they would neatly and conveniently fit into my understanding of salvation. I had one view: Salvation means getting a seat in heaven, and this is how you get in. When it came to Zacchaeus, the rich young ruler, or the weeping woman with the expensive perfume, I had to insert things into the text to make them correspond to my presuppositions. For instance, the woman's tears must have been tears of repentance; and her kneeling at Jesus' feet was her sign of accepting him as Lord; so, clearly, she was going to heaven.

I had explanations like that for every story you can point to. But I was always inserting stuff to make it neater and tidier for God. I believed that the Gospel writers had omitted important details that, if they had just included, would make everything a lot clearer. In the absence of written clarity, I was happy to help out and clear things up. I have since learned that I am not the only person who does this. Lots of people do. And it seems the more people claim to be "Bible-believing Christians," the more apt they are to add material to the text so that it will say what they want it to say.

Therein lies a problem that plagues much of the modern Western church. We are so concerned with having everything neat and tidy, according to our standards, that we distort, add to, insert, adjust, and guess what Jesus and the writers of the New Testament must have "really meant."

It's time we let the New Testament stand on its own. The writers don't need our help, and God certainly doesn't. When we let go of our fetish for control and certainty, we will be able to say that the biblical story is multilayered, ambiguous at times, and even sometimes paradoxical, but it must be allowed to speak.

Only then will we be able to broaden our understanding

of salvation to include a passage such as Matthew 25:35-46. What does it mean that those who are saved and entering the place of eternal life, prepared from the creation of the world, qualified for this eternal life by providing someone a drink of water?

> "'For I was hungry and you gave me something to eat, I was thirsty and you gave me something to drink, I was a stranger and you invited me in, I needed clothes and you clothed me, I was sick and you looked after me, I was in prison and you came to visit me.'
>
> "Then the righteous will answer him, 'Lord, when did we see you hungry and feed you, or thirsty and give you something to drink? When did we see you a stranger and invite you in, or needing clothes and clothe you? When did we see you sick or in prison and go to visit you?'
>
> "The King will reply, 'I tell you the truth, whatever you did for one of the least of these brothers of mine, you did for me.'
>
> "Then he will say to those on his left, 'Depart from me, you who are cursed, into the eternal fire prepared for the devil and his angels. For I was hungry and you gave me nothing to eat, I was thirsty and you gave me nothing to drink, I was a stranger and you did not invite me in, I needed clothes and you did not clothe me, I was sick and in prison and you did not look after me.'
>
> "They also will answer, 'Lord, when did we see you hungry or thirsty or a stranger or needing clothes or sick or in prison, and did not help you?'
>
> "He will reply, 'I tell you the truth, whatever you did not do for one of the least of these, you did not do for me.'
>
> "Then they will go away to eternal punishment, but the righteous to eternal life."

How do we understanding a passage like this according to the "get a seat in heaven" view of salvation we have carried around for so long? Where does helping our neighbors fit into the grand scheme of things? Do you find a passage like this a little troubling? I did. I really struggled with the fact that Jesus wasn't banishing people to eternal fire because they weren't followers, or weren't saved, or weren't born again, but because they chose not to help homeless people, strangers, needy people. A lack of willingness to help those in need was enough to banish someone.

On the flip side, the same principle is true. Those called *righteous* in the passage are those who through their actions help others in need. Again, nothing about spiritual conversion as typically defined in the modern church. But it does echo the two great commandments that Jesus identified: loving God and loving people. Is evidence of these an indication of salvation?

I admit that I have done all sorts of backbends, double somersaults with a twist, and other gymnastics with the text to try to get these passages to fit my preconceived idea of what salvation is and how to get it. But in the end I've found that it's much easier to let the text speak and adjust my views accordingly. Getting the text to say something different from what it obviously says is certainly not a good alternative. God must be free to speak into our ideas and preconceived notions. If he can't, we can never grow, never move toward health, never hear the whole truth.

In our conversations with other people, rather than talking about salvation (a topic with much cultural baggage), I wonder if it wouldn't be better to talk instead about wholeness and wellness—genuine shalom—which is actually what salvation is.

27

An Invitation to the Banquet

The streets of Kathmandu, Nepal, are some of the most interesting places in the world. I have visited many unique places and intriguing countries, but Nepal ranks way up there on the interest scale. I saw temples built in the tenth century, still in use, and old holy men—and I mean they looked ancient—with full body paint, sitting at the entrance to these temples. And I saw people take food offerings to temple or shrine gods made out of concrete and carved stone—something hard to understand from the perspective of a Western Christian. One has to ask, "Do they really think these little stone figurines eat the food they are bringing them?" Come on!

What these food offerings show, from the hands of people so poor they don't have enough to feed their families, is just how important food is in religious settings. Food is also important in the human world of creating bonds. Few things are quite as sacramental as sharing a meal.

I love to cook, so I get to enjoy both sides of the food experience. When I was in college, I had the opportunity to work at a very nice French restaurant. Not only did we get to eat a full meal prior to each shift, we also had the opportunity to take cooking and wine classes from the chef. It would have been pretty hard not to get turned on to the idea that cooking is a lot of fun. And even though cooking is an expensive hobby, you do get to eat what you make—not a bad payout.

Another thing I learned is that great food and a great setting create space for love and life to flow. This is one respect in which other cultures around the world are very different from ours. Meals in Italy, France, Hungary, and Nepal and other parts of Asia are seen more as events, focal gathering spots to connect, debrief, and experience life together. I want to suggest that in some ways this is part of God's original intention for the Garden—the full flow of love, sharing, food, drink, and conviviality that come in that setting.

Meals in the first century were a big deal, far more so than in twenty-first-century America. Early in Matthew's Gospel, we noted the story of Jesus' being called on the carpet for eating with a tax collector, and how incensed the Pharisees were about it. Jesus was breaking long-standing customs that governed who could eat with whom. What we haven't discussed yet is how the idea of the meal and banquet became a fundamental image of salvation for Jesus. To that discussion we now turn.

First-century Jewish culture had elaborate dietary laws, as well as customs about who got to eat with whom and where each person sat at the table. My friend Conrad Gempf says it well: "Supper was not just sustenance; supper was spirituality. Doing lunch was doing theology."[1] Jesus was repeatedly berated by the pastoral theologians of the day for "eating with tax collectors and sinners." We've seen it with Matthew the tax collector, and we saw it with Zacchaeus in Luke 19.[2]

What is going on in these passages where the religious leaders are keeping tabs on Jesus and the people with whom he is eating? Well, you may be surprised, but I think his choice of eating partners and the repeated images of eating and banqueting comprise one of the more profound metaphors for *salvation* and the *shalom* that salvation brings. In Luke 7:33-34, an accusation is made comparing Jesus to John the Baptist: "For John the Baptist came neither eating bread nor drinking wine, and you say, 'He has a demon.' The Son of Man came eating and drinking, and you say, 'Here is a glutton and a drunkard, a friend of tax collectors and "sinners."'"

The reason John and his disciples fasted is an obvious one. For an ascetic like John, fasting and preparation were part and parcel of his life ministry, and thus carried over naturally to his announcement of the coming kingdom. But what about Jesus? A little further along in Luke, Jesus goes on a real tear about the issue of eating. The way Luke records this series of stories unpacks Jesus' intent in a powerful way, as if by linking these stories together, Luke is making sure his readers don't miss the central story line.

> When [Jesus] noticed how the guests picked the places of honor at the table, he told them this parable: "When someone invites you to a wedding feast, do not take the place of honor, for a person more distinguished than you may have been invited. If so, the host who invited both of you will come and say to you, 'Give this man your seat.' Then, humiliated, you will have to take the least important place. But when you are invited, take the lowest place, so that when your host comes, he will say to you, 'Friend, move up to a better place.' Then you will be honored in the presence of all your fellow guests. For everyone who exalts himself will be humbled, and he who humbles himself will be exalted."[3]

Jesus starts the conversation by tapping into a familiar setting. At every wedding, there were certain places where people were to sit. Most people would be in general seating locations, but there were some special seating assignments that would acknowledge the relationship of the guest to the ones hosting the wedding feast. The same is true today; family and close friends have special, reserved seats—it is expected and assumed.

Jesus then invites people to do something counterintuitive

and out of the ordinary. He says, "When heading into a setting like this, always err on the side of taking a humbler seat. You can always accept an upgrade later. But if you take a seat you shouldn't and have to be asked to move, well, that is simply humiliating." The story on its own seems like no big deal—a simple lesson in etiquette and a way to avoid embarrassment. But I want to suggest that this is only the opening conversation of a discourse that probes something more than etiquette. The next story Luke records goes one layer deeper, one step further:

> Then Jesus said to his host, "When you give a luncheon or dinner, do not invite your friends, your brothers or relatives, or your rich neighbors; if you do, they may invite you back and so you will be repaid. But when you give a banquet, invite the poor, the crippled, the lame, the blind, and you will be blessed. Although they cannot repay you, you will be repaid at the resurrection of the righteous."[4]

The directional shift may not be totally obvious at first, but it should give us at least a hint of where Jesus is going with the story. He ups the ante from a concern about where the invited guests will sit to a question of *who* will be invited. Seems kind of strange, doesn't it? One would expect that family, friends, neighbors would be on the guest list. But then Jesus makes an interesting shift in language. He goes from talking about a luncheon or a dinner to talking about a banquet or reception. And then he says, "Invite the poor, the crippled, the lame, the blind," and immediately tells us why: *They* cannot repay you, but you will be repaid.

Is that the point of the story? The context seems to indicate that something else is going on.

Where else have we seen the language that is being echoed here, of the poor, crippled, lame, and blind? Two passages in Luke immediately come to mind. The first one is Luke 4:16-21, where Jesus reads from the scroll of Isaiah, then sits down and says, "This scripture is fulfilled in your hearing." His reading from Isaiah 61 is one of several sections in the book of Isaiah that talk about some sort of reversal—the lame walking, the blind seeing, the deaf hearing, and so on. These reversals were signs of God's kingdom breaking into our realm, hints of the restoration of the Garden shalom.

The second instance is in Luke 7:18-23, when John the Baptist sends two of his disciples to ask Jesus if he is, in fact, the Expected One. John had baptized Jesus and had elevated him to a level of importance, proclaiming that the kingdom of God was about to dawn. But John was eventually arrested by Herod and thrown in prison. And as with all difficult and trying circumstances, what seemed so obvious and clear to John in the light of day was now getting fuzzy in the dark of night. He was quite convinced that Jesus was the Expected One; but if so, why was John in prison? Why was he under the power of someone else if Jesus was going to rule and reign? So John sent his disciples to get some clarification. "Jesus, I thought you were the Expected One; in fact, I was convinced you were. But right now Herod has got my neck and I am wondering, 'Are you really the man?'"

Jesus gives a response that for some may seem illusive and indirect. But for anyone in the first century at all familiar with the Hebrew Scriptures, Jesus' answer—though not explicit—is crystal clear. Jesus tells John's disciples to go tell John about all the reversals they've seen (v. 22). Lame people are walking, blind people are seeing, the deaf are hearing, lepers are clean, the dead are coming to life, and the poor are receiving a newsflash. What is Jesus saying? "Those who have been outcasts and marginalized are experiencing the newsflash of my *shalom*. They are experiencing *restoration* (salvation). Go tell John what you've seen."

By the time we get to Luke 14, we already have a pretty good idea of who the crippled, blind, lame, and poor represent. Jesus now asks his followers to do something and tells them about something he is doing. I think both the asking and the telling are in view here. First, he invites his followers to break with social convention and associate with people who are considered unclean, marginal, and not to be socialized with. To interact with these people would be a big deal. To invite them to your home for a banquet? Unheard of.

Jesus is obviously asserting that he intends to be a boundary breaker, a barrier buster. His ministry will be marked by its offering of shalom to people who currently seem to have the least of it, but who, due to their marginalization, are the most humble, unassuming, and therefore deserving.

Now we come to the real punch line of the story. My guess is that Luke has been laying some careful groundwork as he has gradually built up the story line to this climactic moment.

> One of those at the table . . . said to Jesus, "Blessed is the man who will eat at the feast in the kingdom of God." Jesus replied: "A certain man was preparing a great banquet and invited many guests. At the time of the banquet he sent his servant to tell those who had been invited, 'Come, for everything is now ready.' But they all alike began to make excuses. The first said, 'I have just bought a field, and I must go and see it. Please excuse me.' Another said, 'I have just bought five yoke of oxen, and I'm on my way to try them out. Please excuse me.' Still another said, 'I just got married, so I can't come.' The servant came back and reported this to his master. Then the owner of the house became angry and ordered his servant, 'Go out quickly into the streets and alleys of the town and bring in the poor, the crippled, the blind and the lame.' 'Sir,' the servant said, 'what you ordered has been done, but there is still room.' Then the master told his servant, 'Go out to the roads and country lanes and make them come in, so that my house will be full. I tell you, not one of those men who were invited will get a taste of my banquet.'"

Wow, is this a volatile one! It's tough to swallow whom Jesus includes and excludes here. Apparently, this is a picture of the banquet to occur in the future heaven—the "not yet" part of the kingdom of God. Some of God's kingdom has *already* arrived in Jesus, but it has *not yet* fully come. We are living between the "already" and the "not yet."[5]

In the story, a certain group of people have been invited. In this context, Jesus is clearly referring to the Jewish people—and the Pharisees, as keepers of the law, would expect to be considered part of the "in" group. Of course, from the beginning of Jesus' ministry, they have struggled with the fact that he eats and hangs out with people who are *not* part of the "in" group.

But now, in this story, the "in" group are too busy, too preoccupied, too self-absorbed to attend the feast. What happens? Their invitations are rescinded, and those previously thought to be totally disqualified are now invited in. Anyone and everyone, especially the disenfranchised, are included. Those of mixed ethnicity, any economic class, male, female—all of these are invited to the same table, with no screening interview and no way to make sure the eating rules are observed.

Do you see how this fits into the question of why John and his disciples fasted but Jesus and his disciples didn't? In Jesus' eating overtures, there is an image of salvation and inclusion. His presence doesn't call for deprivation and asceticism; it calls for the bounty and abundance of eating and drinking with the King. Jesus' redefinition of who could be considered an eating partner is a powerful image and symbol of who will be included in the family of God, and this last story about the banquet really drives the point home.

Salvation, shalom, and a banquet in heaven may not be available to those who thought they were going there. The Pharisees were so busy drawing the lines on who was "in" and "out" that they failed to notice that they themselves were on the wrong side of the line, because they were too arrogant, too convinced, too preoccupied.

What if the people all around you, the ones you are convinced aren't going to heaven, actually have an invitation extended to them independent of all the systems and structures you thought were necessary for salvation? What if they have a seat next to yours at the table?

Salvation may be more about the restoration of shalom in people's lives than it is about anything else. Jesus is interested in providing abundant life. He is interested in relationships. But he seems very uninterested in the rote rules and regulations of the Pharisees, who thought they had the power and privilege to define the haves and have-nots. I wonder if Jesus has the same sorts of issues with us in today's church. From my vantage point inside the church as a pastor for almost two decades, it sure seems that a lot of us are all about the rules and regulations. Oh, we've updated them and sanitized them to make them appear more palatable, but they're rules nonetheless, and rules nowhere to be found on the lips of Jesus. Where did we get all these hoops that people have to jump through to belong?

Two of our shiniest hoops are these: If you believe the right things and then behave in the right ways, we just might let you belong. The irony, of course, is that this sounds exactly like the attitude Jesus was trying to deconstruct and fight against most of his ministry. Instead, Jesus said to people, "Come and belong. And as you start on the personal transformational journey, you will naturally have a craving to ask questions about the believing dimension; the character bar will naturally be raised as you spend time with me, doing what I do." That's how it worked with the disciples.

When we look at the disciples in light of "salvation," we're hard pressed to know when they were actually saved. That's because our category of "being saved" is flawed from the very root. If experiencing shalom in our lives is a process (and experience seems to indicate that it is), and if shalom is a good picture of what salvation is, then is it possible our idea of "getting saved" focuses too much on a singular, momentary event?

28

Restoration as a Process

If salvation *is* about experiencing a sense of shalom, a return to the Garden of wholeness and wellness, then it's probably clear that salvation must be more about a process than a point in time. Following Jesus is a process. All relationships are a process. So let's face it: The cut-and-dried approaches we so often gravitate toward in the modern world are simply not very functional when applied to these spongy and soft things called relationships.

Several years ago, our staff at Westwinds was going through a major process of evaluating the modern point-of-sale approach to coming to follow Christ. When I say point-of-sale, it's not out of disrespect for those people who have come to follow Jesus that way or for those who have evangelized people that way. But I say it to distinguish the modern Four Spiritual Laws way of coming to follow Jesus with what, in my own experience, seems to be far more of a process.

I began to notice a very interesting phenomenon in our church. Though we had never had a traditional altar call—as in, come up front and kneel at the altar while someone prays for you—we did give people the opportunity to respond to the message by seeking out someone on the platform or talking to someone in the auditorium after the service or any number of other relatively nonthreatening options. What finally came to my attention, after I had seen it happen about seven or eight times, was that most people who raised their hand or sought out a person to affirm their commitment to follow Christ weren't choosing to do it on that particular day.

Let me give you an example.

Leah came up to me in the lobby after a weekend worship event and whispered in my ear, "I want you to know that I feel this prompting inside me, but I am definitely not ready to 'sell the farm' and commit to following Jesus. I guess I just want you to know I am in the process."

Leah was one of dozens of people who had done this either to me or to one of the other staff members. They felt some interior prompting by the Spirit of God, some "next step" being urged—and so clearly urged that they wanted to share it with somebody—but they were not ready to make a full commitment, to "sell the farm," as Leah put it.

So we did a little homework, and do you know what we discovered? Almost every person "responding" on a given morning really wasn't "getting saved" right then. They said point blank that they were either in the process but felt prompted to be accountable to someone in the process or had started a relationship with Jesus over the past number of months but were clueless as to exactly when "it" happened. Our takeaway? Most people do not experience a moment of conversion. There isn't a point of sale they can point to. The typical experience for the average person is not a Damascus Road experience like the apostle Paul's.

Why is this important? Because the whole notion behind the question "Are you saved?" implies a specific starting point, and many people simply have no reference point for this in their experience. Do a quick survey of your own. You will find lots and lots of people who claim they have a relationship with Jesus who cannot tell you when it began. For those of us who like the tight and tidy categories of who is in and who is out, who has crossed the line, and who we have "won to Christ," this sort of revelation isn't comforting. But it does tell us something about our theology and our methods.

Theology is simply how we think about God. If our theology tells us we get saved at some point in time when we consciously make a decision to do so, then we will have church services, develop evangelism training techniques, and pose questions to people that indicate our theological persuasion. If, on the other hand, we see that a vast number of people experience more of a process than a point of sale, then we will create church experiences and rituals that assist in that process.

Our staff reviewed all the issues biblically and personally, and it was interesting to see their conclusions. We had several staff members from a Lutheran background, and they were very comfortable with the idea of salvation as a process for which a written date in the flyleaf of their Bible was an impossibility. And we had some who were raised as Baptists, who had to admit they weren't sure which campfire meeting or altar call response was their actual time of "getting saved." In the end, they had to admit that even for them, with a very decisive point-of-sale theology, they had come to follow Christ as a process and were still in that process.

The process *is* the point. In John 16, Jesus assures us that the Holy Spirit is at work in the heart of every person who doesn't yet know God. We simply haven't adequately developed our understanding in the church of this preconversion work of the Holy Spirit. Furthermore, we haven't developed effective rituals and steps that people can take to assist them in the journey toward entering a relationship with Christ. The simple question "Are you saved?" is a yes or no proposition. But at what point do we enter a relationship with someone? And at what point is that relationship solid or established?

As I said, I don't think we've done an adequate job of addressing the preconversion work of the Holy Spirit. For the vast majority of people—and it may well be universal, based on John 16—their experience of coming to be "saved" involved a number—sometimes a large number—of interior promptings that slowly prepared, wooed, and drew them into relationship with Jesus. Those interior promptings are sometimes in the form of quiet impressions, self-conversations in which probing questions are raised, or decisive events and challenges that lead to turning points.

These inflection points are mini steps on the pathway of repentance. They are small step-by-step reorientations, often with no fanfare or drama, but are nonetheless decisive in the long run. As part of the pool of experience, they are responsible for drawing the person into relationship with Jesus. This process is so little understood, and yet so necessary to evangelism, that we need to develop full-scale books on postmodern evangelism and the interior yearnings of the heart. One of my next writing projects is to be a part of that conversation.

Though some have already written on this topic, for the most part it has been ignored. Scot McKnight's *Turning to Jesus* is the best single-volume treatment I've seen of the process of salvation. McKnight combines great reflections on the Gospels, an understanding of sociology, and lots of anecdotes and stories from people about their personal processes.[1] Does it make sense that engaging people in a conversation about *process* will be far more fruitful than a conversation about being *in* or *out, saved* or *lost*?

What if we aren't really sure when our relationship with Jesus started, but we're certain we're in one? Are we okay with that? Are we okay with the idea that the way we experience salvation—what I'm calling shalom, wholeness, and wellness—changes as our relationship with Jesus changes? Are we okay with the New Testament referring to salvation using past-, present-, and future-tense verbs, making the question of "Are you saved?" rather irrelevant to the current state of your relationship with Jesus?

Let's not forget the reason for this investigation—indeed, the whole premise of this book. When we go around using "saved" language or asking people if they are saved, we are entering conversations with a sometimes volatile and at least somewhat misleading term. As we've seen, talking about salvation as an entry point to conversations about God that doesn't seem to be what Jesus or any of the New Testament writers did.

So, instead of continuing to pound the old buzzwords such as *gospel, sin, salvation,* and *repentance,* we are trying to come up with language that more closely echoes biblical concepts and more closely connects with human experience. If *salvation* is *shalom,* which we experience by being in a growing and dynamic relationship with Jesus, it makes sense it would be presented in the New Testament as both past, present, and future.[2] Not only that, but creation is also included in salvation, in the experience of the shalom of the Garden. This makes total sense in light of the primary charge given to Adam in the Garden "to work it and take care of it" (Genesis 2:15). Romans 8, penned by Paul, is the clearest biblical statement of creation's need of salvation, restored shalom. Paul says that creation is yearning for Garden restoration to come to her as well (Romans 8:22).

Two other hot-button words that we don't necessarily want to reframe but that we certainly want to put in their proper perspective are *heaven* and *hell.* For so long, the world at large, those people who claim no relationship with Jesus, have been told that if they are not saved they are going to hell. But if they would only follow Jesus, they could be with him forever. Isn't it interesting that heaven and hell are used as the carrot and stick we dangle in front of people's faces? That was certainly my experience at camp, and very possibly yours too. But is all this emphasis on heaven and hell really all that well founded? Did Jesus use the carrot-and-stick approach to get the disciples to follow him? Did he use heaven-or-hell rhetoric to get the woman caught in adultery to shape up? or the woman at the well who had had a bunch of husbands and was "living in sin" with someone else? Did he use this method of persuasion with the paralyzed man who was brought by his friends or with blind Bartimaeus? The answer in every case is no.

Jesus didn't use the carrot of heaven as an incentive package to get people to sign on. Why not? Let me say it again. I don't think he was primarily interested in the question of eternity—at least not nearly as interested as we are. Simply reading the Gospels and noticing where he spoke about heaven and hell should be sufficient proof. When Jesus talked about hell, it wasn't to motivate people to follow him; it was a threat to the religious leaders of the day that they would end up there if they didn't quit being such arrogant dingbats. Read Matthew 23:15, 33, for example.

What if heaven and hell are simply the outflow of our current relationship or lack of relationship with Jesus? If salvation has past-tense and present-tense components, what if eternity with Jesus is nothing more than the obvious future-tense outcome of what we were doing here on earth—experiencing a relationship with Jesus where healing, wholeness, wellness, and shalom are growing and developing? For Jesus, heaven wasn't a motivator to get people to have a relationship with him. You know why? How can you convince people that spending an eternity with Jesus is a huge benefit if they don't want a relationship with him here and now? In other words, an eternity spent doing something you don't want to do for a short time here on earth isn't *heaven*—it's *hell.*

Heaven isn't a carrot. Hell isn't a stick. Those concepts don't resonate with people anymore. Instead, heaven and hell are the obvious future outcomes of what has already happened in our earthly relationship with Jesus. He isn't trying to populate heaven; he's trying to grow his family. Jesus isn't worried about getting people a seat at the table; he's interested in granting them restoration and peace—that is, shalom. When you enter a restored-shalom relationship with Jesus, you are instantly in the process of moving toward the place where the shalom you are tasting now—the pink-spoon sample you are experiencing here on earth—will come to full fruition.

Think about the implications of this shift on our evangelistic efforts—that is, our efforts to broadcast the newsflash. Isn't a winsome relationship far more compelling than simply escaping hell? The old nineteenth-century revivalism scare tactics just don't ring true today. They seem controlling, tribal, even mythical. Isn't it easier to see your friends gravitating toward wholeness? Can't you see them wanting to engage in conversations about wellness as parents, wholeness as families, and shalom in their marriages?

Can you imagine the same interest being generated in a conversation about salvation? "If you get saved, it will improve your marriage, your parenting, and your personal life." That sales pitch is exactly what is wrong with the modern presentation of Christianity. We need to hear what the other person hears in the conversations we try to have with them about religion and Christianity.

29
Do-Over!

When I was in fourth grade, kickball pretty much ruled the world, and recess was clearly the most important part of the day. I'm sure we would all agree that the socialization of learning to play with our friends and learning to include others are the sorts of things that make the world go round. But if the behavior of some adults today is any indication, there are people who missed out on this very important socialization process. Maybe they were recess deprived.

Kickball implies teams, and teams imply captains. The ticket to success in kickball was to be one of those captains, for obvious reasons. Captains chose teams and therefore controlled the destiny of the fourth-grade world. The smart captains, of course, employed Darwin's survival of the fittest in outfitting their teams. The biggest and strongest kids were always picked first; the captains counted on them for home runs. But a well-rounded strategy also included looking for smaller-but-quick kids. They couldn't kick the ball as far, but they could move on the bases. The best captains strategically blended these two important strategies for picking their teams. Thus, with only a fourth-grade-level math background, we were calculating speed, distance, power, and flight long before we reached tenth-grade physics.

Looking back now, I'm not sure who chose the

captains, but I do remember being one of four or five guys who were usually captains. Of course, being a captain carried over into regular fourth-grade life, as well. It was a sort of social position, a status within the fourth-grade social and sports hierarchy. There were other benefits, of course, not the least of which was the impact on female interactions and a host of other complex and nuanced circumstances that most adults can't quite remember. But one of a captain's primary powers, apart from picking the team, was the magical power to call a "do-over." That's right, do-overs.

For those uninitiated into the subtleties of the near-professional sport of fourth-grade kickball, any time players weren't ready, were looking the other way when they shouldn't have been, or were distracted by another ball from another diamond rolling into their field of play, the captain could call a do-over. It was a no-ifs-ands-or-buts-about-it call. If the captain called a do-over, there was going to be a do-over.

Of course, all sorts of captain wannabes attempted to call do-overs, and at times they could get their captain to join them in making the call, thereby activating his power. But most of the time, a wannabe's call was ignored or was greeted with catcalls, and the game would proceed as if nothing had happened. Do-overs were an important part of the game, but only a select few had the privilege of making the call.

What does a kickball captain calling a do-over have to do with salvation? Well, if "getting saved" or "being born again" is simply the language we use to describe the start of a relationship with Jesus, which like all relationships is a *process* that evolves and ebbs and flows, then why is there so much negative press about it?

As far as I know, the phrase *born again* gained currency as part of the "I Found It" evangelism campaign in the 1970s, and it was also the title of Charles Colson's autobiography, which came out around that same time. But even after the evangelism program ran its course, the phrase stuck as a shorthand way for a certain subset of the Christian community to describe itself—we've all heard the phrase "born-again Christian." As a label to describe the in-house experience of the average Christ follower, I suppose it's okay, if you understand what it means. As a term for public discourse, however, I'm pretty sure it's beyond salvage, at least in the short term. Regardless of which side of the fence you're on, the term *born again* has picked up negative associations for many people. I have no particular insight into why the phrase carries such negative connotations in some circles today, but it's hard not to make a connection to the cultural backlash against the so-called religious right. I also know plenty of Christ followers who are just as turned off by the title, due to the cultural baggage that has attached itself to the term.

So what can we do to redeem the concept without using the phrase? And do we have any idea what the concept actually means? Listening to the average sermon on John 3, one might get the impression that Jesus was answering a question posed by Nicodemus about how he could get to heaven at the end of his life. But the text doesn't support such a view. Nevertheless, for many Christ followers, John 3:1-8 has become a watershed passage about salvation. They've been taught that "being born again" is what sets apart those who *really* believe the Bible from those who have gone a bit soft. Following this line of reasoning leads to the inevitable conclusion that those who are "born again" are *in* (as in "going to heaven"), and those who are not are *out*. But before we draw such conclusions, it seems reasonable to ask, "Is Jesus even talking about going to heaven in his conversation with Nicodemus?"

It seems ironic that such hubbub can flow from one brief story recorded in the third chapter of the Gospel of John. The phrase *born again* is used in only one other book in the entire New Testament.[1] So how has this phrase become a defining label for a swatch of Christianity? Furthermore, is the way the term has come to be understood in common public parlance an even remotely accurate reflection of what Jesus meant in his conversation with Nicodemus? Let's take a look at the story.

> Now there was a man of the Pharisees named Nicodemus, a member of the Jewish ruling council. He

> came to Jesus at night and said, "Rabbi, we know you are a teacher who has come from God. For no one could perform the miraculous signs you are doing if God were not with him."
>
> In reply Jesus declared, "I tell you the truth, no one can see the kingdom of God unless he is born again."
>
> "How can a man be born when he is old?" Nicodemus asked. "Surely he cannot enter a second time into his mother's womb to be born!"
>
> Jesus answered, "I tell you the truth, no one can enter the kingdom of God unless he is born of water and the Spirit. Flesh gives birth to flesh, but the Spirit gives birth to spirit. You should not be surprised at my saying, 'You must be born again.' The wind blows wherever it pleases. You hear its sound, but you cannot tell where it comes from or where it is going. So it is with everyone born of the Spirit."[2]

Let's start with what is clear in the story and move toward what is less clear. For starters, the conversation is clearly about the kingdom of God—but here is where many readers make a couple of interpretive leaps that color their understanding of what Jesus says. First, they jump ahead to verse 5 and substitute the word *enter* for the word *see* in verse 3, and then they substitute the word *heaven* for the phrase "kingdom of God." Thus, they take what Jesus says—"No one can see the kingdom of God unless he is born again"—and read it as "No one can enter into heaven unless he is born again." I think this reading of the passage is common and well known, both inside and outside the church. Even if people in our culture don't know the story of Nicodemus, they've probably heard somewhere that the ticket to heaven is this experience that Christians label "being born again."

But what if Jesus isn't talking to Nicodemus about how to get to heaven? What if "kingdom of God," as spoken of here, refers to a present reality rather than to someplace out there after we die?

We've already seen that "kingdom of God" is not synonymous with "heaven," but many people at this point still make a quick and subtle change in the language of the verse. They assume that Jesus is talking to Nicodemus about the place we go when we die. However, from our previous discussion, we know that kingdom language—the language of empire and restoration—has "here and now" dimensions as well as "yet to come" dimensions. Remember that both John the Baptist and Jesus came proclaiming that the kingdom of God was near at hand. In other words, not all kingdom-of-God conversations imply a discussion of the afterlife. On other occasions, Jesus said the kingdom of God is in us, around us, and in our midst.[3]

When Jesus explicitly says that no one can *see* the kingdom of God unless he is born again, what if he is talking about the ability to see, as in "sense" or "be aware of," the kingdom right here and right now? What if Jesus is actually responding to Nicodemus's observation that the miracles were clear indicators that the kingdom of God was at work in their midst? This would be a gutsy observation coming from a Pharisee, which might explain in part why this conversation takes place at night when the other Pharisees would be unlikely to see Nicodemus visiting with Jesus.

We know that when Nicodemus says, "We know you come from God . . . because of the miracles," he is not representing the majority opinion of the Pharisees. In fact, Matthew, Mark, and Luke all record a time when Jesus healed a demon-possessed man, and instead of giving glory to God, the Pharisees said, "He's only able to cast out demons by the power of Beelzebub, the prince of demons."[4] In other words, "He's only able to do that because he's a demon himself."

In that situation, Jesus responded to the Pharisees with his famous statement that a house divided against itself cannot stand (which Abraham Lincoln later used to great effect).[5] Jesus also says, in Matthew 12:28, "But if I drive out demons by the Spirit of God, then the kingdom of God has come upon you."

So when Nicodemus says, "We know you come from

God," he's revealing that, at least at some basic level, he sees the connection between what Jesus does and who Jesus is, contrary to the prevailing view among the Pharisees. That, I believe, is the point that Jesus responds to.

Before we get to the heart of Jesus' response to Nicodemus, we must briefly consider one other important factor—the immediate context of Nicodemus's approach to Jesus. At the end of John 2, we read that "many people saw the miraculous signs he was doing and believed in his name. But Jesus would not entrust himself to them, for he knew all men. He did not need man's testimony about man, for he knew what was in a man" (John 2:23-25). In other words, there were some people who believed or "trusted" in Jesus as a result of the miracles they'd seen, but Jesus wasn't entrusting himself to them because he knew what was truly in their hearts. So, when Nicodemus comes to Jesus and says, "We've seen your miraculous signs, and therefore we know that you must come from God," we can't rule out the possibility that his profession of belief is not entirely trustworthy. He may, in fact, have been simply trying to flatter Jesus. Nevertheless, we can know that Jesus discerned what was truly in Nicodemus's heart and responded accordingly. It's with that context in mind that we turn our attention more specifically to the conversation.

30
Gestation

"Unless one is born again he cannot see the kingdom of God."[6] When I read Jesus' response to Nicodemus, the question that comes to my mind is this: Is Jesus giving him a prescription for something to do—that is, if you want to see the kingdom, you must be born again—or is he describing an existing condition and a process that was already in motion? It seems that Jesus is acknowledging what Nicodemus has said, but then he cuts to the heart of the matter by suggesting that Nicodemus's belief has not yet fully come to term—he's still in gestation, to borrow from the imagery of being born again—he's still in process.

This might rock your boat, but do you see the distinction between one understanding and the other? Is it possible that instead of telling Nicodemus what he must do in order to be saved or get to heaven, as is often taught, Jesus is actually trying to uncover for Nicodemus an internal process that is already taking place but which Nicodemus isn't yet fully aware of? Is it possible that Jesus is pointing out and bringing language to some inklings and promptings that Nicodemus has already felt but has not fully comprehended, even though, as a Pharisee and teacher, he should have understood them by now? Might Jesus be saying that a transformation is already underway, even though it has not yet come into focus for Nicodemus?

What if Jesus is trying to clarify Nicodemus's observation so that his spiritual journey could progress and he could embrace the mysterious wind-blowing of the Spirit of God?

Nicodemus immediately focuses on Jesus' graphic imagery of being "born again." He says, "Hey, I'm an old man. How can I return to the womb?"

Now that Jesus has Nicodemus's attention, he leads him through a transition in his thinking, from flesh to spirit.

Because Nicodemus was a Pharisee, Jesus knew that he had been born into a Jewish family and was circumcised on the eighth day, according to the law. He knew he'd been born into going to the Temple, eating kosher food, and responding to the Sabbath laws and the details of the hundreds and hundreds of purity laws that Nicodemus and his fellow Pharisees believed kept them distinct and separate from the rest of the world. And Jesus also knew that Nicodemus had no choice or control over the circumstances into which he was born. His background simply was what it was.

The same is true for us. When we are born into the world, we are born into certain conditions, situations, circumstances, and understandings. Our background has a huge effect on our view of the world and those around us; it isn't something we've consciously chosen.

Jesus notes that Nicodemus has made some unusual observations. Though many were apparently giving lip service to Jesus because of the signs he performed, not everyone was seeing the miracles as proof that Jesus was from God. In fact, Nicodemus was smack-dab in the middle of a controversy among the Pharisees, most of whom saw Jesus as a threat, not a helper; an antagonist, not a friend; a devil, not someone from God. Jesus knows that Nicodemus has taken a huge risk in coming to see him. He knows that everything Nicodemus had been born into was at stake. But I think Jesus also wants to show him that there's even more at stake—a spiritual dimension that Nicodemus has not yet begun to grasp. Jesus says, in effect, "Despite all you have been born into, you are slowly but surely being born out of it. In order for you to see what you have seen, you must be born out of your conditioning, your heritage, your single-lens perspective that the other teachers of the law are using to view what I am doing. You are being born out of all that into a new kind of *aha*. You are having a do-over, you are experiencing a fresh start. You are being born all over again."

Nicodemus responds with confusion, which is perfectly understandable when one has had his paradigm shifted in such dramatic fashion. He says, "How can this be? How can I go back to the beginning, to being a baby, as if I hadn't lived all these years and learned all these other things?"

Jesus replies, "The truth is, you need both. You need to be born naturally and supernaturally. But don't be surprised by this. This is the work of the Holy Spirit, who cannot be seen—he's like the wind, in that respect—but who makes himself known as he sees fit. Granted, there is a mystery to how the do-over takes root, just as there is a mystery to how the wind blows and where it lands. Nicodemus, you are experiencing God's powerful do-over; it is only the beginning, but the process has begun, the new journey has started. For you to be able to see God at work is an act of the Spirit."

To my way of thinking, this possible reading of the story of Nicodemus is one of the few I've heard that make sense of Nicodemus's comment and Jesus' response. If indeed this is a passage about *seeing* the kingdom of God in our midst, rather than a description of how to get to heaven, it changes our perspective from *point of sale* to *process*. It changes our understanding from *what we have to do* to *what is already happening* when we begin to recognize the presence and activity of Jesus in and around us.

When Nicodemus says, "These miracles you have performed, Jesus, tell me something about you—namely, that God is with you," Jesus replies, "That you can see these things proves that something is going on inside you. Furthermore, it is something you couldn't do for yourself. It is a work of the Spirit."

In John 7, we have further evidence of the process taking place in Nicodemus's heart. When Jesus goes up to Jerusalem for the Feast of Tabernacles, the Jewish leaders send temple guards to arrest him. When the guards come back empty handed, the leaders are outraged, but Nicodemus says, "Does our law condemn anyone without first hearing him to find out what he is doing?" (John 7:51). Here, it seems Nicodemus has come a long way from approaching Jesus under cover of night, to standing up in the assembly of Pharisees to defend Jesus' right to due process.

Later, we're told, Nicodemus helps Joseph of Arimathea prepare Jesus' body for burial after the Crucifixion (John 19:38-40). Moreover, John tells us that the two men had Pilate's permission, which suggests Nicodemus had come to a point where he was willing to associate himself fully with Jesus, even to the point of exposing his loyalties before the Roman governor.

Nicodemus's process of being born again evidently came to a point of birth over time, but when was the point of sale, when was the point of conversion that so many Christians insist is necessary to any true "decision" to follow Jesus? We're not told. What we are told—what Jesus himself told Nicodemus during their nighttime conversation—is that "the wind blows wherever it pleases. You hear its sound, but you cannot tell where it comes from or where it is going. So it is with everyone born of the Spirit" (John 3:8).

So, what are we to take away from our reading of the story of Nicodemus? I see several possibilities.

I believe the story shows the quiet, surprising process that goes on inside people as they find themselves in the mysterious, jarring, even bewildering process of a do-over. The story implies that no matter what we have been born into in our earthly lives, the Spirit of God can bring an altered perspective, a fresh start, a clean slate. Better yet, by the time we realize what is happening, the process is already underway.

The story of Nicodemus is a real-life example of the internal prompting of the Holy Spirit in someone's life, a process that happens in the heart of every person on the planet, though not everyone chooses to respond positively when the wind blows on them.

This story is more about the front-end spiritual process and the mystery and vertigo it creates. It is not about a mandate—be born again or burn in hell—that we are supposed to trumpet to the "unsaved world." If anything, this story is about how we must learn to listen sensitively and with discernment to people as they tell their stories, to hear them narrate their spiritual journeys and to help them by pointing out where we see the wind of the Spirit blowing in their lives. The quiet work of the Holy Spirit in Nicodemus's life and his apparent perplexity are further hints and clues that there is a process at work in people's hearts that needs to be clarified in order for them to grasp the full import of what they are experiencing.

I believe that a careful and reflective reading, one that pays attention to what is said and not said, asked and not asked, will point us to a different understanding, a different conclusion, and a different mandate than perhaps we've heard in sermons about Nicodemus and the catchphrase "you must be born again." Jesus isn't saying, "Here is how to be born again to get to heaven"; rather he is saying, "When you experience these interior insights and promptings, that is the work of the Holy Spirit. Don't be confused by it, but embrace it and go with it."

As we've seen in our journey through the first few verses of John 3, the bad press surrounding the term *born again* is really unwarranted, if we look at the story carefully. I hope this is the real takeaway from this entire volume. We have all sorts of ideas about what we think certain biblical terms and concepts mean—and maybe, just maybe, we don't have the full story. My proposal for a better term, such as *do-over,* in the case of *born again,* grows out of what I think most people in our culture understand and can respond to. The adults with whom I have used the term *do-over* instantly recall some experience like fourth-grade kickball. The idea of a fresh start, a new perspective, a paradigm change, a mental model shift—all these are part of the same complex of ideas. The point is, if we really want to engage people in dialogue, if we really want to understand their world and have them understand ours, then we will have to be masters of language—how it either creates understanding or distorts, dilutes, and misleads. The church has typically not been very careful on this issue. We've persisted in speaking our own language despite the static it creates in our communications.

The more nuanced reading of the story of Nicodemus I have suggested is a call for different sorts of models for telling the story of Jesus—models with far more intuitive soundings; approaches with more sensitivity to the initiation of the person on the quest; better frameworks, where the understanding of *spiritual process,* in all its complexity, individuality, and winsome mystery, is allowed to not only exist but really sing. When we embrace evangelism as a dance or an improvised jazz duet or trio, I think we may find many more people in the conversion process, but maybe not quite ready for the all-or-nothing modern idea of a point-of-sale conversion experience. Are we ready for the honest ambiguity, lack of control, and relational mystery that happens in a human heart wrestling with spiritual murmurings? Or will we one more time return to the highly directive point-of-sale conversion models manufactured in the mechanical world of modernity? I think it is time to reread passages like John 3 and to craft our understandings and our approaches accordingly. We need more writing and reflection on this. And we need it yesterday.

31 Crumpled Napkins

Phil and Jess opened the door to my car and were greeted by the loud snap and crackle of static on the stereo. I had just hit the *on* button but hadn't yet punched the FM frequency into my iPod. When the cable frequency and the stereo frequency are different, watch out; it's nothing but loud noise.

"What the—? You're tunin' down to some loud static, Ron. I like the stereo loud, but I prefer music, not the rock version of Rice Krispies." I can always count on Phil for a touch of sarcasm.

"I'm trying to get the music going to play a new tune I heard last night from Hootie. I thought we could listen as we head over to Outback for your dinner with Marty."

"Ron, thanks for giving us a ride," Jess said as she slipped into the passenger seat. "We didn't want to have to drive two cars to The Fray concert after dinner." She tapped nervously on the dashboard. I could sense she was frustrated. There had been an increasing edge in her voice in recent days about the whole "witnessing" issue.

"What's wrong, Jess?" I glanced at her as I pulled away from the curb.

"Ron, just what are we supposed to say to Marty?" She was looking directly at me now. "If it isn't 'repent, you're on a one-way street in the wrong direction,' if it isn't 'you need to get everything in order so you can get to heaven,' and if it isn't 'Jesus died for you and has a wonderful plan for your life if you will just sign on the dotted line,' then what is it?"

"Slow down, Jess," I started to say, but before I could get it out, she brought the conversation back to the booming static that had greeted them when they got in the car.

"You know," she said, "I feel like I'm the flippin' iPod cable that is on the wrong frequency. I would really like people to hear the music, but I just don't know which FM number I'm supposed to punch into the little gizmo so the music can be heard."

"Jess, I am with you. I often feel the same way. This is not the neat little trite simplistic thing we have often made it to be in our modern world. I'm all for simple and clear, but I'm *not* for simplistic and clichéd."

Phil leaned forward from the backseat. "Ron, you know what we are really struggling with is this major rethinking of what we were convinced we clearly understood. On the one hand, the big picture really hasn't changed. We're still talking about Jesus and connecting people to God. On the other hand, it feels like everything has changed. Last week, when I was really honest with myself, I realized I had reduced God. I had reduced the gospel. I hate admitting that, but it's the honest truth."

"Big growth there, Phil," I kidded him.

Jess kept the thought flowing. "Phil and I were talking last night, knowing that we were going to be getting together with Marty today, and we were trying to come up with what we should tell him, what we should do." She pulled a crumpled piece of paper out of her bag and held it up so I could glance at it while I was driving. Written in black marker was a series of equations:

gospel = newsflash
repent = reorient
kingdom of God = empire of God
sin = shame
salvation = do-over and shalom

☹ Argh!?!?!

At the bottom of the page was a large frowny face with question marks and exclamations next to it.

"Jess, good drawing! But, don't quit your day job." I smiled and looked back at the road. "You know, Jess, all these conversations we've been having haven't been about just replacing one word with another. . . . You know that, don't you? . . . I admit that I have been advocating using words such as *do-over* and *shalom* because I believe these types of words may break through the communication barriers and resonate with more people. But in the end, I'm not sure simply replacing a couple of words will solve everything. What I was trying to say—"

Jess interrupted me with a loud huff and stared out the window. "Sometimes, I wonder whether there is a reason for even talking to Marty about God . . ." Her voice got quieter at the end, which with Jess was usually a verbal cue that she had voiced all she had to say—at least for the moment.

"Come on, you two." I glanced at Phil in the rearview mirror. "You know I feel passionate about connecting with guys like Marty. I realize that when we remove the abbreviated and skewed version of God's story from our minds, we all feel like we're floundering a bit. But what we have in its place is a much fuller and richer story, a far more beautiful, elegant, and powerful story we can invite people into. For so long we have communicated things with such *static*. I really think you're right on that one, Jess." I stole another glance at her while I was turning right onto Main. She was still staring out the window. "We have made unclear what should be crystal clear."

"But, Ron, what is crystal clear?" Jess crumpled up her list of equations and stuffed it into the empty cup holder on the console. "Nothing," she mumbled under her breath and stared accusingly at me.

"Well, the whole and complete story of God," I said. "That's one thing that's clear. Remember when we talked about how we're used to telling a shorter version of it: the Fall and Redemption sound bite? Remember how I said there was a richer story that included Creation, Fall, Redemption, and—"

"—Restoration," Phil interjected from the backseat. "Se-e-e, I was listening."

"That's right, Restoration. As I said, Phil, big-time growth." I could see in the rearview mirror that Phil was grinning.

"But how do I summarize that and explain it to Marty?" Jess was pulling the crumpled paper out of the cup holder and unfolding it.

"Jess, I don't think there are any easy answers, pat formulas, or quick clichés. That's the 'Christian noise' we have to work so hard to cut through. What we have, though, is the wild and woolly complete story of God, as recorded in the Bible. The story tells us about who God is and how he relates to real, often complex, people in a variety of different circumstances. It's a complex story because it's a real story about a real God. It can't be stripped down, reprocessed, repackaged, and served to us with fries on the side. It's a multicourse dinner at Outback that we spend time to enjoy—not a McDonald's Value Meal we gulp down in minutes."

I paused, and Phil made a sarcastic comment about how they should be meeting Marty at McDonald's instead of Outback.

"It takes time to tell a really good story about characters we care about. Think about it. We allow George Lucas to spend over twelve hours of our time telling the visual story of *Star Wars*. But we want to stuff the story of God into a five-minute conversation. There's intriguing variety within God's story that can't be summarized in five minutes. Remember when we talked about the intertwined story lines of Exodus, Exile, and the sacrificial worship system? All this helps us paint the full, grand story of God. Our job is to highlight the parts of the story that connect to people like Marty in a special way—and ultimately draw them closer to God."

"Ron, that's sounds so-o-o eloquent," Jess said. "But how is Marty going to be interested in that? Come on. He'll be more interested in what songs The Fray are playing tonight than in all the fancy words you can put together right now." She was tapping nervously on the dashboard again, clearly exasperated with me. "Ron, aren't you discouraging people from talking about God at all with their friends by making it so complicated?"

"Jess, I'm going to be completely honest with you. So try to take this the right way." I reached for the crumpled paper that was resting in her hand. "I really think you're upset that I'm not giving you another diagram you can memorize and then sketch on a napkin for Marty."

"So what? I want to be prepared to explain and defend what I believe. Doesn't the Bible tell us to be prepared?"

"Sure it does. That's what these conversations we've been having are all about. But, isn't the diagram really for *you*? Don't you really want a new diagram for your napkin so you can feel good about presenting it to Marty? So that you can feel good about what you did with Marty over dinner at the Outback? You can check it off your Palm Pilot's to-do list and then move on to the next to-do item."

I could see a slight smile forming on Jess's face. She was starting to get it, so I continued. "Bottom line, I don't think anyone falls in love with a formula written on a napkin. And, the Martys I meet today know deep down that the complexities of life can't fit on a single crumpled-up napkin. Believe me, I've tried that approach."

I paused in order to make a left turn in the face of oncoming traffic. The only sound in the SUV was the accelerating V-8 engine. The Hootie song had ended, and I was fighting the urge to punch up another song on my iPod. Yet, background music somehow didn't seem right for the moment. I waited a little to let Phil and Jess process what I was saying. Then, I broke the silence. "So, in the end, what did the formula accomplish? Is Marty any closer to loving God after your five-minute presentation?"

Jess let out a big sigh and turned toward me. "Okay, okay, there's no diagram. I get it. But when, Ron, are you going to answer my question: What, then, do we talk to Marty about?"

"Good question. I believe that Marty, like just about everyone, has some fundamental *core yearning,* something he's on a quest for. I think we have to listen for hints to what he's looking for. That's one way to connect Marty to the story of God. Find out where Marty has felt those Garden longings—those glimpses of God in his life."

"Well-l-l, he loves all kinds of music—jazz, r & b, rap, and alternative," Phil interjected.

"Yeah, but, Ron, what do we *tell* Marty?" Jess was nothing if not persistent. We were a mile away from Outback now. She was feeling that the impending encounter was just minutes away, and she was trying to hasten us along.

"How about nothing?" I asked.

"What?" Jess stopped tapping on the dashboard and slapped her hand on her knee.

"How about listening for the 'hints' in the conversation? How about a commitment not to tell Marty anything for a while? What if we decided to learn how to ask good questions first? And what if we decided to listen carefully? What might happen?" I glanced at Jess and Phil, indicating that I wanted a response. "Really, what might happen?"

"Well, Marty might not shut down like the last time I brought the subject up," Phil said from the backseat.

Jess let out a sigh. "Isn't that *really* just giving up, Ron?"

"Or is it *really* learning to love Marty?" I countered. "Learning to appreciate him? Learning to discover who Marty is? Is it learning to look for God, who is already at work in Marty's life? Is it *really* the more difficult work of connecting a real person—with his own issues and problems, emotions and pet peeves, challenges and potential—to God? Okay, I admit it, Jess. It's not easy and quick. It doesn't fit on a napkin. It's not a sound bite. But it may be what's required. If we don't do that, then we may miss what God is doing long-term in Marty's life. We may miss the variety of ways in which God wants to connect to all the different 'Martys' he has placed on Main Street, in Jackson, or wherever."

I paused to switch on my turn signal. "Isn't that *really* what God did anyway? Why do you think God hasn't beamed down a formula to us from heaven? Why did he send his Son instead?"

I paused. Once again, there was dead silence in the car. Jess was staring out the window. "Okay, Ron, I get what you're saying. . . . It's just so much more difficult than I first thought. . . . Okay, we'll listen. And we'll ask good questions. . . . But, Ron, you must make a deal with us. We need your help in thinking aloud about these 'core yearning' things you are talking about."

"And the wild, complete story." Phil leaned forward again.

"And how to connect that story to the lives of our

friends," Jess added. "I think we've just scratched the surface of that."

"Deal," I said as I pulled into the parking lot at the Outback Steakhouse. "I will talk to you two later. I'm headed over to the golf course to meet my own 'Marty' for a little twilight golf game, lots of listening—and lots of pars and birdies, I hope."

"*I* just hope you're not taping these conversations for your next book," Phil joked as he slid out of the backseat.

"You never know what these gizmos can do." I grabbed my BlackBerry from the center console, waved it at him, and then slipped it into my pocket.

Notes

Foreword

1. This word of advice appears on a list of recommendations for new Christians who want to *deepen* their life in Christ, in ***Steps to Peace with God,*** by Billy Graham (Minneapolis: Billy Graham Evangelistic Association, 1998). The text can also be found online: http://www.billygraham.org/SH_StepsToPeace.asp.

Chapter 1 Pheidippides Was a Wimp

1. Frederick W. Dankes, *Jesus and the New Age: A Commentary on St. Luke's Gospel* (Philadelphia: Fortress, 1988), 54.

Chapter 5 A First-Century Newsflash

1. William L. Lane, "The Gospel According to Mark," in *The New International Commentary on the New Testament* (Grand Rapids: Eerdmans, 1974), 42.
2. Ibid., 43.

Chapter 8 Reorienting the Compass

1. Two sources that provided background information for this section are N.T. Wright, *Jesus and the Victory of God* (Minneapolis: Fortress, 1996), 250–254; and Scot McKnight, *A New Vision for Israel: The Teachings of Jesus in National Context* (Grand Rapids: Eerdmans, 1999), 172-175.

Chapter 9 High Stakes and Juicy T-Bones

1. Peter Farb and George Armelagos, *Consuming Passions: The Anthropology of Eating* (Boston: Houghton Mifflin, 1980), 4, 211.

Chapter 13 Four Views of the Kingdom

1. For further reading on the kingdom of God, see George Eldon Ladd, *A Theology of the New Testament* (Eerdmans, 1974), especially chapter 3; Richard A. Horsley, *Jesus and Empire* (Fortress, 2003); and Richard A. Horsley, *The Message and the Kingdom* (Fortress, 2002).

Chapter 16 All Riled Up

1. John 3:16, emphasis added.

Chapter 17 Pink-Spoon Samples

1. N.T. Wright, *Jesus and the Victory of God* (Minneapolis: Fortress, 1996), 332.

Chapter 19 Freedom, Favor, and Fake IDs

1. Joel Green and Mark Baker, *Recovering the Scandal of the Cross* (Downers Grove, Ill.: InterVarsity, 2000), 20.

Chapter 20 Hungarian Goulash

1. Sallie McFague, *Speaking in Parables: A Study in Metaphor and Theology* (Philadelphia: Fortress, 1975).

Chapter 21 Soaking in a Sin Solution

1. For well done treatments on sin that open up various nuances, see Ted Peters, *Sin: Radical Evil in Soul and Society* (Wipf and Stock, 1998); and Mark Biddle, *Missing the Mark: Sin and Its Consequences in Biblical Theology* (Abingdon, 2005).
2. http://web.uvic.ca/wguide/Pages/LTHamartia.html. See also http://en.wikipedia.org/wiki/Hamartia.
3. Richard Rohr, *The Enneagram: A Christian Perspective* (New York: CrossRoad, 2004), 34.
4. Ibid., 34–35.
5. See the great exchange that Scot McKnight has with Mark Biddle's book on sin, *Missing the Mark*, at http://www.jesuscreed.org/index.php?s=mark+biddle
6. Joel Green and Mark Baker, *Recovering the Scandal of the Cross* (Downers Grove, Ill.: InterVarsity, 2000), 55.
7. For the good, quick overview of Old Testament meta-stories, see Gerhard Hasel, *Old Testament Theology: Basic Issues in the Current Debate* (Eerdman's, 1991).

Chapter 22 A Garden-Variety Longing

1. I have already mentioned Scot McKnight's blog, www.jesuscreed.org, and you can find similar discussions on www.theooze.com, www.emergentvillage.com, www.next-wave.org, and www.nextreformation.com, and that is just a brief sampling. Start there and you can link to others.
2. See, for example, Steven Chalke and Alan Mann, *The Lost Message of Jesus* (Zondervan, 2003); and for the not faint of heart, Anthony Thistleton offers a rather sophisticated and more dense understanding into the postmodern psyche and self-understanding in *Interpreting God and the Postmodern Self* (Eerdman's, 1995).

Chapter 23 Recentering Our Storytelling

1. Stephen Pattison, *Shame: Theory, Therapy, Theology* (Cambridge: Cambridge University Press, 2000), 71.
2. Joel Green and Mark Baker, *Recovering the Scandal of the Cross* (Downers Grove, Ill.: InterVarsity, 2000), 153ff.
3. C. Norman Kraus, *Jesus Christ our Lord: Christology from a Disciple's Perspective* (Scottdale, Pa.: Herald Press, 1990), 223–227.
4. Gershen Kaufman, *The Psychology of Shame* (London: Routledge, 1993), 17.
5. Joel Green and Mark Baker, *Recovering the Scandal of the Cross* (Downers Grove, Ill.: InterVarsity, 2000), 23.
6. See passages such as Ephesians 1 and Colossians 2. For other resources developing this theme, see Alan Mann, *The Atonement for a "Sinless" Society* (Paternoster, 2005); and Gustaf Aulén, *Christus Victor: An Historical Study of the Three Main Types of the Idea of the Atonement* (Wipf and Stock, 2003). For an outstanding synthesis of several positions, see Colin E. Gunton, *The Actuality of Atonement: A Study of Metaphor, Rationality and the Christian Tradition* (Edinburgh: T&T Clark, 2003).
7. The resources available on narrative therapy are numerous, but a helpful framework with full case studies showing how it actually works can be found in Michael White and David Epston, *Narrative Means to Therapeutic Ends* (New York: Norton, 1990).

Chapter 24 Not There Yet

1. This quote is widely attributed to Winston Churchill. I ran across it in a photo essay book called *A Tribute to Golf* (Harbor Springs, Mich.: Stewart Hunter and Associates, 1990).

Chapter 25 The Quintessential Question

1. NKJV.
2. Luke 2:8-14.

Chapter 26 Everything

1. Luke 7:44-48.

Chapter 27 An Invitation to the Banquet

1. Conrad Gempf, *Meal Time Habits of the Messiah* (Grand Rapids: Zondervan, 2005), 133.
2. See also Matthew 11:18-19 and Mark 2:18.
3. Luke 14:7-11.
4. Luke 14:12-14.
5. Luke 14:15-24.

6. For further reading on the "'already' and 'not yet'" aspects of the kingdom of God, see George Eldon Ladd, "The Need of the Kingdom: The World and Humanity," in *A Theology of the New Testament* (Eerdmans, 1974), 42–53.

Chapter 28 Restoration as a Process

1. Scot McKnight, *Turning to Jesus: The Sociology of Conversion in the Gospels* (Westminster/John Knox, 2002).
2. For example, we see the *past* element in Ephesians 2; the *present* element in Philippians 2; and the *future* element in Romans 8.

Chapter 29 Do-Over!

1. See 1 Peter 1:3, 23 (NASB).
2. John 3:1-8.
3. See Luke 10:9-11; 11:20; 17:20-2.
4. See Matthew 12:22-28; Mark 3:22-30; Luke 11:14-20.
5. Matthew 12:25; Mark 3:24-25; Luke 11:17.
6. John 3:3, NASB. The syntax of the *New American Standard Bible*'s rendering of John 3:3 more closely matches the original.

About the Author

Dr. Ron Martoia is a transformational architect. His mission is to help followers of Jesus design, build, and experience revolutionary change as they seek to understand and interact with the new culture in which they live. Over the past two years, Ron has spoken to more than 25,000 leaders, in a variety of conference settings, on the new and shifting intersection between church and culture. He helps churches consider how they can shift their theological outlook, which in turn will adjust their ministry trajectory and cultural interface. Through his speaking, consulting, writing, and acting as a "distant staff member" to a number of churches, Ron uses his cultural intonation to help churches shift paradigms from the old Newtonian world to the Quantum world of the twenty-first century.

He is the author of numerous articles and a chapter in *Great Preaching* titled "Preaching to Postmoderns." His first book project, *Morph!,* a volume to help leaders do good self-leadership as they foster creative and compelling environments, was welcomed with widespread critical acclaim.

Ron facilitates a new experimental learning community model, called Vortex, in Jackson, Michigan. Meeting in an arts enclave, Vortex hosts weekly conversations on everything from string theory and the origins of the universe to the insights of Aristotle on personal development, as well as theological discussions about world religions and global spiritual formation models. Vortex hopes to be part of shaping a new learning container for twenty-first-century spiritual and personal formation.